ENGLISH IS BROKEN HERE

ENGLISH

COCO FUSCO

IS BROKEN HERE

NOTES ON CULTURAL FUSION IN THE AMERICAS

THE NEW PRESS : NEW YORK CITY

95 96 97 98   9 8 7 6 5 4 3 2 1

ISBN 1-56584-245-6

LIBRARY OF CONGRESS CATALOG CARD NUMBER 95-67818

PUBLISHED IN THE UNITED STATES BY THE NEW PRESS, NEW YORK

DISTRIBUTED BY W. W. NORTON & COMPANY, INC., NEW YORK, NY 10110

ESTABLISHED IN 1990 AS A MAJOR ALTERNATIVE TO THE LARGE, COMMERCIAL PUBLISHING HOUSES, THE NEW PRESS IS THE FIRST FULL-SCALE NONPROFIT AMERICAN BOOK PUBLISHER OUTSIDE OF THE UNIVERSITY PRESSES. THE PRESS IS OPERATED EDITORIALLY IN THE PUBLIC INTEREST, RATHER THAN FOR PRIVATE GAIN; IT IS COMMITTED TO PUBLISHING IN INNOVATIVE WAYS WORKS OF EDUCATIONAL, CULTURAL, AND COMMUNITY VALUE THAT, DESPITE THEIR INTELLECTUAL MERITS, MIGHT NOT NORMALLY BE COMMERCIALLY VIABLE. THE NEW PRESS'S EDITORIAL OFFICES ARE LOCATED AT THE CITY UNIVERSITY OF NEW YORK.

BOOK DESIGN BY PAUL CARLOS

PRODUCTION MANAGEMENT BY KIM WAYMER

PRINTED IN THE UNITED STATES OF AMERICA

CONTENTS

PURA BICULTURA:
AN INTRODUCTION

Y POOR GRANDMOTHER. By the time she arrived in New York from Havana via Madrid, American cartoons and daily trips to Washington Square Park had turned my brother and me into nasty little *yanquis*. We answered back—in English. We turned her Spanish admonitions into puns. We liked to shock adults with bad words. She made sure, however, that we called her *mamá*, instead of disrespectfully reminding her of her age by calling her grandma. But it wasn't long before she began to complain to her daughter. "*No puedo con estos niños,*" she would say. "*Estan demasiado americanizados.*" (I can't deal with these kids. They're too Americanized.)

What could my mother say? Teachers were warning her that our learning abilities would be impaired by our being subjected to more than one language at home. She and my father were more worried about racial questions than linguistic ones. They were frantically looking for a decent school in New York where we wouldn't be bothered continually for being *mulatos*. They pumped our egos like crazy to give us a defense against the idiocies of a racist world. We became expert mimics, aping the melodiously accented English of our elders, on the one hand, and spoofing the attempts of Americans to pronounce Spanish words on the other. (*I Love Lucy* was of course, our favorite TV program.) We also became great shape shifters, turning on Latin politeness to impress our American friends' parents, and then reverting to little *yanqui* brats when we wanted to bewilder the latest nana. One of them, Rufina, fled the house after my parents refused to heed her pleas that we children be exorcised. "*Traen el diablo por dentro,*" she cried. (They're possessed by the devil.)

Like most immigrant kids, we slid into the gap between languages and cultures with ease. The world around us was already communicating to us that we were better than our relatives because we had English under our belts. Then there were the other markers that distinguished us. *We* didn't live in a barrio, my mother fiercely reminded us, though she had hidden from the real estate agents so that we could get into the neighborhood. Just in case anyone passing by dared to get any wrong ideas, my mother regularly scrubbed the steps and sidewalk in front of the house. My father unrolled an American flag on the appropriate holidays. We went to church with the Irish on Sundays and prayed in English, and we kids went to a mostly Jewish school during the week. Thanks to my parents, I was fairly oblivious to the implications of the looks and comments that show people's prejudice, and, in any case, we somehow managed to believe that we weren't really in America, or that we got here by mistake. "I *did* apply for other visas…," my mother would say.

America, we believed, was somewhere else. It was in any direction going away from New York. There wasn't anything good to eat there. My mother had spent two years upstate before I was born and still complained that no one there ate garlic or onions and that the people didn't care about other places. They thought all foreign films were pornographic, the kids were ruder than we were, and they didn't even wash their sneakers. That was the North, but we could also forget about the South. One of the first news stories my mother heard when she arrived in the United States was about Emmet Till. We couldn't even think of traveling to a place where black boys got lynched for whistling at white ladies. If we went there, we'd end up in jail or something, I used to imagine.

Behind the walls of our home, walls that shielded us from that America, we made a world where people and things from all different kinds of places met. To us it seemed that someone was always just arriving from somewhere, which meant we had to celebrate. Maybe it was that immigrants and outsiders share certain experiences that tend to make socializing among themselves easier. Maybe it was that recently arrived relatives and friends would descend on us for weeks at a time, providing us with playmates. Visiting could last a day or several weeks, during which time our friends and cousins became our English pupils while we absorbed their nostalgia for a place we'd never seen. As kids, we might have believed that we were better because of our command of English, but people and things from far away attracted us.

The taste we had for the foreign had been cultivated long before we became immigrants. Cuban exiles in Miami embraced American consumerism in their violent rejection of *el comunismo,* but there was an older tradition, maintained by many, of always looking outward for culture—to France, preferably, but most places on "the continent" would do. We could go to school in America, if necessary, but to be truly worldly, we had to learn European ways. When, as a young adult, I returned from a semester's study in Paris, my aunt took out her finest china to serve me coffee and sweets. Eight months away and suddenly I was a specially honored guest. My newly acquired French impressed everyone much more than my English ever had. I didn't realize at the time that in their minds I had fulfilled an entirely *criollo* dream.

There was a moment when I thought that I had emptied the Spanish from my mind to make room for all the information I'd had to absorb as a college student.

Academic learning had seemed to demand so much effort that I underestimated how much knowledge I had soaked up without trying. I could act the part of a thoroughly assimilated American and block out all my other resources. If I put the two worlds I had lived between side by side in my mind, there were good reasons for my adolescent self to favor things American. The America I had grown to like seemed less strict to me; I saw in it fewer social rules, more physical freedom for the young, fewer constraints on me as a woman than Latin Catholics sought to impose. But such acts of psychic amputation would prove to have their price. I would be forced to pay by being subjected to an American view of my difference as irreducibly racial; the richness of the cultures I had been raised in would be lost or forever misunderstood. To this day I despise having people, especially those who claim some intelligence, ask me what I "really" feel that I am, or begin to question the authenticity of my claims on the basis of some eugenics equation. In the 1970s, that was always a losing proposition for me, since I didn't look oppressed enough for white liberals or black enough for cult nats. I just signaled confusion for most back then. I could not have predicted that the political and cultural shifts of the 1980s would thrust me into a world of hybrids and clashing signals that, with the passing of each year, was becoming more uncannily reminiscent of the one in which I had begun.

The *diálogo* between Cuban exiles and nationals that began in the late 1970s brought about the possibility of travel back to the island to be reunited with relatives for the first time in nearly twenty years. It also made already existent divisions within communities and family more visible. My aunt and cousins went back first. Then my mother. They came back loaded with stories. Years after my father's death, my mother's new curiosity about the country she'd left seemed to yank her out of mourning. In the middle of this came the Mariel boat lift that brought 125,000 Cubans to the Florida shores, and relatives we hadn't heard from in ages washed ashore. I was incredibly impressed by the young cousins of mine who arrived around that time. My brother took them to a Spielberg film, and they came back unfazed, commenting only that it was just a bunch of superficial special effects that had nothing to do with reality. *They* hadn't wasted their childhoods on pinball games and cheesy TV, I remember thinking.

While some Cubans were brought closer by the family unification initiatives that came out of the *diálogo*, leftist insurgency in Central America, coupled with the United States's military support to suppress it, put things Latin back into the American popular imagination. Solidarity movements drew hundreds of artists and intellectuals to Central America, as the Nicaraguan bourgeoisie went into exile, leaving their lavish homes to the *internacionalistas* and press corps. Meanwhile, the United States military actively sought out Latino boys to fight the Red Menace to the south. One of my brothers, Arturito, was among the casualties of 1984. According to the official reports, his motorboat hit a mine in Laguna de Brus, Honduras. No one could explain to us why he didn't have a radio. I heard from his platoon mates that he used to crack them up by reading my mother's letters aloud, imitating her accent, and that he would slip jugs of gasoline reserved for the Navy to the locals. He had visited my mother less than a month before his death, devastated by the nightmares he had witnessed. I remember finding a little drawing among his belongings that he had made of himself as an older man, with a boatman's cap, a tattooed arm, and a big cigar. Underneath he had written, cryptically, "hiding somewhere in Latin America in the year 2000." For months I would stare at newspaper and magazine pictures of crowds in Central America, as if I believed I might see him there.

Tragedies such as this were we could survive, but never forget. My somewhat innocent and abstract sense of politics was gone. The turbulent, violence-ridden world my family had fled from was banging on our door. It shook me to the bone to face my participation in the cynical game that used affirmative-action success stories as window dressing while turning the less fortunate into cannon fodder. The shock forced me out of a perplexed state brought on by too much theory too young. Grief can make you isolate yourself, or it can humble you. It made me more aware of how my life was bound up with those of others, subject to forces beyond my control.

Had I been another sort of person, I might have involved myself in some political cause or charitable endeavor. Long before, however, I had turned the pressure that was put on me to be cultured into an obsession with culture, and couldn't have shed it even if I had tried. I decided that I wanted to make sense out of the clashes between cultures that cause so many of us so much trouble and pain, but I chose to do so within the realm of art. I began with an interest in the radical possibilities of independent media to open our minds to distant or hidden realities, and wove my way through media-based art, performance, and other experimental forms that dramatize, in their production and reception, the process of cultures meeting, clashing, and mixing.

I ceded to the impulse to become the kind of cultural translator that life seemed to be preparing me for. As if guided by some inner compass, I set off in search of my tribe, and found it—in London, Havana, Brooklyn, San Francisco, Merida, Paris, San Antonio, Chicago, Berlin, Montreal, Miami, Santiago, Denver, Managua, Barcelona, San Juan, Mexico City, Toronto, and Porto Alegre, among other places. A friend in Chile named his clan the children of the Cold War, while one in Cuba called his the children of utopia, and then the children of William Tell. In el D.F., or Mexico City, they're the first generation of gringos born in Mexico, according to cultural critic Carlos Monsivais. I say we're caught between two worlds—at least two. That's *pura bicultura* for me. We didn't theorize postcoloniality after the fact, learn about it from a workshop, or wait for multiculturalism to become foundation lingo for "appreciating diversity"—we lived it and still struggle to make art about it.

The writings brought together in this volume are the traces of many of those journeys. They are also the result of tremendously enriching dialogues. Artists, I am glad to say, have taught me more about art, particularly about contemporary art, than any long-winded treatise or intricate theory. I am tremendously indebted to all the artists and writers who have shared their work with me over the years; some of my attempts to grasp what their work is about are in this book. I would like to extend special thanks to many friends who have opened doors, asked the right questions, and showed faith: John Akomfrah, Hilton Als, Josefina Alcázar, Candida Alvarez, Martina Attille, Cameron Bailey, Juan Pablo Ballester, Roger Bartra, Catherine Benamou, Dawoud Bey, Consuelo Castañeda, Magdalena Campos, Papo Colo, Ernesto de la Vega-Pujol, María Elena Escalona, Raul Ferrera-Balanquet, Nereida Garcia-Ferraz, Lina Gopaul, Ada Griffin, Jeanette Ingberman, Isaac Julien, Leandro Katz, Pervaiz Khan, Liz Kotz, Agustin Lao, Iñigo Manglano-Ovalle, Tracey Moffatt, Celeste Olalquiaga, Osvaldo Sanchez, Kim Sawchuk, Ella Shohat, Kendall Thomas, Nena Torres, and Michele Wallace.

I would also extend my thanks to those who have edited, and in some cases first commissioned, these and other texts: Jean Fisher, Kurt Hollander, Steve Gallagher, Martha Gever, Thelma Golden, Inverna Lockpez, Lynn Schwarzer, Elizabeth Sussman, David Trend, Brian Wallis, and Jeff Weinstein. My very special thanks I offer to Dawn Davis at The New Press for giving me the opportunity to bring these writings together and for her guidance at each step. I am also indebted to my friend and colleague, Carolyn Wendt, for her editorial assistance. Finally, I thank all the artists and photographers who graciously loaned me reproductions of their work for this volume.

To my partner and collaborator Guillermo Gómez-Peña, I owe indescribable thanks. My artistic and intellectual journeys of the past decade have been profoundly influenced by our joint endeavors; thus, this book includes a record of what we have created together, against all odds.

I dedicate this book to my family, with the greatest of hopes for the living, and in loving memory of the dead.

Los Angeles
August 1994

PART I

AT THE CROSSROADS
BETWEEN
NORTH AND SOUTH

EL DIARIO DE MIRANDA/
MIRANDA'S DIARY

AMERICANS OFTEN ASK ME WHY CUBANS, exiled or at home, are so passionate about Cuba, why our discussions are so polarized, and why our emotions are so raw after thirty-three years. My answer is that we are always fighting with the people we love the most. Our intensity is the result of the tremendous repression and forced separation that affects all people who are ethnically Cuban, wherever they reside. Official policies on both sides collude to make exchange practically impossible. Public debate is extremely limited in the United States and on the island. Only extreme positions get attention; any other stance is recast as what Cubans call "ideological diversionism," a pejorative way of characterizing those who stray from the official view of things. Travel is severely restricted by the United States and Cuban governments, making contact difficult and allowing exaggerated rumors to pass for truth. Communication, when it does happen, is often strained.

The main players in this game—the Cuban government, the Miami-based Cuban right, and the Cuban supporters in the United States—are all suspicious of Cuban border crossers: People who allow ethnic, kinship, and emotional ties to override ideological difference; people whose intellectual and political perspective is less nationalist and less invested in fictions of separate development. The Cuban government has no official policy vis-à-vis the liberal/progressive sectors of *la comunidad*, which allows the prejudices of individual bureaucrats to determine action and allows easy erasure of any real distinction between extremist anti-Castro terrorists and proponents of dialogue. The Cuban right wing uses its economic clout and political ties to the United States government to proclaim that it speaks for all Cubans. Pro-Cuba intellectuals of the international left, or *cubanólogos*, as some of us lovingly refer to them, can use the convenient stereotypes about Cubans outside Cuba—*gusanos*,

This essay first appeared in *The Subversive Imagination* and the *Michigan Quarterly Review* in 1994.

colonizados, and *fanáticos*—to maintain a paternalist attitude toward all exiles and Cuban Americans, reject all their criticism of the Cuban government, and justify not sharing power with them. None of these sectors has effectively dealt with the complexities of the situation. The Revolution and the Cold War created a separate nation, but never completely succeeded in dividing a people.

I am the daughter of a Cuban who emigrated to the United States in 1954 and who was deported in 1959, shortly after the triumph of the Revolution. My mother hid from the INS (Immigration and Naturalization Service) until after my birth. She then returned to the island with me. My United States citizenship enabled my mother to return to New York City within weeks, while the lines of Cubans seeking exit visas at the American Embassy in Havana grew and grew. In the decade that followed, my mother's sisters, brother, parents, nieces, and nephews all emigrated, and my home became a way station. At the age of eight, I was teaching English to my cousins and translating for older relatives; at school, I would hide this side of

Nena Torres, Horacio García Mendietá, and Fusco in Havana, 1990.
PHOTO COURTESY OF THE AUTHOR.

my life to downplay my difference from the rest of the children, and look embarrassed when adults asked me what I thought of Fidel Castro. Yet, as a child among foreigners, I grew accustomed to living with the presence of an imaginary country in my home; it spoke to me in another language, in stories, rhymes, and prayers; it smelled and tasted different from the world beyond the front door. Still, unlike other immigrants who could return and replenish their repertoire of cultural references, we could not. For many exiles, the real Cuba had died with the Revolution and would live on only in their minds.

The Cuban children of my generation didn't choose to leave or to stay—the wars that shaped our identities as Cuban or American are ones we inherited. There are those among us who have made quiet pilgrimages back to the island as a way of reconciling ourselves to the paradoxical familiarity and distance that mark our connections to our origins. That decision to reestablish contact with Cuba is often looked upon as an act of treason—we are traitors to the exile community's extremists and ungrateful to our parents, who saved us from the Caribbean "gulag." When I began to travel to Cuba in the early 1980s, I was naive enough to believe that I could slip past the watchful eye of *la comunidad*. I was soon forced to realize that my decision to return defined me in ways that went far beyond my power to determine my own life; it also opened the door to understanding myself as a child of diaspora, of the Cold War, of the Civil Rights movement, of the Black Caribbean, of Cuba, and of the United States.

None of this would have been possible were it not that Cuban culture didn't die with the Revolution, as the exiles would have had it. The neocolonial world of the middle and upper classes had simply diminished in importance, as different notions of the popular moved into the foreground. I went there ostensibly to confront Cuban culture in the present, but returning enabled me to face and come to know my counterparts, the children (now grown) who had also had no choice, but who had stayed in Cuba. Although history had intervened to separate us, we shared a healthy

"suitcase #4: Cuba," by Ernesto de la Vega-Pujol, 1994.
PHOTO BY OREN SLOR.

skepticism toward the nationalist rhetoric of our parents' generation and a growing curiosity about one another.

The following is a collection of my reflections on my experiences traveling to Cuba since 1985. I chose to write it in diary form because of the fleeting nature of those encounters with the island. I also wanted to stress the subjective dimension of those experiences, rather than "speak for Cuba," as I had done as a journalist to gain entry into the country. The account is not chronological—instead, I piece together memories of them all to find the logic that links disparate events. This way of thinking reminds me of conversations I have had late at night on the island: with so little information circulating officially, our favorite pastime was to drink coffee and chew over the details each member of the group provided to figure out what the government was up to.

I call my essay "Miranda's Diary" (referring to Prospero's daughter, Miranda, in Shakespeare's *The Tempest*) because of the host of allusions to *The Tempest* in Latin

American intellectual history and postcolonial thought. Shakespeare's drama, set on an island, is thought to have been inspired by accounts of voyages and shipwrecks during the early colonial period. Among the drama's many characters, the patriarchal magician Prospero, his indigenous slave Caliban, and his ethereal assistant Ariel have become, in nineteenth- and twentieth-century Latin American thought, symbols of colonial relations and of struggles to forge identity. In 1900, following the transfer of Cuba, Puerto Rico, and the Philippines to the United States as "protectorates," the Uruguayan writer José Enrique Rodó published "Ariel," an essay that depicts an allegorical conflict between two versions of modernity.[1] In it, the United States is a chaotic and materialistic Caliban whose influence threatens Latin America; Ariel is envisioned as a neoclassical, orderly, and ideal world.

In the postcolonial period, Latin American and Caribbean intellectuals began to recast this allegory, shifting their identification from Ariel to Caliban. In 1960, George Lamming championed Caliban's ability to reshape his master's language in "The Pleasures of Exile;" in 1969, Aimé Césaire wrote "A Tempest: An Adaptation of Shakespeare's *The Tempest* for a Black Theatre." Then, in 1971, the Cuban writer Roberto Fernandez Retamár published his "Caliban: Notes on a Discussion of Culture in Our America,"[2] transforming the slave into an admirable combination of defiant Carib and New World Man, and identifying him with the island, the Revolution, and even Fidel.

These writers concentrate little attention on Miranda, *The Tempest's* only significant female character. They only take note of Caliban's attempt to seduce her shortly after she arrives on the island with Prospero. Psychoanalytic theorists Octave Mannoni and Frantz Fanon underscore the implications of this; in *Prospero and Caliban: The Psychology of Colonization,*[3] Mannoni coined the term "Prospero complex" to describe the psychology of the colonial patriarch whose racism is manifested in his obsessive fear that his daughter's virginity is threatened, especially by the hypersexualized New World Man.

Miranda's name literally means "wonder." In Shakespeare's play she is a young woman whose arrival to the island marks the beginning of a process of self-discovery. In the opening scenes of the drama, Prospero reveals to her the secret of her birth, and she confesses to having already been haunted by the memory of belonging to another family. Her initial attitude toward the island is one of compassion and curiosity, and it is actually she who teaches Caliban the language of the master. Her relationship with Caliban is immediately sexualized, which provides the pretext for Prospero's intervention to save her "purity," resulting in her redirected attention to a more "appropriate" form of courtship. It would seem, then, that the knowledge Miranda gains in her symbolic loss of a father figure is too dangerous for her to have—it makes her too independent, or too vulnerable, depending on whose perspective one takes. It was traveling to another place that allowed the original Miranda to understand her identity as different from the fiction that had been propagated by her symbolic father. The Mirandas of the present, myself among them, continue to undertake these journeys, straying far from the fictions of identity imparted to us by our symbolic fathers. What was once a potential sexual threat is now a matter of political transgression. As the Cold War, that modern-day tempest, subsides, it seems logical that Miranda's story would emerge.

NOVEMBER 1991: While hundreds of international visitors flock to Havana to attend the country's fourth art biennial, the passports of two art professionals waiting for visas to attend the event sit on desks at the Cuban embassy in Mexico City and the Cuban Interests Section in Washington, D.C. Despite frequent phone calls, faxes, and letters, no official move is ever made to accept or deny these visa requests. The biennial passes and neither of them is able to attend.

JANUARY 1988: After weeks of waiting, I receive the news that two Cuban artists whom I have invited to New York City for the opening of a group exhibition in which they are participating will not be able to attend because they do not have visas to enter the United States. U.S.-based Cuba supporters urge me to lodge a formal complaint against the U.S. State Department.

DECEMBER 1990: I am walking down the street with a relative of mine whom I've just met in a provincial city in southeastern Cuba. I have a new electrical fan in my hand that I have just bought from a *diplo-tienda,* a hard-currency store for foreigners. My relative looks uneasy. Outside Havana, that fan is like a red flag. "What will I say if I get stopped with you?" he asks.

"Tell them I'm your cousin," I say.

"No," he says. "Then they'll know that the fan is for me."

"OK, tell them I'm a journalist and that I asked you for information about music."

"No good," he says. "They'll say I should have taken you to talk to my professors. Look," he finally says, "if I walk away at any point, just meet me in a half hour in the main plaza, OK?"

No one in Havana has ever expressed such worries about being seen in public with me or about owning appliances from the *diplo-tienda.*

JANUARY 1986: My first radio program about Cuban film airs on a community radio station in New York. The next day, my mother receives a phone call from a Cuban colleague who tells her that I should try living in a Cuban prison for a while before talking "communist propaganda" on the radio.

JULY 1991: I receive a letter from a friend telling me that an article I published in *The Nation,* in which I criticized an exhibit of art from Cuba in the United States for occluding the current complexities and political tensions in the art world there, has caused quite a stir in Havana. According to the letter, a faculty member at the Higher Institute of Art was brought in to make an official translation for Wifredo Lam Center director Llilian Llanes and members of the Party leadership.

NOVEMBER 1987: I stop in Miami to see old family friends before traveling to Havana. The father of the family, a Cuban exile, takes me outside to tell me that it's a bad idea to go to Cuba. He says I will be kidnapped by the secret police and forced to be a prostitute for visiting Russians. His oldest daughter asks me to visit their old house and take pictures. She says she'd like to go with me, but can't because she might get fired from her job for doing so.

NOVEMBER 1991: One of the professionals whose visa was held up is Nina Menocal, a Cuban-born Mexican resident who owns and manages Ninart, a gallery promoting Cuban art in Mexico City. For exhibiting and selling the artwork of Cuban nationals, she has incurred the ire of sectors within the Cuban cultural ministry (for not splitting the profits with the Cuban government) and the Miami-based Cuban right (for allegedly aiding the island "regime" by supporting the artists). The other person whose entry to Cuba was effectively blocked is me, a Cuban American writer and media artist who has spent at least one month a year there since 1984.

JANUARY 1992: Sufficient confusion was created by conflicting reports that manage to obfuscate the deep-rooted reasons for my visa problem. Cuban artists who ask about me during the event receive blank stares from the biennial organizers. A biennial committee member who inquired on my behalf was told definitively by Llilian Llanes that "there simply were no more visas to give out." A Cuban American political scientist who sought information about my case in Havana received the explanation from a local specialist on Cuban relations with the exile community that my request was trapped in a temporary visa war with the United States, in which Cuba stopped giving press visas because the United States had denied entry to two Cuban journalists.

This does not explain why Nina Menocal's visa never arrived. When she questions Luis Camnitzer, a U.S.-based Uruguayan artist and critic who had a solo exhibition at the 1991 biennial and has served as adviser to two previous ones, he tells her that it was logical that our visas would be denied since we "both have problems with Cuba." This response expresses a familiar double standard: The same leftists who defend Cubans' right to enter the United States often find many reasons to justify the exclusion from the island of those deemed undesirable to Cuba. None of the Americans who attends the biennial makes any public statement of dissatisfaction over our having been denied entry.

NOVEMBER 1991: In Mexico City, the first exhibition of art by Cuban nationals and exiles to take place since 1959 opened in mid-November at Ninart, entitled *15 Cuban Painters*. All the Cuban nationals in the exhibition have established temporary residence in Mexico, while the exiles were from the United States. On the island, there were no Cuban American participants in the biennial exhibition, although there were some other diasporic and ethnic minority populations included, such as Chicanos and Canadian artists of color. U.S. art historian Shifra Goldman delivers a paper that touches on work by Cuban exiles and her mention of Cubans outside the island is met with favorable response. Several cultural ministry officials publicly express regret to biennial visitors that an initiative such as Nina Menocal's to join nationals and exiles in one exhibit had not been organized by Cuba.

DECEMBER 1991: In Miami, the Cuban exiles who participated in the Ninart exhibition are criticized for aiding the "Castro regime" through their collaboration. One of them had already been counseled by his U.S. gallery representative that such activities would lower his prices. On the other side, the Cuban government sends the Vice Minister of Culture to Mexico to proclaim that the show is a "Miami plot" to compromise the young Cuban nationals politically.

In Mexico City, dozens of Cuban artists tighten their belts and enjoy the pleasure of painting to pay the rent. Those in Spain, France, and Germany get a taste of racism from the new xenophobic European Community, a confusing experience for those Cubans who are, at least visibly, white. They are living what artist Arturo Cuenca calls "low-intensity exile," living abroad without defecting.

Several Cuban cultural ministry officials announce their intentions to visit Mexico City to interview Cuban artists and determine how these artists can contribute (financially) to the Revolution from abroad.

DECEMBER 1990: A meeting takes place in Havana between UNEAC (Unión Nacional de Artistas y Escritores Cubanos) officials, U.S.-based foundation representatives, and visiting Cuban Americans. The Cuban Americans insist that dialogue and cultural exchange between the two sides be resumed with official blessings. They are effectively stonewalled. A foundation representative who approaches Llanes to suggest that a Cuban American component to the 1991 biennial might be eligible for financial support is politely rebuffed.

JANUARY 1992: One month after the biennial, a rally takes place in New York City to support ending the U.S. blockade against Cuba. The several thousand people who pack Nassau Coliseum are joined by several thousand more who form a counter-demonstration led by Cuban right-wing leader Jorge Más Canosa. The morning of the rally, my mother receives a phone call from a Más Canosa supporter threatening that if I show my face at the rally I will be severely beaten. I had just published an article in the *Village Voice* about Ninart's show in Mexico City last November.

AUGUST 1991: At the Festival Latino opening in New York City, a crowd of anti-Castro protesters who are frustrated because they can't find Gabriel García Márquez, known to be a friend of Fidel's, hurl curses at me as I enter the theater. "*¡Coco Fusco! ¡Puta! ¡Traidora!*" they yell, then push toward me and physically attack the two male friends who try to protect me. The police intervene to break up the struggle.

AUGUST 1989: I arrive in Brasilia on a U.S. Information Agency-sponsored lecture tour and am taken to the home of the U.S. cultural attaché, where I am questioned for over an hour in an intrusive manner about my trips to Cuba, my activities there, and my relatives on the island. My head is pounding from trying to resist his questions. He tells me with a smirk at the end of our discussion that he is going back to the States to run Tele-Martí, the anti-Castro television station based in Key West.

A few days later, his Brazilian assistant lets me know that my FBI file was scrutinized carefully by the embassy because, according to him, I was labeled "sympathetic to leftist movements" and "travels to Cuba."

DECEMBER 1986: After working as a coproducer of a documentary shot during the 1986 biennial, I am brought to the office of Wifredo Lam Center director Llilian Llanes, where she and her assistant, Jorge Ayala, question me for two hours about the material that was shot. They demand copies of all rushes, which I do not provide.

NOVEMBER 1987: During a phone conversation between myself and a U.S.-based Cuba supporter, he criticizes the video documentary for depicting Havana as run-down and unattractive. I explain to him that the permission to shoot outside was granted only two days before our departure, limiting our ability to capture the variety of the city's landscape. "Oh," he says, "I didn't know you needed permission to film outside." This person has been an official guest of the Cuban cultural ministry several times and is writing a book about contemporary Cuban culture.

DECEMBER 1987: At the Havana Film Festival, the second screening of my documentary is mysteriously canceled at the last minute. During a screening of a rough cut several months earlier, several Cuban artists defended the piece in a closed meeting with officials from the cultural ministry and the Wifredo Lam Center. A Cuban friend who accompanies me to the airport is questioned by police after I leave.

MARCH 1988: The video master of the documentary sits locked in a secret vault in Budapest, Hungary, where it was edited. A letter was sent from Cuban officials to the Hungarian Minister of Culture, denouncing the material and demanding that it be confiscated as a gesture of socialist solidarity. We succeed in bribing someone to remove it from the vault and having it sent to the United States, where it is sold to public television.

FEBRUARY 1992: A recently emigrated Cuban artist is yelling at me on the phone in disagreement over the article I have written for the *Village Voice* about the Cuban artists in Mexico. "You weren't critical enough," he says.

"I can't write based on speculation," I retort. "I have to respect people's right to represent themselves how they choose."

"Of course people don't really tell you how bad things are," he screams. "They think you're from the CIA, no matter what they tell you to your face."

APRIL 1989: A *marielito* completing graduate work in the Midwest comes to see me at my office. As soon as I shut the door, he begins to speak to me with tears in his eyes. "I saw your work, and I know you can go to Cuba," he says. "I want to go home. I made a mistake. I can't stand not being able to be in my country. Can you help me?"

MARCH 1993: Two Cuban American colleagues call me from Miami, where they have been waiting for four months for entry visas to go to Havana. "The head of the Interests Section called early this morning," says one of them. "He told me there was another delay, but not to worry, because that doesn't mean I'm being rejected. Who is he kidding?" We laugh uncomfortably.

APRIL 1991: One of the artists I invited to the U.S. in 1988 who was not able to enter is now living in Miami. He learned before processing his visa that his first request three years ago was never completed in Cuba, although the cultural ministry had told him at the time that his visa had been denied by the U.S. State Department.

JUNE 1992: I've waited a good six months to write anything about Cuba since my visa to travel was denied. I think I was afraid of becoming a knee-jerk "counter-revolutionary," or at least feared that people might see me that way if I complained. Putting my own dilemma into a broader context becomes my way of depersonalizing a rather painful experience of rejection.

Global politics have changed since the fall of the Berlin Wall, and Cuba's future is uncertain. Cultural debates on postcolonialism and about the relationship between other U.S.-based Latinos and the populations and cultures of their homelands have matured significantly in the last decade. These factors, together with the new migration of 1980s-generation artists and intellectuals and the existence of a postexile generation of moderate Cuban-Americans, contribute to conditions that demand a paradigm shift in the way we think about Cuban culture, Cuban cultural identity, and "revolutionary" cultural activity. We must rethink our priorities and define alliances on the basis not of territory but of shared interests. Nationality has been a Cold War game. Identity, for Cubans, goes far beyond it.

Cuba still operates in the American imagination as the last great mythic terrain of the Cold War. U.S. efforts to isolate Cuba have stepped up and are conveniently justified by "evidence" of intensified repression on the island: the execution of Arnaldo Ochoa, the quarantining of people with AIDS and those diagnosed as HIV-positive, the frequent use of physical violence by police against protestors, the arrest of human rights activists, and most recently the execution of Cuban exile infiltrators and the United Nations declaration that put Cuba on the human rights violators list. On the other hand, the U.S. government's sabotage efforts are continuously frustrated by Cuba's maintenance of a higher standard of living than most of her neighbors, despite crippling food and energy shortages; the island's growing tourist and bioengineering industries; the commercial and critical successes of several Cuban artists and entertainers who have not defected; and Fidel Castro's uncanny ability to maintain international media popularity, even as communism goes out of fashion.

In such a politically charged context, art making for Cubans in Cuba is like walking in a mined desert. Supplies are hard to come by. Anything that might spark unrest or a public manifestation of discontent is considered dangerous. The economic and political factors mentioned above have led to the silent exodus of many of Cuba's best and brightest artists and intellectuals. Over sixty visual artists and writers are in temporary residence in Mexico; among them are José Bedia, Osvaldo Sanchez, Consuelo Castañeda, Glexis Novoa, Ruben Torres Llorca, Leandro Soto, and Alejandro Aguilera. María Magdalena Campos-Pons, Arturo Cuenca, Dania del Sol, Tomás Esson, Florencio Gelabert Soto, Carlos Rodriguez Cardenas, Ana Albertina

Delgado, and Armando Correa are among those who have recently moved to the United States. More are scattered throughout Spain, France, Belgium, and Germany; among them are Ricardo Rodriguez Brey, Flavio Garciandia, Humberto Castro, Ivan de la Nuez, Gustavo Acosta, and Juan Pablo Ballester. The majority of them have opted out of the Havana vs. Miami conflict and look instead for neutral territory to wait out the last gasp of the Cold War.

In the 1980s, a growing number of younger Cuban Americans expressed interest in open engagement with Cuban nationals. Many of them are post-*diálogo*, post–Antonio Maceo Brigade types, who are less interested in the Revolution and more concerned with multicultural activism, cultural identity, Santería, Caribbean culture, contemporary Cuban art and cinema, etc. Some of them organize activities to bring

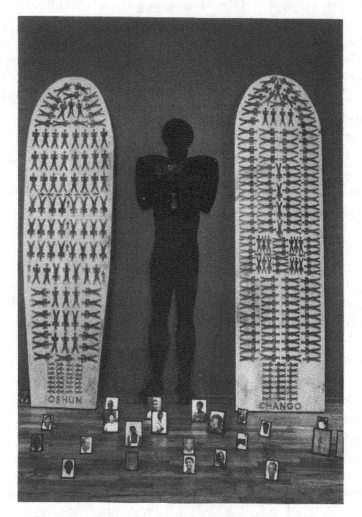

Installation detail of "The Seven Powers Come by the Sea,"
by Maria Magdalena Campos-Pons, 1993.
PHOTO COURTESY OF INTAR GALLERY.

Cubans to the United States or to help support them during their visits here. Some visit Cuba and begin collaborations with Cuban artists and writers. Most of their activity goes on through unofficial channels, although official bureaucratic demands must occasionally be met to justify travel and stay out of trouble. Some, like Nereida García-Ferraz and Raul Ferrera Balanquet, have developed an entire body of work around their status as displaced Cubans. Others, such as Ricardo Zulueta, Ana María Simo, Carmelita Tropicana, Felix Gonzalez-Torres, and Eduardo Aparicio, might refer to Cuba in their work and maintain varying degrees of political "neutrality" with respect to the revolutionary government, but they are also engaged with lesbian and gay politics and culture in the United States. Still others, like César Trasobares, Felix Gonzalez-Torres, and Luis Cruz Azaceta, have stuck their necks out and broken taboos by exhibiting with Cuban nationals.

Not only have attitudes toward Cuban nationals begun to change, but the exile community itself has evolved to the extent that monolithic descriptive models simply do not work anymore. A class and cultural divide becomes increasingly apparent in Miami. Most of the most recent immigrants from Cuba (Mariel and its aftermath) to Miami are not accepted by the Cuban aristocracy. Like the Cuban American second generation intellectuals and artists, many are more politically moderate. Many are lesbian and gay and are out. Many are not white. Together with the first and second generation moderates who reside for the most part outside Miami, they make up an informal support network for visiting Cubans and information exchange with the island. They assist in obtaining visas, provide housing and extra money for visitors, take mail and medicine to and from Cuba, organize receptions, assist the recently arrived in finding employment, etc. The most famous story about this network comes from the Tropicana Nightclub's visit to New York, when the same *marielitos* who picketed the entertainers from "Castro's Cuba" would run around to the dressing rooms to greet old friends and bring them *pastelitos*.

JUNE 1992: At a party in New York City, Carmelita Tropicana laments that her work is not well received by the Cuban upper crust in Miami. "They tell me I must be Puerto Rican," she says, "because they don't think that Cubans could be into kitsch."

JUNE 1992: Over the last six months, I have made dozens of lists in my mind of the conditions for rapprochement between two sides of a divided population. Culture is at the center of this issue, since it is precisely that which has bound a people otherwise split by geography and ideology. Art is also a symbol of Cuban people's creative possibilities, a barometer of "freedom," that ideologically charged word.

For three decades, two forms of "liberty" stood at odds: On the one hand, the opportunity to have access to free art education and a state infrastructure that allows an artist to carry out his or her métier—with occasional strings attached; on the other, the unlimited availability of an art market open to those who can afford to educate and produce artwork with practically no hope of subsidy. Cultural politics on both sides determined the value of the art produced. Until recently, the differences were easy to define: If you were in Cuba and made art about identity and popular culture, it was very likely to be supported and receive critical attention, and if you made nonfigurative art that was also fine, but it might not benefit from the Euro-American interest in Third World exoticism. If you were in Miami and made nonfigurative or surrealist work, you might sell to the local market, but you would not receive a tremendous amount of critical attention. If cultural or sexual politics entered into your work, you would probably have to move to another part of the country, where you would be likely to receive some degree of support—but not from Cubans. Now there are Cubans making art about the island from a variety of political perspectives and locales. Some travel with Cuban passports, others with American or European ones. The majority do not live on the island. Who can say whose art is more or less Cuban?

DECEMBER 1992: I visit Nina Menocal at her gallery in Mexico. She is making preparations to take a group of "her" Cuban artists to the Art Miami fair in January. She is extremely worried because she has been receiving calls from Miami warning her that someone is going to give her an unpleasant surprise.

JANUARY 1992 – MARCH 1993: I have reviewed several articles and catalogue essays by the newly migrated young Cubans. These are the same people who put spirit and intellectual rigor into their arguments against reductive nationalism in the conceptualization of Cuban identity, who posited a cultural politics of "appropriation" based on Cuban cultural history, and who explained the role of popular culture and ritual in the reclaiming of public space for personal expression in the 1980s. New arguments emerge: If these Cubans could make whatever they appropriated Cuban by virtue of that act, then they can also take their culture to another place. Cuban culture throughout history, they argue, has been influenced by contact with other countries; Wifredo Lam, Alejo Carpentier, Amelia Pelaez, Raul Martinez, José Martí—even Fidel—spent time abroad. Dámaso Perez Prado created an entire genre of Cuban music—in Mexico.

A new chapter in the theorization of exile.

JULY 1992: I'm in Mexico City, having lunch with a Cuban art critic now living there. "It's one thing to talk about broadening notions of identity on the island," I tell him. "It's quite another to redefine exile when there are at least three decades of exile culture preceding you."

"We're just beginning," he says.

"That's fine," I say, "but you might want to consider getting to know all the other Cuban artists out here if you're going to continue using national paradigms to define the work you're talking about." I have this feeling he's not really listening to me.

DECEMBER 1990: I'm sitting in a conference room at UNEAC in a meeting with Cubans, Cuban Americans, and U.S. foundation representatives. UNEAC president Abel Prieto starts off by suggesting "that the Cubans introduce themselves." He means the islanders. Raul Ferrera-Balanquet, a *marielito* exile and video artist, immediately interjects that Prieto's suggestion only enforces polarization and that he

(Raul) considers himself Cuban too. Cuban American Roly Chang concurs. Prieto clears his throat and begins discoursing on the "inauthenticity" of Oscar Hijuelo's novel, *The Mambo Kings Play Songs of Love.*

JANUARY 1993: I meet up with a Cuban painter friend who has lived in Chicago since she was a teenager. She has just come back from the Art Miami fair. "I saw all our friends from *la colonia cubana de México*," she said. "I couldn't help noticing their surprise at the fact that my work was selling like mad. I think they respect me a little more now."

JUNE 1992: Is there any difference, I wonder, between the fights Cubans and Cuban Americans have and the ones Chicanos and Puerto Ricans have with their homeland-based populations? Because of the upper- and middle-class composition of the mass Cuban migration of the 1960s, and because of the ideological tone of the derogatory terms for exiles, the homeland's image of the immigrant community has a different gloss on it. The problem, however, is fundamentally the same. It's real identity versus fake identity, original versus copy, upper class versus working class, good Spanish versus bad Spanish.

The 1980s generation in Cuba made enormous contributions to politicizing debates on appropriation and postmodernism, and created an internal critique of the iconography and rhetoric of the Cuban Revolution that had been entrenched since the 1960s. There are, however, several aspects of progressive cultural politics that developed in other parts of the Americas during this same period that Cuban artists have not participated in and toward which they still display suspicion. I am thinking here of critical social and political movements in North America in which culture has played an enormous role: black cultural politics, the Chicano movement, multiculturalism, feminism, lesbian and gay liberation, and AIDS activism. From the point of view of leftist traditions within Latin America, with their deeply ingrained universalist rhetoric and patriarchal and authoritarian tendencies, these movements could easily be dismissed as sectarian and inconsequential. But underneath the frequent rejection of these politics is an old-school brand of Marxism rearing its head. That and some old-style *machista* and Catholic resistance to taking radicalism into the privacy of the bedroom.

Cuban artists for whom the celebration of cultural identity was experienced as official policy of the State, and for whom radicalism could be measured in terms of one's distance from official policy, tend to look upon the identity politics of the new New Left with skepticism, if not disdain. Multiculturalism more often than not spells manipulation of art for political ends to them. While their evaluations of mainstream institutional paternalism and exoticizing attitudes toward marginal cultures are often prescient, they have difficulty acknowledging the grass-roots dimension of efforts toward cultural pluralism in the North and do not recognize the advantages of an alliance based on a shared interest in cultural democracy.

MAY 1992: A Cuban artist in Spain shows me a letter from another Cuban artist who is living in Europe: "It's incredible," writes the artist, "that when I am in Cuba, the Europeans who visit us love my work because it's made on the island, '*dentro de la revolución*,' even if the materials are lousy. Nobody's interested in what I make as a Cuban in Europe."

DECEMBER 1993: A longtime U.S. Cuba supporter calls me, and I share with her the news that another Cuban artist has won a Guggenheim fellowship. "We're in a very difficult situation with these artists," she says. "There are a couple of us who are very angry, because some of these artists are asking us for letters of support and then they're defecting. Now, I still support Cuba's right to exist…"

I listen quietly. I've learned to say nothing.

MARCH 1993: UNEAC continues to send messages expressing their interest in organizing cultural exchange between Cubans and Cuban Americans. And yet not even Abel Prieto, who in addition to being the president of UNEAC is a member of the Central Committee of the Cuban Communist Party, seems to be able to guarantee a visa. There will be those on both sides who will not see this dialogue as a priority or who find any kind of politicized cultural gesture suspicious. It would be naive to think that after over three decades of psychological warfare, everyone would just jump at the opportunity to convene with the enemy; and it would also be naive to think that a little individualism on the part of the artists might not be a necessary antidote to an overdose of revolutionary sacrifice. Many artists are startlingly candid about their objectives. Some want the comfort that money brings, not just the honor that critical acclaim offers; others want peace and distance.

MAY 1993: I'm in Cologne to give a lecture and unexpectedly run into a Cuban artist who is opening a show there that same evening and then driving back to his home in Belgium, where he has lived for three years. Over coffee, we swap stories and I watch his eyes widen as I list all the peers of his who have ended up in Miami. He confesses that he's glad to be far away from it all. "I saw it coming, and I knew it was time to go. You know what that means, Coco, because you saw us when we were living that utopian moment. At least growing up amidst underdevelopment teaches you how to survive. You'll see how we all manage."

JULY 1992: I receive news from Mexico; the Museo del Chopo is planning an exhibition of Cuban artists. The curators, one Cuban and one Mexican, intended to include works by Tomás Esson, Florencio Gelabert Soto, Arturo Cuenca, and Dania del Sol, four recent defectors to the United States. They receive word from the Foundation for Cultural Goods (the marketing arm of the Ministry of Culture) that all works promised from Cuba will be pulled from the exhibition if the defectors participate.

In mid-June, the Club Ateneo de Fotografía in Mexico sponsored an exhibit entitled *150 Years of Cuban Photography*, to be donated to the University of Guadalajara. In the show was a piece by Arturo Cuenca. Just before the opening, Nina Menocal was informed by the club president, Jesus Montalvo, that Cuba had threatened to withdraw the entire exhibit if Cuenca's work was included. Cuenca's photo was promptly returned to Ninart.

AUGUST 1992: I receive word from *Third Text* in England that they cannot publish this piece as I have written it. The editors send me a fax stating that all the names must be removed, and that all personal information about my experiences in Cuba must also be excised. I argue by fax for weeks and succeed only in getting them to add a line explaining that Nina Menocal and I were both denied visas to attend the 1991 biennial. I have also sent this piece (in an earlier form) to *La Jornada Semanal* in Mexico, where it is published with no significant editorial changes.

"Soy balsero y trabajo por comida. Ayúdame."

Yo llegué aquí el 14 de noviembre. Un hombre ahí me dijo que eso era un mal ejemplo para los cubanos porque yo estaba pidiendo trabajo por comida. Yo le dije que yo no sé hacer otra cosa. Yo no sé robar. No sé quitarle la cartera a una vieja. No ssé vender drogas. En Cuba yo trabajaba en abono químico. Soy de Regla y no tengo familia. Allá yo no podía vivir porque el régimen está muy malo.

"I am a boat person and I work for food. Help me."

I got here on the 14th of November. A man told me that I was giving Cubans a bad name because I was asking for food in exchange for work. I told him I didn't know how to do anything else. I don't know how to rob. I don't know how to steal an old woman's handbag. I don't know how to sell drugs. In Cuba, I worked in the chemical fertilizer industry. I'm from Regla and I don't have any relatives. I couldn't live there because the regime is very bad.

Julio Ramírez Marques
Desempleado (Unemployed), Miami, Florida, 1993

"Julio Ramirez Marques," from the *Fragments from Cuban Narratives* series by Eduardo Aparicio, 1993.

MARCH 1993: "There's a guy visiting from the island whom you have to meet," says a Cuban artist living in Massachusetts. We're sitting down to dinner and in walks a man who looks no more than twenty-five. He entertains us throughout the meal with stories about the new tourist complexes in Varadero Beach. The Fondo de Bienes Culturales has installed a gallery/boutique in every hotel, where tourists can buy Cuban art with U.S. dollars. Fondo representatives with budding entrepreneurial leanings (like himself) could seek out and contract local artists for exclusive representation at one store or another. "I've got five new artists from Matanzas who'll do anything on order," he announces proudly. I ask him how he thinks that these marketing strategies will affect creative output, but he avoids my question. "And if you come down, I can also make arrangements for you to have a driver and maybe take you to a real *toque de santo*. Here's my card."

FEBRUARY 1993: I'm sitting in the living room of a New York City apartment sublet to a Cuban artist for the duration of his Guggenheim fellowship. "What I saw in Miami was so depressing I can hardly talk about it," he says. "The *chusmeria* that we wanted to get away from—the paranoia, the accusations—it's all been brought over to Miami. Everybody's accusing the next guy of being an '*infilitrado*' just to damage them professionally."

APRIL 1993: An American woman comes up to me at a Cuban artist's opening in SoHo. "Coco Fusco? I wrote to you last fall to tell you about the Cuban artist (she gives his name) who's in New York, and you never answered." I apologize awkwardly, but am wondering who this artist is. "Well," she says, "here he is."

A young man steps forward with a broad smile, offers me his hand, and then gives me a business card. The woman hands me a photo album and asks me to look at pictures of his work. Under duress, I flip through and see baskets. Glancing at his card, I notice that he gives folkloric dance classes. We chat for a moment. "Did you study at the Art Institute?" I ask.

"Well, no, actually, I didn't," he admits without missing a beat. "In Cuba, I used to be an engineer."

MAY 1993: At the Barcelona apartment of two young Cubans who have been in Spain for over a year on mysterious scholarships, a group of us sit on the floor, eating pizzas, drinking wine, smoking cigarettes, and arguing. We take photos and make jokes about which archives they'll end up in. At one point, one of the women turns to me and says, "Ay, Coco, I remember when you used to come to Havana. Whenever people from outside would arrive, we would look at them and notice how pretty they looked. When they would say they were going to Paris or Rio next, I would think, Oh, what nice lives they have. Now I just came back from Paris, where I spent a month washing dishes. We're even thinking about running a Cuban food stand on the weekends to make money. I didn't know what things were like out here."

JUNE 1993: I'm standing in the ground floor passageway of the Museum of Modern Art in New York City, at the opening of *Latin American Artists of the 20th*

Century. There are Cuban artists and art lovers of all kinds all around me, ranging from American-raised YUCAs (Young, Urban Cuban Americans) to about-to defectors. We're laughing and hugging, and everything feels very euphoric. Cuban Americans I've never seen or heard of before come up to me and tell me that they're writing articles about Cuban art or opening galleries to show it. *The Miami Herald*, a friend whispers, is still trying to foment discord by attempting to pit José Bedia and Luis Cruz Azaceta, the two living Cuban artists in the exhibition, against each other. Ironically, the Cuban government's undisputed "art star" and one of the exile community's finest painters are represented by the same New York gallery. Their sales are booming and they make a point of being photographed together.

I can't help but notice that Llilian Llanes is standing at the other side of the passageway, staring at us all, but unwilling to join our little party. Strange, I think. She's jumped on the bandwagon and is now pushing for an encyclopedic *Cuban Art: Inside and Out* exhibition, for which the preliminary proposal has just been mailed to me by friends on the West Coast. But the sight of us mingling is still shocking enough to keep her at a distance.

This story continues. As Cuba's uncertain future unfolds, Cubans everywhere continue to argue over which direction things will take. In the post–Cold War era, the U.S. press is approaching the Cuba question from every possible angle, singling out potential converts to capitalism among young Party officials, casting an occasionally skeptical glance at Más Canosa while giving space to views of moderate dissenters and chiseling away at views that cast the exile community as monolithic. As usual, however, the politicians on both sides still lag behind, evincing unfailing rigidity. Complain, joke, or speculate as we may, the Cuban American National Foundation, on the one hand, and Fidel and the Central Committee on the other, still call the shots. The blockade has been tightened since the end of the Cold War, not loosened. In addition, the Mexican government has grown tired of providing a safe haven for Cubans in limbo; wanting neither an immigration nor a diplomatic crisis, it has curtailed entry by Cubans into Mexico, prompting many more to flee to Miami.

That a generational split distinguishes political and cultural sensibilities inside and outside Cuba is now undisputable; those involved in culture are not waiting for political change to happen first. Many of the older, more established exiled intellectuals have either passed away or taken a backseat in cultural debates, ceding somewhat to the vitality of the heterogeneity of perspectives brought by successive immigrations of younger Cubans to the United States. What isn't always as clearly recognized, however, is just how instrumental the voices of those marginalized by the official discourse of both sides have been in keeping doors open all along.

Among those who have consistently attempted to lessen the polarizations that have reified those discourses, many have been women. On *la comunidad* side, women such as Lourdes Casals, Dolores Prida, Ana María García, María Torres, and Nereida García-Ferraz were key in establishing the Antonio Maceo Brigade and in initiating the *Diálogo* that resulted in family reunification. Ana Mendieta broke ground by reestablishing links between artistic communities. Nina Menocal was the first to exhibit artists from both sides. The cubanía evoked by Cristina García in her novel *Dreaming in Cuban* floats effortlessly across borders, as family members separated by geography, politics, and even death communicate with one another.

This is not to say that all Cuban women dissent from official points of view on Cuba. However, given that the areas that kept Cubans bound *despite* politics are primarily those of family and culture, and that women have traditionally been ascribed the role of their keepers, it doesn't surprise me that women would take the lead in these areas or that they would cast a skeptical eye toward a political sphere that excluded them before the Revolution, as well as outside the island. Furthermore, while official channels of communication remain blocked or clogged by empty rhetoric, the kinds of exchange that have gone on across borders take forms usually associated with feminine discursive practices: home gatherings, letters, gossip, and other intimate forms of conversation. Long before Radio Martí transmitted news from abroad, *Radio Bemba* (word of mouth) was known to be the best source of information from within.

As more and more Cubans of all persuasions settle in Miami, the culture and the politics of exile will continue to change dramatically. As they do, where will the Mirandas go? Just yesterday, I bought a ticket to Miami to visit artists who have just defected—people who eight years ago could barely tolerate the sight of a foreigner. "We're reliving our childhood by watching them arrive," a friend told me a few months ago. Another Miranda from the Midwest recently rented a pied-à-terre in La Fla, as we now call it, to be in the middle of it all. South Beach is beginning to feel like *la Habana Vieja*, complete with *jineteros* who peddle stolen goods at cut-rate prices right at your doorstep. Sometimes I jokingly tell friends that Cuba will end up in Miami and Miami in Cuba. At the rate we're going, it could very easily happen.

PAN-AMERICAN POSTNATIONALISM: ANOTHER WORLD ORDER

I N CUBA, WHERE the black people in my family spent a couple of centuries before coming to the United States, there is a popular refrain from the Abakua religion: "*Chivo que rompe tambor, con su pellejo paga,*" which literally translates as "the goat who breaks the drum will have to pay with his skin." But it can also mean that the troublemaker turns him- or herself into the instrument so that the music can go on. I keep thinking about that refrain as I listen to how and why black vernacular cultures have so many explanations for the critical positions black people adopt within identity and community. Black popular cultures, especially musical cultures, have generated an abundance of archetypes that embrace dissonance and contend with internal differences, these I take to be semantic residues of histories of contradiction and conflict. Maybe one of these days our intellectual debates will catch up with our popular cultural ability to engage with dissent, without the defensiveness that continuously rears its head in other spheres.

In the course of this conference ["*Black Popular Culture,*" DIA Foundation, New York City, December 1991], it has become increasingly apparent to me that "doing the right thing" could easily have been the title of the entire event. Postnationalism, essentialism, and black cultural criticism, rather than simply being the topics of this panel, are, in actuality, the terms that have been defined and redefined throughout the last three days of discussion. Clearly, all of us who have engaged in the racial and cultural "wars of position" have unsavory recollections of the punitive injunctions against artists and intellectuals (especially feminists, lesbians, and gay men) who have "done the wrong thing." The notions of identity, culture, and community invoked by such gestures can feel like a burden, if not a muzzle. Yet, our continued engagement with these ideas would indicate that we are not ready to give them up—for such divestment still appears too similar to the racial violence that has robbed black peoples

This essay first appeared in *Black Popular Culture* in 1992.

of the right, first to be considered human beings, and then to have access to political power. For black peoples, at this historical moment, the postmodern fetishizing of the exchange of cultural property seems less like emancipation and more like intensified alienation.

In this country, the black cultural critic's ethical responsibility to do the right thing frequently generates public displays of anxiety (Did I do the right thing?), opportunism (Only I can do it), and theatrical exercises in defensive authoritativeness (Only I can tell you how to do it). These positions point to a paradox at the heart of nationalist and essentialist ideas of identity—for while they invoke an absolute, preexisting blackness, they also characterize it as performative. To *be* black, we must understand, doesn't just mean to do the *right* thing, but also to *do* it. Yet, the complete transfer of identity from essence to action, from innate property to consumable or reproducible activity, without any ethical referent or political grounding, is a form of cultural politics few blacks would benefit from, given the political and economic inequalities that continue to divide American society along racial lines. As we have argued these issues, it has been apparent throughout that this particular group of black cultural critics does not think of culture and identity without asking about politics—that is, about relations of power—and about ethics—that is, about responsibility. We cannot confuse the appearance of access created by the commodification of ethnicity and, as Hazel Carby noted, the celebration of diversity, with the decentralization of wealth and the democratization of political power that have yet to take place in this country.

I see some very good signs in these debates. The ease and vitality of the dialogue between black American and black British cultural critics and media artists is, for me, a reason to reflect for a moment on the past, a source of hope, and a cause for joy (a word for Cornel West)—joy, because among other things it signals the waning of the isolationist view of culture characteristic of postwar American thought. That distinctly American chauvinism (which is a kind of nationalism in patriotic disguise) was present in many of the initial responses in this country to the black British cultural renaissance of the 1980s.

During that time, I was motivated to take on work as a cultural critic because I thought contending with different black cultures outside the United States would help to make more space for the differences within and among black cultures at home. I also thought it would eventually curtail the impulse on the part of blacks and whites to treat any one individual or diasporic culture as a prototype of blackness. At the time, it seemed of particular political importance to insist that this encounter be orchestrated by and among black people (with a glance to their cultural politics), to avoid retracing the "intercultural" patterns established by modernism, surrealism, and ethnography, which had positioned white avant-gardes, for decades, as the gatekeepers of otherness and arbiters of aesthetic value. It was a difference that made a difference, not because of some kind of romantic essentialism about black unity, but because of a strategic need to distinguish between ideology and politics, between multicultural rhetoric and desegregation in American culture. And like all the other goats in this room who have beat their drums too loudly, I paid the price for having done so. But, if I had to, I would do it again.

I now reflect on this because I continue to believe that doing cultural criticism necessarily involves interpreting and contributing to such transformations as these. Ultimately, I hope that the de-essentializing logic of this postnationalist dialogue will eventually lead to another—one that will eliminate, or at least diminish, the linguistic and historical barriers which have impeded black critical dialogue between the Anglo-American and Latin American worlds. We are living in a moment in which these populations are coming together with greater frequency and in increasing numbers. In addition, as American mass culture deepens its entrenchment in the South, the experience of "blackness" in Latin America becomes increasingly influenced, if not dominated by, the mainstream media's versions of black American popular culture.

The dialogue I am hoping for will not only require getting around accents and the differences between internal and external migrations. It will also mean breaking down the jingoistic English-only barriers that essentialize language as if it were some kind of impenetrable, irreducible difference. It calls for the refusal to lapse into the bad habits which have enabled the U.S. government and the American media to turn hundreds of ethnic groups into one—Hispanic, Latino, you name it—and systematically promote its misinterpretation as a racial term, for the benefit of a segregationist system that sees only in black and white, no matter what the other's color is. It also involves comprehending how the respective colonialisms of the North and the South engendered different social constructions of race, despite shared legacies of slavery, sexual exploitation of black and indigenous women by white men, and segregationist legislation.

In the North, a combination of prolonged legal and social segregation and a deeply embedded ideology of essentialist separatism, supported by the pragmatist stronghold on American philosophy, has continuously deferred recognition and affirmation of this country's and its people's racial and cultural hybridity. In the South, at least two centuries of ideological celebration of hybridity (the many discourses of *mestizaje*) often brings Latin American intellectuals to reject binary understandings of race. Latino cultural critics tend to insist on the historical difference of a more variegated racial classification system, claiming that class counts more than race, that Latinos have always had a higher rate of interracial unions and a progressive, nationalist, anticolonialist tradition, which is, at least in theory, integrationist. Although it is true that the independence struggles and nationalist discourses of the Spanish Caribbean stipulated racial equality whereas the American Revolution did not, it is also true that no multiracial Latin American society has eliminated racial inequity. What is often left out of these equations are the similarities between northern and southern segregationist legislation, social practices, and economic hierarchies. What is also occluded is the political manipulation of hybridity, by Latin American official cultures in the nineteenth century, which encouraged miscegenation (without legitimating interracial marriage) as a strategy for diminishing the threat of black political power. Finally, in the twentieth century, this rhetoric has been used both to mask racialized economic disparities and to fuel the popular conception that blackness is something Latinos get rid of with socialization, miscegenation with whites, and hair straightener.

I hear echoes of that strategy in the deployment of contemporary multicultural rhetoric in this country—an official celebration designed to contend with white fears of a growing nonwhite population and to hide increasing economic polarization. And, as U.S. late capitalism begins to resemble late feudalism, I perceive greater and greater similarities between the deplorable living conditions and excessive policing of people of color in the South and that in the North. The national and linguistic differences between them don't really make that much of a difference anymore.

The black British–black American dialogue has helped to highlight the historical contradictions that forged an oppositional relationship between race and nationality in the Anglophone contexts. It has extended a debate on black hybridity, both racial and cultural, that had already been broadened by the feminisms of such writers as Michele Wallace and Angela Davis. I firmly believe that this debate can be enhanced only if recast as a pan-American dialogue, taking into account the complementary discourses on race and nation in Latin America that began five hundred years ago and have informed revolutionary political movements and cultural syncretism in the region's multiracial societies.

While the advanced technologies of contemporary societies have facilitated popular cultural dialogue between geographically disparate black populations, it is also true that the concurrent postwar immigrations of black Americans, Afro-Caribbeans, Puerto Ricans, Dominicans, and Cubans to the inner cities of the United States are creating the conditions for the production of hybrid black/latino, english/spanish/spanglish cultures. Not even the social engineering that demands conveniently absolutist, but pseudoscientific, distinctions between black Americans and Caribbean Latinos can completely suppress the history of over a century of cultural and political dialogue between jazz musicians and *soneros*, between Cuban revolutionaries and civil rights leaders, between Young Lords and Black Panthers. Those dialogues resonate in the exchanges between black and Latino rappers who hail from the barrios of New York, Los Angeles, São Paulo, and San Juan, and in the formation of pan-Caribbean syncretism in Brooklyn and the Bronx. Those interactions are transforming what was once a largely Caribbean phenomenon into the seeds of America's cultural present and future.

PASSIONATE IRREVERENCE:
THE CULTURAL POLITICS
OF IDENTITY

H ARDLY A WEEK has passed in the last two years without public attention being drawn to yet another battle over identity and culture. Behind each debate linger fears and hopes about the image this country projects to its people(s) and to the rest of the world. *Who are we?* asked *Time* magazine, as statistics point to the changing (i.e. increasingly nonwhite) ethnic make-up of American society. *Whose values?* asked *Newsweek,* as many reel and others applaud at the radical Right's neofascist, universalist rhetoric. These questions have spilled over into the world of art in several interrelated and volatile debates over censorship, cultural property, and cultural equity. *Whose museums and whose aesthetics?* asks a new generation of critics, curators, and artists. *Whose icons?* wonder multicultural theorists and activists, as familiar elements of foreign worlds are absorbed with increasing speed by American consumer culture. *Whose image?* argue the lawyers involved in the lawsuit against Jeff Koons who, in the eyes of the law, "appropriated" and, in doing so, capitalized on another artist's photograph by reinterpreting it as sculpture without acknowledging a "source".

Where are we? We are in America, five hundred years after the beginning of the conquest and colonization of the New World, five years after the beginning of sweeping transformations in the socialist world, and eight years from the end of the millennium. The last great empires of this century—the United States and the Soviet Union—are on the decline as superpowers, their respective economies tip into tail-spins, and their international work forces become migratory "social problems." With the unravelling of these systems, the concept and reality of the unified, homogeneous nation-state and national culture become highly contested terrains. To these political and ideological changes we must add the fact that advances in technology have disrupted geographical, political, and cultural boundaries forever.

This essay first appeared in the 1993 Whitney Biennial catalog.

The collectively experienced anxiety provoked by these transformations has generated a plethora of identity-related conflicts, from geopolitical boundary disputes and the resurgence of ethnic tensions in Europe, to the concomitant racial unrest of North America. In Europe, these issues are being fought over principally in the geopolitical sphere; in the United States, we find ourselves in more of an ideological battle over symbolic representation. This does not mean, however, that the battles in America are any less political; on the contrary, culture in this country is a critical, if not the most crucial, area of political struggle over identity. While the tensions in the East and the West do differ, they are nonetheless driven by the same underlying contradictory forces: On the one hand, economic internationalization and the formation of "global culture" (symbolized by the European Economic Community and the North American Free Trade Agreement); and, on the other, political fragmentation based on regionalism, ethnic separatism, and extreme economic polarization. We struggle to preserve distinctions that, for some, can no longer be taken for granted, and, for others, appear for the first time to be within reach.

These conditions shape much of the art and the cultural debates of our historical moment. Physical and cultural dislocation characterizes the daily lives of many, if not most, of the people of the world. Those in a position of privilege live this condition by choice, conducting international business, using advanced technology, or playing virtual reality games; others who are less privileged are compelled to live this sense of dislocation without respite as migrant workers, immigrants, exiles, refugees, and homeless people. Diasporic cultures rival those of the homelands in size and complexity. Exile communities often provide crucial economic support to imperiled "centers." Exile, and the split sense of self it entails, are paradigmatic experiences of identity for millions. Some nations exist without a place, while others exist only through authoritarian enforcement. The hegemony of national cultures is perpetually disrupted by "foreign" information, media, consumer items, and people. The once colonial condition of having to adjudicate between local and outside cultures and power structures has not been swept away by the postcolonial age; in fact, it bears resemblance to daily life in postindustrial societies, where advanced technologies facilitate continuous transmission of information and commodities to different ends of the globe. Nonetheless, for some, these transformations do not necessarily signal greater availability of resources—only more intrusions into their lands and their lives.

In such a state of things, the very notion of cultural purity can seem like something of a nostalgic fantasy, one that not even "non-western" societies can provide proof of any longer. Yet these issues continue to trouble many and are central to cultural debates about the condition of subaltern peoples in the United States. Our continued engagement with questions of identity would indicate that not even a shifting of borders will bring us to relinquish them altogether. Unlike many other interpretations of postmodernity that have suggested that the accelerated flow of cultural property has nullified fixed identities and power relations between them, subaltern theory and cultural practice have maintained the need to account for distinctions between political power (i.e., the ability to make things happen and how those with political power see themselves) and symbolic exchange of cultural symbols. While other schools of thought associated with postmodernism have interpreted identity as pure process, and as infinitely transformable and essentially performative, subaltern discourses have looked upon these positions as volunteerist characterizations that do not account for controlling forces that affect identity, such as racism and the determining force of collective historical experience. Such elisions still appear too similar to the racial violence that has robbed many in this country of the right, first to be considered human beings, and then to have access to political power. At this historical moment, then, the postmodern fascination with the exchange of cultural property and with completely deracinated identity can seem for many people of color less like emancipation

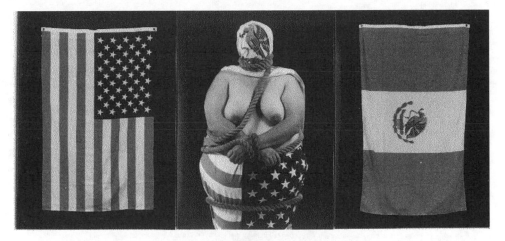

"Three Eagles Flying," by Laura Aguilar, 1990.

and more like intensified alienation. Instead, for many, the times demand what Gayatri Spivak has called "strategic essentialism," that is, a critical position that validates identity as politically necessary but not as ahistorical or unchangeable.

Cultural identity and values are politically and historically charged issues for peoples in this country whose access to exercising political power and controlling their symbolic representations has been limited within mainstream culture. While some might look upon the current wave of multiculturalism as inherently empowering and/or new, others look upon the present in relation to a long tradition of "celebrating" (or rather, objectifying) difference as light but exotic entertainment for the dominant culture. From the perspective of those who have been geographically, politically, culturally, and economically marginalized in and by the United States, these celebrations and the curiosity that drives them are not necessarily disinterested or inherently progressive phenomena. They are, instead, potentially double-edged swords, signaling both the exercising of control over cultural difference through the presentation of static models of diversity and the potential opportunity to transform the stereotypes that emerge with the imposition of control.

Those stereotypes that have grown ingrained over time cannot be easily dismissed and then simply cast off; they are both reminders of a painful legacy of bigotry and disempowerment that has fueled their systematic misrepresentation, *and* the starting point for understanding the racially inflected, voyeuristic impulses in Euro-American and other colonizing cultures. "Appropriation," a favorite buzzword of the 1980s art elite, isn't just about disinterested pastiche or tracing one's creative bloodlines to Marcel Duchamp and Andy Warhol; it is also about reckoning with a history of colonialist power relations vis-à-vis non-Western cultures and peoples to contextualize certain forms of appropriation as symbolic violence. In other words, although appropriation may not connote power inequities when conceived within other strains of

James Luna as "The Shame Man," 1993.
PHOTO BY FRANCISCO DOMINGO.

postmodern culture, its historical and political implications in relation to European colonialism and American expansionism cannot be ignored, because the erasure of authorship and the exchange of symbols and artifacts across cultural boundaries have never been apolitical or purely formalist gestures. That mainstream culture has periodically expressed desire for subaltern art has never obligated anyone to deal with subaltern peoples as human beings, compatriots, or artists. That is, perhaps, until now.

While the claims to absolute authority in issues of cultural identity and property are at times problematic (since no one, in the end, speaks for every member of a group), the ways that these dealings are represented in the mainstream media and even most of the art press are invariably tendentious. Little effort has been made to distinguish between dominant cultural attempts to curtail an artist's right to express his or her aesthetic sensibility and a subaltern critique of institutionalized racism and privilege; in fact, the blurring of these distinctions has fueled the debates over political correctness during recent years. Nonetheless, many if not most of the criticisms leveled at those who raise questions about cultural appropriation are hardly substantive; rather, masked by platitudes about quality and freedom, they are often expressions of displeasure that heretofore underheard sectors of society choose to have opinions about culture at all. As the Left and Right invoke "imagined communities" of "the audience" to justify their assuming the authority to speak, this "audience" is

"La Cucaracha," by Lalo Alcaraz from POCHO Magazine, 1993.

deemed either too sensitive and innocent or much too smart to mistake evil for good. Anyone who challenges an entrenched power structure's absolute "freedom" to make money or meaning in whatever way it finds desirable can be labeled anti-American, socially backward, and artistically ignorant. Any subaltern question or protest, even if its aim is not to curtail but to contextualize, can be perceived as threatening to the current cultural order of things.

For privileged purveyors of culture in this country—be they artists, teachers, critics, collectors, benefactors or exhibitors—confronting the limitations of one's knowledge and relinquishing authority can be seen as a challenge or a crushing blow. This prospect has generated another spate of defensive retaliation in the past two years, using very old tactics. In the summer of 1992, when hundreds of Chicano actresses in California protested the production of a film about Frida Kahlo because its producers refused to hire a Latina actress for the lead—claiming that "there weren't any big names"—many mainstream reports presented the protestors as having interfered with basic artistic freedoms. The Chicana position was seen as subjective and partisan and as a personal attack against the director. Such an analysis could not take into consideration that decades of absence of a substantial role for a Latina actress in Hollywood might not be the result of pure coincidence but of an unwritten and unchallenged policy. Nor could it, for that matter, stress an awareness of the sense of disempowerment provoked by the knowledge that rampant commodification of one's cultural heroes does not necessarily lead to gaining access to cultural resources for oneself or for one's community. On the contrary, the mainstream appropriation of subaltern *cultures* in this country has historically served as a substitute for ceding to those peoples any real political or economic power.

Had it been the 1960s, and had the protestors been male, they might have been lauded as the leaders of a new lobbying group in Hollywood and protagonists of a chapter on Chicano history. Instead, they have been largely represented outside the Chicano community as the latest in a line of politically correct feminists to appear on the horizon. The commercial impetus and concentration of wealth of the movie industry have made it perhaps the toughest cultural arena in which to fight, particularly for women artists of color, who have benefitted the least from the latest round of investment in commercial films about African Americans and Latinos. This is perhaps the saddest lesson about identity politics that we have learned in the aftermath of the Civil Rights movement and the backlash against the policies it inspired that the Reagan and Bush administrations have fueled: that superficial assimilation through consumerism and tokenism can be lauded as a sign of the mainstream's acquiescence, while the fundamental changes needed to bring out a more profound form of equity are still thwarted at every turn.

On the other hand, the world of the visual arts at times evinces more conciliatory signals. For example, amid the countless Native American art showcases opening throughout the Midwest in the fall of 1992 as liberal-minded counter-quincentennial gestures, a conflict erupted at a Minneapolis art museum over the proposed exhibition of Native American pipes that are considered sacred by many indigenous peoples. It was only after lengthy discussion among Native elders, artists, activists, and museum staff that the institution was convinced of its error, a position that might not have been taken had it not been for years of debates about the ownership of Native artifacts, and for the fact that around the same time the American Indian Movement filed a suit against the Washington Redskins for the team's use of a racial slur as its name.

Another indicator of this changing tide is that recent complaints in New York City over representations of blacks and Latinos in public art by white artists have been met with unprecedented willingness to pay them heed. Such communally oriented and ethnically divided discussions of the role and quality of public art strike at the core of the radical individualism that characterizes the mainstream's notion of the artist in this society. These discussions also test the limits of power of dominant cultural institutions and curators, whose long-standing authority to act as arbiters of taste is now being continually questioned by "lay" critiques of their notions of aesthetic value and realism. I cannot say that I have always found these criticisms to be devoid of extra-artistic motives—some have been used as indirect attacks on politicians, for example. Furthermore, these criticisms would be more convincing if they were more systematic, more clearly directed at perceived misrepresentations in the commercial media, and not only the arts. Nonetheless, these protests offer a critical opportunity to reconsider relationships among culture, art making, community, and public space. However they may be manipulated by the press, these encounters are multicultural identity politics made manifest in everyday life. They speak to the complexities of negotiating diverse views on culture and identity in our society. Together with public actions by such groups as the AIDS activists of ACT UP (AIDS Coalition to Unleash Power), the feminists of WAC (Women's Action Coalition) and Guerrilla Girls, and the artists of color of PESTS, they constitute some of the most interactive public engagements with the media and the arts that have emerged in the past decade. Each, in its own way, seeks to redress inequities by taking its concerns to the street and other public spaces, merging activism with spectacle.

These conflicts over a person's right to define his or her culture and icons resonate with similar battles from the past, but in the late 1980s and early 1990s, they have become increasingly concentrated within the arts, the media and education, and have taken on a particularly strident tone. They signal a growing awareness of symbolic representation as a key site of political struggle. These conflicts also herald important shifts in how we must understand postmodernism and "difference." By giving abstract concepts and formal operations more overt social content, these conflicts localize, politicize, and historicize postmodern cultural debates that had been at one time excessively formalist and ethnocentric, even in the characterization of difference itself.

At the heart of these other postmodernisms lies an insistence that art and politics are never truly extricable. While a more formalist approach to appropriation and pastiche characterized much of the art and art criticism of the early 1980s, the subaltern cultural strategies that have gained attention more recently foreground the connection between the political and the symbolic. The surrounding debates also involve explicit critiques of liberal humanist claims that legal equality ends significant difference between peoples, and of the relativist postures of certain strains of poststructuralism and their accompanying volunteerist propositions for understanding identity. Scores of feminists and postcolonial theorists have rejected formulations of poststructuralism that declare the death of the subject, the end of meaning, the decline of the social, and the failure of political resistance; these proclamations, they argue, speak only to the realities of those few who once could claim absolute rights, absolute truth, and absolute authority. They also turn a skeptical eye to popular interpretations of the poststructuralist stress on the performative dimension of identity that reduce subjectivity to pure and self-determined artifice. Despite cataclysmic changes in the ways that communities are defined and information circulates, only an infinitely small sector of society actually chooses freely where they are, who they are, and how they live. Even the limited ability one might acquire to alter aspects of one's identity cannot completely obfuscate the impact of outside social, political, and economic factors in the constitution of the self. To paraphrase the cultural theorist Stuart Hall, not all symbols and exchanges are interchangeable—there still are differences that make a difference. What emerges, however, is not a romantic form of essentialism, but a fluid notion of identity that is imbedded in but not mechanistically determined by history.

Within the realm of culture, then, two interrelated but seemingly contradictory struggles are in the foreground. One, waged in the realm of political representation, is an interracial, intercultural battle in the public sphere over appropriation, in which people of color are demanding the right to determine the meaning of their culture and delimit its identity—or, rather, to point to borders that still exist. This is a battle that seeks to resolve a legacy of inequity by addressing the power relations involved in symbolic representation. On the other hand, the artistic outpourings from these same communities in recent years have stressed hybridity as a cultural experience and as a formal strategy. Performance artist and musician Alvin Eng, for example, sets his experimental video about being Asian, *Rock Me Gung Hey*, in Chinatown, but tells his story in rap idiom. Interestingly, rap music, which is often characterized as the expression of black male youth, is perhaps today's most resonant crosscultural American language for defiant self-affirmation; its use has spread to Chicanos such as Keith Frost and the groups A Lighter Shade of Brown and Aztlan Nation, to Cuban Americans such as Mellow Man Ace, and to Nuyoricans such as Latin Empire—as well as dozens of young black women in the United States whose voices often counter the male-centeredness of the practice, and to other young people throughout the world.

Although some might cling to the idea that all artists are bound to a specific, group-oriented mandate, or a fixed notion of community, the most intriguing work takes these very assumptions apart and presents new possibilities for old terms. Adrian Piper's media installation *Cornered*, for example, is an indictment of American prejudice that demonstrates how the legal definition and social understanding of the term "black" are incompatible, compelling us to rethink our own understanding of our racial makeup. Rather than celebrating the survival of a "pure" tradition, James Luna's moving performance, *The Shame Man*, depicts some of the most saddening aspects of contemporary Native American experience, inviting us to enter into a poignant and enriching process of redefining his culture.

Perhaps the best result of the cultural climate of the past decade has been the flourishing of a *variety* of artistic practices and perspectives, which testifies to the impossibility of reducing cultural identity to a simplistic paradigm. It appears that we have worked away from the once widely held belief that artists of color must all be engaged in what Stuart Hall has called the act of imaginative recovery of a singular, unifying past in order for their work to be valid. No longer bound to a sense of having to restrict one's focus, materials, or genre, many contemporary artists of color move back and forth between past and present, between history and fiction, between art and ritual, between high art and popular culture, and between Western and non-Western influence. In doing so, they participate in multiple communities. Artists such as Fred Wilson and Renée Green excavate the European and Euro-American colonial past, drawing our attention to often horrifying elements many ignore or take for granted, but also underscoring our attraction to and even fascination with the artifacts and documents themselves. Pepón Osorio's ornate and intricately redesigned domestic objects and theater sets blur commonly held distinctions between original and copy, and between reliquary and sculpture, forcing us to redefine Euro-American notions of taste and originality.

These artists reflect the hybrid experiences that shape so much of contemporary life. They emerge from the dynamics of moving between worlds, and feeling at home and not at home in more than one. They use different languages, and cross-aesthetic genres as they follow ideas through multiple media. They express the ambivalence produced by being out of sync with dominant media constructs and yet being fascinated with images and with the creative possibilities for their recontextualization. Similarly, they look at Western history and art history not to excise its racism but to excavate and play with symptomatic absences and stereotypes, creating a counter history by bouncing off negative images and teasing out hidden stories. Rather than reject dominant culture for its exclusionary tendencies and retreating, literally or figuratively, many artists of color who have matured in the last decade are forcefully engaged with it in ways that make it new. I am reminded here of the New York–based Palestinian filmmaker Elia Suleiman's description of his own strategy of creating a new visual syntax out of bits of footage from television: " In a war in which you have no weapons, you must take those of your enemy and use them for something better—like throwing them back at him. "

The strategy of taking elements of an established or imposed culture and throwing them back with a different set of meanings is not only key to guerilla warfare; the tactics of reversal, recycling, and subversive montage are aesthetics that form the basis of many twentieth-century avant-gardes. Nonetheless, a more profound understanding of the influences affecting many artists of color demands that we also perceive their connections to the semiotics characteristic of the colonial condition. Syncretism, or the fusion of different forms of belief or practice, enabled disempowered groups to maintain their outlawed or marginalized traditions. It also paved the way for a host of cultural recycling methods that infuse old icons with new meanings. Symbolic action, in the form of spirituality and art, has for centuries been a critical arena for self-definition by politically disenfranchised peoples. One might recall the importance of

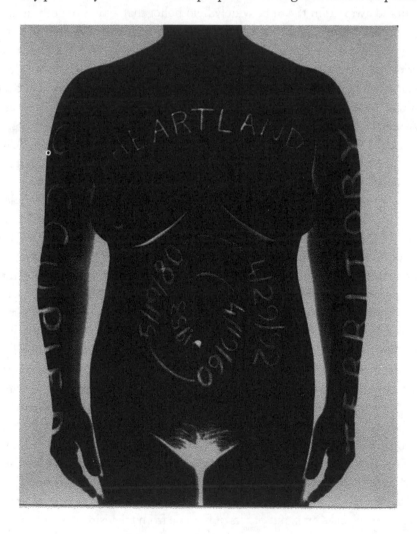

"Defining Moments," by Yong Soon Min, 1992.
PHOTO BY ALLAN DE SOUZA.

African American spirituals in the Civil Rights movement, or the role of the *corridos* for Chicanos in the Southwest as conveyors of a history suppressed by the dominant Anglo society. Culture and communal self-expression are perhaps most important sites of resistance, the signs in everyday life of an ongoing political struggle. Yet, resistance within a colonial context is rarely direct, overt, or literal; rather, it articulates itself through semantic reversals, and through the process of infusing icons, objects, and symbols with different meanings. As Henry Louis Gates has argued in his analyses of African American *signifyin'*, it is in these dynamics that one finds echoes of the creative defense of the enslaved against his or her master. They are among the many ways oppressed peoples have developed to take their identity back.

"Skin/Deep," by Allison Saar, 1993.
Ceiling tin, nails, and copper. Figure with fifty-three nails of varying length.
Collection of the Whitney Museum of American Art
(purchase, with funds from the Painting and Sculpture Committee).
PHOTO BY GEOFFREY CLEMENTS.

However bittersweet, they are also, often, very humorous. Parody, satire, and car-nivalesque unsettling of established orders continue to thrive as creative strategies for temporarily subverting authority. Not surprisingly, the sixteenth-century government of the Viceroyalty of Peru issued a law to outlaw comedy, out of fear of its potential political repercussions. Today, those who identify with the established order of things respond in a literal-minded manner to the playfulness and double entendres of sub-altern creative expression by reading only at face value. They insist that art should not "offend," that sophisticated appreciation must be distanced and reverent, and that serious criticism be dispassionate and "objective." What these dismissive attitudes cannot understand is that the irreverence and exuberant energy of these aesthetic strategies is evidence of the survival of subaltern practices that have created the conditions for spiritual and cultural renewal, as well as critical reinterpretations of the world in which we live.

The identity battles of recent years are among the variety of ways that the peoples of this country are transforming our vision of America and its cultures. What are sur-facing in the process are the histories that have circulated until now in marginalized communities. In the debates and art emerging from the tumult of the present are reflections of the many legacies of the conquest and colonization of the Americas, among them, its limiting views of art and culture. Although American society has defined progress as a focus on the future, we must now return to the past in order to place ourselves in that history and understand how we got to where we are. As we try to grasp at crucial parallels and tease new stories out of them, new alternative chronicles surface; these are the latest examples of how collective memories, those storehouses of identity, once activated, become power sites of cultural resistance.

THE OTHER HISTORY
OF INTERCULTURAL
PERFORMANCE

IN THE EARLY 1900S, Franz Kafka wrote a story that began, "Honored members of the Academy! You have done me the honor of inviting me to give your Academy an account of the life I formerly led as an ape."[1] Entitled "A Report to an Academy," it was presented as the testimony of a man from the Gold Coast of Africa who had lived for several years on display in Germany as a primate. That account was fictitious and created by a European writer who stressed the irony of having to demonstrate one's humanity; yet it is one of many literary allusions to the real history of ethnographic exhibition of human beings that has taken place in the West over the past five centuries. While the experiences of many of those who were exhibited is the stuff of legend, it is the accounts by observers and impresarios that constitute the historical and literary record of this practice in the West. My collaborator, Guillermo Gómez-Peña, and I were intrigued by this legacy of performing the identity of an Other for a white audience, sensing its implications for us as performance artists dealing with cultural identity in the present. Had things changed, we wondered? How would we know, if not by unleashing those ghosts from a history that could be said to be ours? Imagine that I stand before you then, as did Kafka's character, to speak about an experience that falls somewhere between truth and fiction. What follows are my reflections on performing the role of a noble savage behind the bars of a golden cage.

Our original intent was to create a satirical commentary on Western concepts of the exotic, primitive Other; yet, we had to confront two unexpected realities in the course of developing this piece: 1) a substantial portion of the public believed that our fictional identities were real ones; and 2) a substantial number of intellectuals, artists, and cultural bureaucrats sought to deflect attention from the substance of our experiment to the "moral implications" of our dissimulation, or in their words, our

This essay first appeared in *The Drama Review* in 1994.

"misinforming the public" about who we were. The literalism implicit in the interpretation of our work by individuals representing the "public interest" bespoke their
investment in positivist notions of "truth" and depoliticized, ahistorical notions of
"civilization." This "reverse ethnography" of our interactions with the public will,
I hope, suggest the culturally specific nature of their tendency toward a literal and
moral interpretation.

When we began to work on this performance as part of a counter-quincentenary
project, the Bush administration had drawn clear parallels between the "discovery" of
the New World and his "New World Order." We noted the resemblance between
official quincentenary celebrations in 1992 and the ways that the 1892 Columbian
commemorations had served as a justification for the United States' then new status as
an imperial power. Yet, while we anticipated that the official quincentenary celebration
was going to form an imposing backdrop, what soon became apparent was that
for both Spain and the United States, the celebration was a disastrous economic
venture, and even an embarrassment. The Seville Expo went bankrupt; the U.S.
Quincentenary Commission was investigated for corruption; the replica caravels were
met with so many protestors that the tour was canceled; the Pope changed his plans
and didn't hold mass in the Dominican Republic until after October 12; American
Indian Movement activist Russell Means succeeded in getting Italian Americans in
Denver to cancel their Columbus Day parade; and the film super-productions
celebrating Columbus—from *1492: The Discovery* to *The Conquest of Paradise*—were
box office failures. Columbus, the figure who began as a symbol of Eurocentrism and
the American entrepreneurial spirit, ended up being devalued by excessive reproduction and bad acting.

As the official celebrations faded, it became increasingly apparent that Columbus
was a smokescreen, a malleable icon to be trotted out by the mainstream for its
attacks on "political correctness." Finding historical justification for Columbus's "discovery" became just another way of affirming Europeans' and Euro-Americans' "natural right" to be global cultural consumers. The more equitable models of exchange
proposed by many multiculturalists logically demanded a more profound understanding of American cultural hybridity, and called for redefinitions of national identity and national origins. But the concept of cultural diversity fundamental to this
understanding strikes at the heart of the sense of control over Otherness that
Columbus symbolized, and was quickly cast as un-American. Resurrecting the collective memory of colonial violence in America that has been strategically erased
from the dominant culture was described consistently throughout 1992 by cultural
conservatives as a recipe for chaos. More recently, as is characterized by the film
Falling Down, it is seen as a direct threat to heterosexual, white male self-esteem. It is
no wonder that contemporary conservatives invariably find the focus on racism by
artists of color "shocking" and inappropriate, if not threatening to national interests,
as well as to art itself.

Out of this context arose our decision to take a symbolic vow of silence with the cage performance, a radical departure from Guillermo's previous monologue work and my activities as a writer and public speaker. We sought a strategically effective way to examine the limits of the "happy multiculturalism" that reigned in cultural institutions, as well as to respond to the formalists and cultural relativists who reject the proposition that racial difference is absolutely fundamental to aesthetic interpretation. We looked to Latin America, where consciousness of the repressive limits on public expression is far more acute than it is here, and found many examples of how popular opposition has for centuries been expressed through the use of satiric spectacle. Our cage became the metaphor for our condition, linking the racism implicit in ethnographic paradigms of discovery with the exoticizing rhetoric of "world beat" multiculturalism. Then came a perfect opportunity: In 1991, Guillermo and I were invited to perform as part of the Edge '92 Biennial, which was to take place in London and also in Madrid as part of the quincentennial celebration of Madrid as the capital of European culture. We took advantage of Edge's interest in locating art in public spaces to create a site-specific performance for Columbus Plaza in Madrid, in commemoration of the so-called Discovery.

Our plan was to live in a golden cage for three days, presenting ourselves as undiscovered Amerindians from an island in the Gulf of Mexico that had somehow been overlooked by Europeans for five centuries. We called our homeland Guatinau, and ourselves Guatinauis. We performed our "traditional tasks," which ranged from sewing voodoo dolls and lifting weights to watching television and working on a laptop computer. A donation box in front of the cage indicated that, for a small fee, I would dance (to rap music), Guillermo would tell authentic Amerindian stories (in a nonsensical language), and we would pose for Polaroids with visitors. Two "zoo guards" would be on hand to speak to visitors (since we could not understand them), take us to the bathroom on leashes, and feed us sandwiches and fruit. At the Whitney Museum in New York we added sex to our spectacle, offering a peek at authentic Guatinaui male genitals for $5. A chronology with highlights from the history of exhibiting non-Western peoples was on one didactic panel and a simulated Encyclopedia Britannica entry with a fake map of the Gulf of Mexico showing our island was on another. After our three days in May 1992, we took our performance to Covent Garden in London. In September, we presented it in Minneapolis, and in October, at the Smithsonian's National Museum of Natural History. In December, we were on display in the Australian Museum of Natural History in Sydney, and in January 1993, at the Field Museum of Chicago. In early March, we were at the Whitney for the opening of the biennial, the only site where we were recognizably contextualized as artwork. Prior to our trip to Madrid, we did a test run under relatively controlled conditions in the Art Gallery of the University of California, Irvine.

Our project concentrated on the "zero degree" of intercultural relations in an attempt to define a point of origin for the debates that link "discovery" and

"Otherness." We worked within disciplines that blur distinctions between the art object and the body (performance), between fantasy and reality (live spectacle), and between history and dramatic reenactment (the diorama). The performance was interactive, focusing less on what we did than on how people interacted with us and interpreted our actions. Entitled *Two Undiscovered Amerindians Visit…*, we chose not to announce the event through prior publicity or any other means, when it was possible to exert such control; we intended to create a surprise or "uncanny" encounter, one in which audiences had to undergo their own process of reflection as to what they were seeing, aided only by written information and parodically didactic zoo guards. In such encounters with the unexpected, people's defense mechanisms are less likely to operate with their normal efficiency; caught off guard, their beliefs are more likely to rise to the surface.

Buffalo Bill and his Wild West Show performers visit Venice, 1890.
PHOTO COURTESY OF THE DENVER PUBLIC LIBRARY, WESTERN HISTORY DEPARTMENT.

Our performance was based on the once popular European and North American practice of exhibiting indigenous people from Africa, Asia, and the Americas in zoos, parks, taverns, museums, freak shows, and circuses. While this tradition reached the height of its popularity in the nineteenth century, it was actually begun by Christopher Columbus, who returned from his first voyage in 1493 with several Arawaks, one of whom was left on display at the Spanish Court for two years. Designed to provide opportunities for aesthetic contemplation, scientific analysis, and entertainment for Europeans and North Americans, these exhibits were a critical component of a burgeoning mass culture whose development coincided with the growth of urban centers and populations, European colonialism, and American expansionism.

In writing about these human exhibitions in America's international fairs from the late nineteenth and early twentieth centuries, Robert W. Rydell (author of *All the World's a Fair; Visions of Empire at American International Exhibitions, 1876-1916* explains how the "ethnological" displays of nonwhites—which were orchestrated by impresarios but endorsed by anthropologists—confirmed popular racial stereotypes and built support for domestic and foreign policies.[2] In some cases, they literally connected museum practices with affairs of state. Many of the people exhibited during the nineteenth century were presented as the chiefs of conquered tribes and/or the last survivors of "vanishing" races. Ishi, the Yahi Indian who spent five years living in the Museum of the University of California at the turn of the century, is a well-known example. Another lesser-known example comes from the U.S.-Mexico War of 1836, when Anglo-Texan secessionists used to exhibit their Mexican prisoners in public plazas in cages, leaving them there to starve to death. The exhibits also gave credence to white supremacist worldviews by representing nonwhite peoples and cultures as being in need of discipline, civilization, and industry. Not only did these exhibits reinforce stereotypes of "the primitive" but they served to enforce a sense of racial unity as whites among Europeans and North Americans, who were divided strictly by class and religion until this century. Hence, for example, at the Columbian Exhibition of 1893 in Chicago, ethnographic displays of peoples from Africa and Asia were set up outside "The White City," an enclosed area celebrating science and industry.

INTERCULTURAL PERFORMANCE

Performance Art in the West did not begin with Dadist "events." Since the early days of European "conquest," "aboriginal samples" of people from Africa, Asia, and the Americas were brought to Europe for aesthetic contemplation, scientific analysis, and entertainment. Those people from other parts of the world were forced first to take the place that Europeans had already created for the savages of their own Medieval mythology; later with the emergence of scientific rationalism, the "aborigines" on display served as proof of the natural superiority of European civilization, of its ability to exert control over and extract knowledge from the "primitive" world, and ultimately, of the genetic inferiority of non-European races. Over the last 500 years, Australian Aborigines, Tahitians, Aztecs, Iroquois, Cherokee, Ojibways, Iowas, Mohawks, Botocudos, Guianese, Hottentots, Kaffirs, Nubians, Somalians, Singhalese, Patagonians, Tierra del Fuegans, Kahucks, Anapondans, Zulus, Bushmen, Japanese, East Indians, and Laplanders have been exhibited in the taverns, theaters, gardens, museums, zoos, circuses, and world's fairs of Europe, and the freak shows of the United States. Some examples are:

1493:   An Arawak brought back from the Caribbean by Columbus is left on display in the Spanish Court for two years until he dies of sadness.

1501:   "Eskimos" are exhibited in Bristol, England.

1550s: Native Americans are brought to France to build a Brazilian village in Rouen. The King of France orders his soldiers to burn the village as a performance. He likes the spectacle so much that he orders it restaged the next day.

1562:   Michel de Montaigne is inspired to write his essay *The Cannibals* after seeing Native Americans brought to France as a gift to the king.

1613:   In writing *The Tempest* Shakespeare models his character Caliban on an "Indian" he has seen in an exhibition in London.

1617:   Pocahontas, the Indian wife of John Rolfe, arrives in London to advertise Virginia tobacco. She dies of an English disease shortly thereafter.

1676:   Wampanoag Chief Metacom is executed for fomenting indigenous rebellion against the Puritans, and his head is publicly displayed for 25 years in Massachusetts.

1788:   Arabanoo of the Cammeraigal people of North Sydney, Australia, is captured by Governor Phillip. At first Arabanoo was chained and guarded by a convict; later he was shown off to Sydney society. He died a year later from smallpox.

1792:   Bennelong and Yammerawannie of the Cadigal people of South Sydney travel to England with Governor Phillip where they are treated as curiosities. Yammerawannie dies of pneumonia.

1802:   Pemulwuy, an Aboriginal resistance fighter from the Bidgegal people, is shot by white settlers in Australia. His head is cut off, preserved, and sent to England to be displayed at the London Museum.

1810-1815: "The Hottentot Venus" (Saartje Benjamin) is exhibited throughout Europe. After her death, her genitals are dissected by French scientists and remain preserved in Paris's Museum of Man to this day.

1822:   "Laplander" family is displayed with live reindeer in the Egyptian Hall in London.

1823:   Impresario William Bullock stages a Mexican "peasant" diorama in which a Mexican Indian youth is presented as ethnographic specimen and museum docent.

1829:   A "Hottentot" woman exhibited nude is the highlight of a ball given by the Duchess du Barry in Paris.

1834:   After General Rivera's cavalry completed the genocide of all the Indians in Uruguay, four surviving Charrúas are donated to the Natural Sciences Academy in Paris and are displayed to the French public as specimens of a vanished race. Three die within two months, and one escapes and disappears, never to be heard from again.

1844:   George Catlin displays "Red Indians" in England.

1847:   Four "Bushmen" on exhibit at the Egyptian Hall in London are written about by Charles Dickens.

1853:   Thirteen Kaffirs are displayed in the St. George Gallery in Hyde Park, London.

1853:   "Pygmies" dressed in European garb are displayed playing the piano in a British drawing room as proof of their potential for "civilization."

1853–1901: Maximo and Bartola, two microcephalic San Salvadorans, tour Europe and the Americas, and eventually join Barnum and Bailey's Circus. They are billed as "the last Aztec survivors of a mysterious jungle city called Ixinaya."

1878:   The skeleton of Truganini, a Tasmanian Aborigine, is acquired by the Royal Society of Tasmania. Her remains are displayed in Melbourne in 1888 and 1904 and then returned to the Hobart's museum where they are displayed from 1904 until the mid-1960s.

1879:   P. T. Barnum offers Queen Victoria $100,000 for permission to exhibit captured warrior Zulu Chief Cetewayo, and is refused.

1882:   W. C. Coup's circus announces the acquisition of "a troupe of genuine male and female Zulus."

1893:   The skeleton of Neddy Larkin, an Aborigine from New South Wales, is sold to the Harvard University Peabody Museum together with a collection of stuffed animals, stones, tools, and artifacts.

1898:   At the Trans-Mississippi International Exposition in Omaha, Nebraska, a mock Indian battle is staged, and President William McKinley watches.

1905:   The sole surviving member of the Yahi tribe of California, Ishi, is captured and displayed for the last five years of his life at the Museum of the University of California. Presented as a symbol of the U.S.'s defeat of Indian nations, Ishi is labeled the last Stone Age Indian in America.

1906:   Ota Benga, the first Pygmy to visit America after the slave trade, is put on display in the primate cage of the Bronx Zoo. A group of black ministers protest the zoo's display, but local press argue that Ota Benga was probably enjoying himself.

1911:   The Kickapoo Indian Medicine Company is sold for $250,000, after thirty days of performances in the United States. 150 shows include one or more Kickapoo Indians as proof that the medicines being hawked were derived from genuine Indian medicine.

1931:   The Ringling Circus features fifteen Ubangis, including "the nine largest-lipped women in the Congo."

1992:   A black woman midget is exhibited at the Minnesota State Fair, billed as "Tiny Teesha, the Island Princess."

In most cases, the human beings that were exhibited did not choose to be on display. More benign versions continue to take place these days in festivals and amusement parks with the partial consent of those on exhibit. The contemporary tourist industries and cultural ministries of several countries around the world still perpetrate the illusion of authenticity to cater to the Western fascination with Otherness. So do many artists.

Emerging at a time when mass audiences in Europe and America were barely literate and hardly cognizant of the rest of the world, the displays were an important form of public "education." These shows were where most whites "discovered" the non-Western sector of humanity. I like to call them the origins of intercultural performance in the West. The displays were living expressions of colonial fantasies and helped to forge a special place in the European and Euro-American imagination for nonwhite peoples and their cultures. Their function, however, went beyond war trophies, beyond providing entertainment for the masses and pseudoscientific data for early anthropologists. The ethnographic exhibitions of people of color were among the many sources drawn on by European and American modernists seeking to break with realism by imitating the "primitive." The connection between West African sculpture and Cubism has been discussed widely by scholars, but it is the construction of ethnic Otherness as essentially *performative* and located in the body that I here seek to stress.

The interest that modernists and postmodernists have had in non-Western cultures was preceded by a host of references to "exotics" made by European writers and philosophers over the past five centuries. The ethnographic shows and the people brought to Europe to be part of them have been alluded to by such writers as William Shakespeare, Michel Montaigne, and William Wordsworth. In the eighteenth century, these shows, together with theater and popular ballads, served as popular illustrations of the concept of the Noble Savage so central to Enlightenment philosophy. Not all the references were positive; in fact, the nineteenth-century humanist Charles Dickens found that the Noble Savage as an idea hardly sufficed to make an encounter with Bushmen in the Egyptian Hall in 1847 a pleasurable or worthwhile experience:

> Think of the Bushmen. Think of the two men and the two women who have been exhibited about England for some years. Are the majority of persons—who remember the horrid little leader of that party in his festering bundle of hides, with his filth and his antipathy to water, and his straddled legs, and his odious eyes shaded by his brutal hand, and his cry of "Qu-u-u-u-aaa" (Bosjeman for something desperately insulting I have no doubt)—conscious of an affectionate yearning towards the noble savage, or is it idiosyncratic in me to abhor, detest, abominate, and abjure him? I have never seen that group sleeping, smoking, and expectorating round their brazier, but I have sincerely desired that something might happen to the charcoal therein, which would cause the immediate suffocation of the whole of noble strangers.[3]

Dickens's aversion does not prevent him from noting, however, that the Bushmen possess one redeeming quality: their ability to break spontaneously into dramatic reenactment of their "wild" habits. By the early twentieth century, the flipside of such revulsion—in the form of fetishistic fascination with exotic artifacts and the "primitive" creativity that generated them—had become common among the members of the European avant-garde. The Dadaists, often thought of as the originators of performance art, included several imitative gestures in their events, ranging from dressing up and dancing as "Africans," to making "primitive-looking" masks and sketches. Tristan Tzara's dictum that "Thought is made in the mouth," a performative analog to Cubism, refers directly to the Dadaist belief that Western art tradition could be subverted through the appropriation of the perceived orality and performative nature of the "non-Western." In a grand gesture of appropriation, Tzara anthologized African and Southern Pacific poetry culled from ethnographies into his book, *Poèmes Nègres,* and chanted them at the infamous Cabaret Voltaire in Zurich in 1917. Shortly afterward, Tzara wrote a hypothetical description of the "primitive" artist at work in *Notes on Negro Art*, imputing near-shamanistic powers to the Other's creative process:

> My other brother is naive and good, and laughs. He eats in Africa or along the South Sea Islands. He concentrates his vision on the head, carves it out of wood that is hard as iron, patiently, without bothering about the conventional relationship between the head and the rest of the body. What he thinks is: man walks vertically, everything in nature is symmetrical. While working, new relationships organize themselves according to degree of necessity; this is how the expression of purity came into being. From blackness, let us extract light. Transform my country into a prayer of joy or anguish. Cotton wool eye, flow into my blood. Art in the infancy of time, was prayer. Wood and tone were truth...Mouths contain the power of darkness, invisible substance, goodness, fear, wisdom, creation, fire. No one has seen so clearly as I this dark grinding whiteness.[4]

Tzara is quick to point out here that only he, as a Dadaist, can comprehend the significance of the "innocent" gesture of his "naive and good" brother. In *The Predicament of Culture*, James Clifford explains how modernists and ethnographers of the early twentieth century projected coded perceptions of the black body—as imbued with vitalism, rhythm, magic, and erotic power, another formation of the "good" versus the irrational or bad savage.[5] Clifford questions the conventional mode of comparison in terms of affinity, noting that this term suggests a "natural" rather than political or ideological relationship. In the case of Tzara, his perception of the "primitive" artist as part of his metaphorical family conveniently recasts his own colonial relation to his imaginary "primitive" as one of kinship. In this context, the threatening reminder of difference is that the original body, or the physical and visual presence of the cultural Other, must be fetishized, silenced, subjugated, or otherwise controlled to be "appreciated." The significance of that violent erasure is diminished—it is the "true" avant-garde artist who becomes a better version of the "primitive," a hybrid or a cultural transvestite. Mass culture caged it, so to speak—while artists swallowed it.

This practice of appropriating and fetishizing the primitive and simultaneously erasing the original source continues into contemporary "avant-garde" performance art. In his 1977 essay "New Models, New Visions: Some Notes Toward a Poetics of Performance," Jerome Rothenberg envisioned this phenomenon in an entirely cele-bratory manner, noting correlations between Happenings and rituals, meditative works and mantric models, Earthworks and Native American sculptures, dream-works and notions of trance and ecstasy, bodyworks and self-mutilation, and perfor-mance based on several other variations of the shamanistic premise attributed to non-Western cultures. Rothenberg claims that unlike imperialism's models of domi-nation and subordination, avant-garde performance succeeded in shifting relations to a "symposium of the whole," an image strikingly similar to that of the world-beat multiculturalism of the 1980s. Referring to Gary Snyder's story of Alfred Kroeber and his (unnamed)Mojave informant in 1902, Rothenberg notes Snyder's conclusion that "The old man sitting in the sand house telling his story is who we must become—not A. L. Kroeber, as fine as he was."[6] Rothenberg goes on to claim that artists are to crit-ics what aborigines are to anthropologists, and therefore suffer from the same mis-representation. "The antagonism of literature to criticism," he writes, "is, for the poet and artist, no different form that to anthropology, say, on the part of the Native American militant. It is a question in short of the right to self-definition."[7]

Redefining these "affinities" with the primitive, the traditional, and the exotic has become an increasingly delicate issue as more artists of color enter the sphere of the "avant-garde." What may be "liberating" and "transgressive" identification for Europeans and Euro-Americans is already a symbol of entrapment within an imposed stereotype for Others. The "affinity" championed by the early moderns and postmodern cultural transvestites alike is mediated by an imagined stereotype, along the lines of Tzara's "brother." Actual encounters could threaten the position and supremacy of the appropriator unless boundaries and concomitant power relations remain in place. As a result, the same intellectual milieus that now boast Neoprimitive body piercers, "nomad" thinkers, Anglo *comadres*, and New Age earth worshippers continue to evince a literal-minded attitude toward artists of color, demonstrating how racial difference is a determinant in one's relation to notions of the "primitive." In the 1987 trial of minimalist sculptor Carl Andre—accused of murdering his wife, the Cuban artist Ana Mendieta—the defense continually suggested that her earthworks were indicative of suicidal impulses prompted by her "satanical" beliefs; the references to Santería in her work could not be interpreted as self-conscious. When Cuban artist José Bedia was visited by the French curators of the Les Magiciens de la Terre exhibition in the late 1980s, he was asked to show his private altar to "prove" that he was a true Santería believer. A critically acclaimed young African American poet was surprised to learn last year that he had been promoted by a Nuyorican Poet's Cafe impresario as a former L.A. gang member, which he never was. And while performing *Border Brujo* in the late 1980s, Gómez-Peña encountered numerous presenters and audience members who were disappointed that he was not a "real shaman" and that his "tongues" were not Nahuatl but a fictitious language.

Our cage performances forced these contradictions out into the open. The cage became a blank screen onto which audiences projected their fantasies of who and what we are. As we assumed the stereotypical role of the domesticated savage, many audience members felt entitled to assume the role of the colonizer, only to find themselves uncomfortable with the implications of the game. Unpleasant but important associations have emerged between the displays of old and the multicultural festivals and ethnographic dioramas of the present. The central position of the white spectator, the objective of these events as a confirmation of their position as global consumers of exotic cultures, and the stress on authenticity as an aesthetic value, all remain fundamental to the spectacle of Otherness many continue to enjoy.

The original ethnographic exhibitions often presented people in a simulation of their "natural" habitat, rendered either as an indoor diorama, or as an outdoor recreation. Eyewitness accounts frequently note that the human beings on display were forced to dress in the European notion of their traditional "primitive" garb, and to perform repetitive, seemingly ritual tasks. At times, nonwhites were displayed together with flora and fauna from their regions, and artifacts, which were often fakes. They were also displayed as part of a continuum of "outsiders" that included "freaks," or people exhibiting physical deformities. In the nineteenth and early twentieth centuries, many of them were presented so as to confirm social Darwinist ideas of the existence of a racial hierarchy. Some of the more infamous cases involved individuals whose physical traits were singled out as evidence of the bestiality of nonwhite people. For example, shortly after the annexation of Mexico and the publication of John Stephens's account of travel in the Yucatan, which generated popular interest in pre-Columbian cultures, two microcephalics (or "pinheads") from Central America, Maximo and Bartola, toured the United States in P. T. Barnum's circus; they were presented as Aztecs. This set off a trend that would be followed by many other cases into the twentieth century. From 1810–1815, European audiences crowded to see the Hottentot Venus, a South African woman whose large buttocks were deemed evidence of her excessive sexuality. In the United States, several of the "Africans" exhibited were actually black Americans, who made a living in the nineteenth century by dressing up as their ancestors, just as many Native Americans did dressing up as Sioux whose likenesses, thanks to the long and bloody Plains Wars of the late nineteenth century, dominate the American popular imagination.

For Gómez-Peña and myself, the human exhibitions dramatize the colonial unconscious of American society. In order to justify genocide, enslavement, and the seizure of lands, a "naturalized" splitting of humanity along racial lines had to be established. When rampant miscegenation proved that those differences were not biologically based, social and legal systems were set up to enforce those hierarchies. Meanwhile, ethnographic spectacles circulated and reinforced stereotypes, stressing that "difference" was apparent in the bodies on display. Thus they naturalized fetishized representations of Otherness, mitigating anxieties generated by the encounter with difference.

In his essay, "The Other Question" Homi Bhabha explains how racial classification through stereotyping is a necessary component of colonialist discourse, as it justifies domination and masks the colonizer's fear of the inability to always already know the Other.[8] Our experiences in the cage suggested that even though the idea that America is a colonial system is met with resistance—since it contradicts the dominant ideology's presentation of our system as a democracy—the audience reactions indicated that colonialist roles have been internalized quite effectively.

The stereotypes about nonwhite people that were continuously reinforced by the ethnographic displays are still alive in high culture and the mass media. Imbedded in the unconscious, these images form the basis of the fears, desires, and fantasies about the cultural Other. In "The Negro and Psychopathology," Frantz Fanon discusses a critical stage in the development of children socialized in Western culture, regardless of their race, in which racist stereotypes of the savage and the primitive are assimilated through the consumption of popular culture: comics, movies, cartoons, and so forth.[9] These stereotypical images are often part of myths of colonial dominion (for example, cowboy defeats Indian, conquistador triumphs over Aztec Empire, colonial soldier conquers African chief, and so on). This dynamic also contains a sexual dimension, usually expressed as anxiety about white male (omni)potence. In *Prospero and Caliban: The Psychology of Colonization*, Octave Mannoni coined the term "Prospero complex" to describe the white colonial patriarch's continuous fear that his daughter might be raped by a nonwhite male.[10] Several colonial stereotypes also nurture these anxieties, usually representing a white woman whose "purity" is endangered by black men with oversized genitals, or suave Latin lovers, or wild-eyed Indian warriors; and the common practice of publicly lynching black men in the American South is an example of a ritualized white male response to such fears. Accompanying these stereotypes are counterparts that humiliate and debase women of color, mitigating anxieties about sexual rivalry between white and non-white women. In the past, there was the subservient maid and the overweight and sexless Mammy; nowadays, the hapless victim of a brutish or irrational dark male whose tradition is devoid of "feminist freedoms" is more common.

These stereotypes have been analyzed endlessly in recent decades, but our experiences in the cage suggest that the psychic investment in them does not simply wither away through rationalization. The constant concern about our "realness" revealed a need for reassurance that a "true primitive" *did* exist, whether we fit the bill or not, and that she or he visually identifiable. Anthropologist Roger Bartra sees this desire as being part of a characteristically European dependence on an "uncivilized other" in order to define the Western self. In his book *El Salvaje en el Espejo/The Savage in the Mirror,* he traces the evolution of the "savage" from mythological inhabitants of forests to "wild" and usually hairy men and women who even in the modern age appeared in freak shows and horror films.[11] These archetypes eventually were incorporated into Christian iconography and were then projected onto peoples of the New World, who were perceived as either heathen savages capable of reform or incorrigible devils who had to be eradicated.

While the structure of the so-called primitive may have been assimilated by the European avant-garde, the function of the ethnographic displays as popular entertainment was largely superseded by industrialized mass culture. Not unsurprisingly, the popularity of these human exhibitions began to decline with the emergence of another commercialized form of voyeurism—the cinema—and the assumption by ethnographic film of their didactic role. Founding fathers of the ethnographic filmmaking practice, such as Robert Flaherty and John Grierson, continued to compel people to stage their supposedly "traditional" rituals, but the tasks were now to be performed for the camera. One of the most famous of the white impresarios of the human exhibits in the United States, William F. "Buffalo Bill" Cody, actually starred in an early film depicting his Wild West show of Native American horsemen and warriors, and in doing so gave birth to the "cowboy and Indian" movie genre, this country's most popular rendition of its own colonial fantasy. The representation of the "reality" of the Other's life, on which ethnographic documentary was based and still is grounded, is this fictional narrative of Western culture "discovering" the negation of itself in something *authentically* and *radically* distinct. Carried over from documentary, these paradigms also became the basis of Hollywood filmmaking in the 1950s and 1960s that dealt with other parts of the world in which the United States had strategic military and economic interests, especially Latin America and the South Pacific.

The practice of exhibiting humans may have waned in the twentieth century, but it has not entirely disappeared. The dissected genitals of the Hottentot Venus are still preserved at the Museum of Man in Paris. Thousands of Native American remains, including decapitated heads, scalps, and other body parts taken as war booty or bounties, remain in storage at the Smithsonian. Shortly before arriving in Spain, we learned of a current scandal in a small village outside Barcelona, where a visiting delegation had registered a formal complaint about a desiccated, stuffed Pygmy man that was on display in a local museum. The African gentleman in the delegation who had initiated the complaint was threatening to organize an African boycott of the 1992 Olympics, but the Catalonian townspeople defended what they saw as the right to keep "their own black man." We also learned that Julia Pastrana, a bearded Mexican woman who was exhibited throughout Europe until her death in 1862, is still available in embalmed form for scientific research and loans to interested museums. This past summer, the case of Ota Benga, a Pygmy who was exhibited in the primate cage of the Bronx Zoo in 1906 gained high visibility as plans for a Hollywood movie based on a recently released book were made public. And at the Minnesota State Fair last summer, we saw "Tiny Teesha, the Island Princess," who was in actuality a black woman midget from Haiti making her living going from one state fair to another.

While the human exhibition exists in more benign forms today—that is, the people in them are not displayed against their will—the desire to look upon predictable forms of Otherness from a safe distance persists. I suspect after my experience in the cage that this desire is powerful enough to allow audiences to dismiss the possibility of self-conscious irony in the Other's self-presentation; even those who saw our performance as art rather than artifact appeared to take great pleasure in engaging in the fiction, by paying money to see us enact completely nonsensical or humiliating tasks. A middle-aged man who attended the Whitney Biennial opening with his elegantly dressed wife insisting on feeding me a banana. The zoo guard told him he would have to pay $10 to do so, which he quickly paid, insisting that he be photographed in the act. After the initial surprise of encountering caged beings, audiences invariably revealed their familiarity with the scenario to which we alluded.

We did not anticipate that our self-conscious commentary on this practice could be believable. We underestimated public faith in museums as bastions of truth, and institutional investment in that role. Furthermore, we did not anticipate that literalism would dominate the interpretation of our work. Consistently from city to city, more than half of our visitors believed our fiction and thought we were "real"; at the Whitney, however, we experienced the art world equivalent of such misperceptions: some visitors assumed that we were not the artists, but rather actors who had been hired by another artist. As we moved our performance from public site to natural history museum, pressure mounted from institutional representatives obliging us to didactically correct audience misinterpretation. We found this particularly ironic, since museum staffs are perhaps the most aware of the rampant distortion of reality that can occur in the labeling of artifacts from other cultures. In other words, we were not the only ones who were lying; our lies simply told a different story. For making this manifest, we were perceived as either noble savages or evil tricksters, dissimulators who discredit museums and betray public trust. When a few uneasy staff members in Australia and Chicago realized that large groups of Japanese tourists appeared to believe the fiction, they became deeply disturbed, fearing that the tourists would go home with a negative impression of the museum. In Chicago, just next to a review of the cage performance, the daily *Sun-Times* ran a phone-in questionnaire asking readers if they thought the Field Museum *should* have exhibited us, to which forty seven percent answered no, and fifty-three percent yes.[12] We seriously wonder if such weighty moral responsibilities are leveled against white artists who present fictions in nonart contexts.

Lest we attribute the now infamous confusion we generated among the general public to some defect of class or education, let it also be known that misinterpretation filtered into the echelons of the cultural elite. *Cambio 16,* a left-leaning news magazine in Spain, ran a newsbrief on us as two "Indians behind bars" who had conducted a political protest.[13] Though ironic in tone, the story only referred to us by our first names, almost as if to make us seem like the latest exotic arrival to a local zoo. The trustees of the Whitney Museum questioned curators at a meeting prior to the Biennial asking for confirmation of rumors that there would be "naked people screaming obscenities in a cage" at the opening. When we arrived at the University of California/ Irvine last year, we learned that the Environmental Health and Safety Office had understood that Gómez-Peña and I were anthropologists bringing "real aborigines" whose excrement—if deposited inside the gallery—could be hazardous to the university. This was particularly significant in light of the school's location in Orange County, where Mexican immigrants are often characterized by right-wing "nativists" as environmental hazards. Upon request from the art department, the office sent several pages of instructions on the proper disposal of human waste and the over thirty diseases that were transmitted through excrement. Interestingly, those institutional representatives who responded to our performance with moral indignation also saw us as dangerous, but in the more ideological sense of being offensive to the public, bad for children, and dishonest subverters of the educational responsibilities of their museums.

I should perhaps note here the number of people who encountered this perfor-

"Two Undiscovered Amerindians Visit Madrid,"
a performance by Coco Fusco and Guillermo Gómez-Peña, 1992.
PHOTO BY PETER BARKER.

mance. We do not have exact figures for Columbus Plaza and Covent Garden, which are both heavily trafficked public areas; however, we do know that 1,000 saw us in Irvine; 15,000 in Minneapolis; approximately 5,000 in both Sydney and Chicago; and 120,000 in Washington, D.C. Audience reactions of those who believed the fiction occasionally included moral outrage that was often expressed paternalistically (i.e., "Don't you realize," said one English gentleman to the zoo guards in Covent Garden, "that these poor people have no idea what is happening to them?"). The Field Museum in Chicago received forty-eight phone calls, most of which were from people who faulted the museum for having printed misinformation about us in their information sheet. In Washington, D.C., an angry visitor phoned the Humane Society to complain and was told that human beings were out of their jurisdiction. However, the majority of those who were upset remained so for only about five minutes. Others said they felt that our being caged was justified because we were, after all, different. A group of sailors who were interviewed by a Field Museum staff member said that our being in a cage was a good idea since we might otherwise have become frightened, and attacked visitors. One older African American man in Washington asserted quite angrily that it would have been all right to put us in a cage only if we had had some physical defect that classified us as freaks.

For all the concern expressed about shocking children, we found that young people's reactions have been the most humane. Young children invariably got the closest to the cage; they would seek direct contact, offer to shake our hands, and try to catch our eyes and smile. Little girls gave me barrettes for my hair and offered me their own food. Boys and girls often asked their parents excellent questions about us, prompting ethical discussions about racism and treatment of indigenous peoples. Not all parents were prepared to provide answers, and some looked very nervous. A woman in London sat her child down and explained that we were just like the people in the displays at the Commonwealth Institute. A school group visiting Madrid told the teacher that we were just like the Arawak Indian figures in the wax museum across the street. Then there have been those children who are simply fascinated by the spectacle; we heard many a child in Sydney, where our cage sat in front of an exhibit featuring giant mechanized insects, yelling "Mommy, Mommy, I don't want to see the bugs. I want to stay with the Mexicans!"

The tenor of reactions to seeing "undiscovered Amerindians" in a cage changed from locale to locale; we noted, for example, that in Spain, a country with no strong tradition of Protestant morality or empirical philosophy, opposition to our work came from conservatives who were concerned with its political implications, and not with the ethics of dissimulation. Some patterns, however, repeated themselves. Audience reactions were largely divisible along lines of race, class, and nationality. Artists and cultural bureaucrats, the self-proclaimed elite, exhibited skeptical reactions that were often the most anxiety-ridden. They sometimes expressed a desire to rupture the fiction publicly by naming us, or arrived armed with skepticism as they searched for the "believers," or parodied believers in order to join the performance. At the Whitney Biennial the performers of DanceNoise and Charles Atlas, among others, screamed loudly at Gómez-Peña to "free his genitalia" when he unveiled a crotch with his penis hidden between his legs instead of hanging. Several young artists also complained to our sponsors that we were not experimental enough to be considered good performance art. Others at the Whitney and in Australia, where many knew that we were part of the Sydney Biennale dismissed our piece as "not critical." One woman in Australia sat down with her young daughter in front of the cage and began to apologize very loudly for "having taken our land away." Trying to determine who really believed the fiction and who didn't became less significant for us in the course of this performance than figuring out what the audience's sense of the rules of the game and their role in it was.

People of color who believed, at least initially, that the performance was real, at times expressed discomfort *because* of their identification with our situation. In Washington and London, they made frequent references to slavery, and to the mistreatment of Native peoples and blacks as part of their history. Cross-racial identification with us among whites was less common, but in London a recently released ex-convict who appeared to be very drunk grabbed the bars and proclaimed to us with tears in his eyes that he understood our plight because he was a "British Indian." He then took off his sweater and insisted that Gómez-Peña put it on, which he did. In general, white spectators tended to express their chagrin to our zoo guards, usually operating under the assumption that we, the Amerindians, were being used. They often asked the zoo guards if we had consented to being confined, and then continued with a politely delivered stream of questions about our eating, work, and sexual habits.

Listening to these reactions was often difficult for the zoo guards and museum staff people who assisted us. One of our zoo guards in Spain actually broke down and cried at the end of our performance, after receiving a letter from a young man condemning Spain for having colonized indigenous Americans. One guard in Washington and another in Chicago became so troubled by their own cognitive dissonance that they left the performance early. The director of Native American programs for the Smithsonian told us she was forced to reflect on the rather disturbing revelation that while she made efforts to provide the most accurate representation of Native cultures she could, our "fake" sparked exactly the same reaction from audiences. Staff meetings to discuss audience reactions were held at the Smithsonian, the Australian Museum, and the Field Museum. In all the natural history museum sites, our project became a pretext for internal discussions about the extent of self-criticism those museums could openly be engaged in. In Australia, our project was submitted to an aboriginal curatorial committee for approval. They accepted, with the stipulation that there be nothing aboriginal in the cage, and that exhibition cases of aborigines be added to our chronology.

Other audience members who realized that we were artists chastised us for the "immoral" act of duping our audiences. This reaction was rather popular among the British, and emerged also among intellectuals and cultural bureaucrats in the United States. I should here note that there are historical precedents for the moralistic responses to the ethnographic display in Britain and the United States, but in those cases, the appeal was to the inhumanity of the practice, not to the ethics of fooling audiences, which the phony anthropologists who acted as docents in American Dime Museums often did. A famous court case took place in the early nineteenth century to determine whether it was right to, exhibit the Hottentot Venus, and black ministers in the U.S. in the early twentieth century protested Ota Benga's being exhibited in the Bronx Zoo. Neither protest triumphed over the mass appeal of the spectacle to whites.

The literalism governing American thought complements the liberal belief that we can eliminate racism through didactic correctives; it also encourages resistance to the idea that conscious methods may not necessarily transform unconscious structures of belief. I believe that this situation explains why moralizing interpreters shifted the focus of our work from audience reactions to our ethics. The reviewer sent by the *Washington Post*, for example, was so furious about our "dishonesty" that she could barely contain her anger and had to be taken away by attendants. A MacArthur Foundation representative came to the performance with his wife and they took it upon themselves to "correct" interpretations in front of the cage. In a meeting after the performance, the Foundation representative referred to a "poor Mexican family" who was deeply grateful to his wife for explaining the performance to them. After receiving two written complaints and the *Washington Post* review, the director of public programs for the Smithsonian Natural History Museum gave a talk in Australia severely criticizing us for misleading the public. We have heard that he has since changed his position. What we have not yet fully understood is why so many of these people failed to see our performance as interactive, and why they seem to have forgotten the tradition of site-specific performance with which our work dovetails, a historical development that preceded performance art's theatricalization in the 1980s.

On the whole, audience responses tended to be less pedantic and more outwardly emotional. Some people who were disturbed by the image of the cage feared getting too close, preferring instead to stay at the periphery of the audience. Barbara Kruger came to see us at the University of California, Irvine and went charging out of the gallery as soon as she read the chronology of the human display. Claes Oldenberg, on the other hand, sat at a distance in Minneapolis, watching our audiences with a wry smile on his face. The curator of the Amerindian collection at the British Museum came to look at us. As she posed for a photo, she conceded to one of our Edge Biennial representatives that she felt very guilty. Her museum had already declined to give us permission to be displayed. Others found less direct ways of expressing such anxiety. A feminist artist from New York questioned us after a public lecture we gave on the performance in Los Angeles last year, suggesting that our piece had "failed" if the public misread it. One young white woman filmmaker in Chicago who attended the performances showed up afterward at a class at the University of Illinois and yelled at Gómez-Peña for being "ungrateful" for all the benefits he had received thanks to multiculturalism. She claimed to have gone to the performance with an African American man who was "equally disturbed" by it. Gómez-Peña responded that multiculturalism was not a "gift" from whites, but the result of decades of struggle by people of color. Several feminist artists and intellectuals at performances in the United States approached me in the cage to complain that my role was too passive, and berated me for not speaking but only dancing, as if my activities should support their political agenda.

Whites outside the U.S. were more ludic in their reactions than American whites, and they appeared to be less self-conscious about expressing their enjoyment of our

Maximo and Bartola, "the last Aztec survivors of a mysterious jungle city called Ixinaya."
PHOTO BY CHARLES EISENMAN, COURTESY OF THE BECKER COLLECTION, SYRACUSE UNIVERSITY LIBRARY,
DEPARTMENT OF SPECIAL COLLECTIONS.

spectacle. For example, businessmen in London and Madrid approached the cage to make stereotypical jungle animal sounds; however, not all the reactions were light-hearted. A group of skinheads attacked Gómez-Peña in London and were pulled away by audience members; scores of adolescents in Madrid stayed at the cage for hours each day, taunting us by offering beer cans filled with urine and other such delicacies. Some of those who understood that the cage piece was performance art made a point—in private—of expressing their horror at others' reactions to us, per-haps as a way of disassociating themselves from their racial group. One Spanish busi-nessman waited for me after the performance was over to congratulate me on the performance, introduced me to his son, and then insisted that I agree that the Spaniards had been less brutal with the Indians than had the English. The over-whelming majority of whites who believed the piece, however, did not complain or express surprise at our condition in a manner that was apparent to us or the zoo guards. No American ever asked about the legitimacy of the map (though two Mexicans did), or the taxonomic information on the signs, or Gómez-Peña's made-up language. An older man at the Whitney told a zoo guard that he remembered our island from *National Geographic*. My dance, however, was severely criticized for its inauthenticity. In fact, during the press review at the Whitney, several writers simply walked away just as I began.

The reactions of Latin Americans differed according to class. Many upper-class Latin American tourists in Spain and Washington, D.C., voiced disgust that their part of the world should be represented in such a debased manner. Many other Latin Americans and Native Americans immediately recognized the symbolic significance of the piece, expressing solidarity with us, analyzing articles in the cage for other audience members, and showing their approval to us by holding our hands as they posed for photographs. Regardless of whether they believed or not, Latinos in the United States and Europe and Native Americans never criticized the hybridity of the cage environment and our costumes for being "unauthentic." One Pueblo elder from Arizona who saw us in the Smithsonian went so far as to say that our display was more "real" than any other statement about the condition of Native peoples in the museum. "I see the faces of my grandchildren in that cage," he told a museum repre-sentative. Two Mexicans who came to see us in England left a letter saying that they felt that they were living in a cage every day they spent in Europe. A Salvadoran man in Washington stayed with us for an extended period, pointing to the rubber heart suspended from the top of the cage, saying, "That heart is my heart." On the other hand, white Americans and Europeans have spent hours speculating in front of us about how we could possibly run a computer, own sunglasses and sneakers, and smoke cigarettes.

In Spain there were many complaints that our skin was not dark enough for us to be "real" primitives. The zoo guards responded by explaining that we live in a rain forest without much exposure to the sun. At the Whitney, a handful of older women also complained that we were too light-skinned, one saying that the piece would only be effective if we were "really dark." These doubts, however, did not stop many from taking advantage of our apparent inability to understand European languages; many men in Spain made highly charged sexual comments about my body, coaxing others to add more money to the donation box to see my breasts move as I danced. I was also asked out on dates a few times in London. Many other people chose a more discreet way of expressing their sexual curiosity, by asking the zoo guards if we mated in public in the cage. Gómez-Peña found the experience of being continually objectified more difficult to tolerate than I did. By the end of our first three days in Madrid, we began to realize not only that people's assumptions about us were based upon gender stereotypes, but that my experiences as a woman had prepared me to shield myself psychologically from the violence of public objectification.

I may have been more prepared, but during the performances, we both were faced with sexual challenges that transgressed our physical and emotional boundaries. In the cage we were both objectified, in a sense, feminized, inviting both male and female spectators to take on a voyeuristic relationship to us. This might explain why women as well as men acted upon what appears to be the erotic attraction of a caged primitive male. In Sydney, our sponsoring institution, the Australian Museum of Natural History, was approached by a female reporter from a soft-porn magazine who wanted to do a photo spread in which she would appear topless, feeding us bananas and watermelon. She was refused by the museum publicist. Interestingly, women were consistently more physical in their reactions, while men were more verbally abusive. In Irvine, a white woman asked for plastic gloves to be able to touch the male specimen, began to stroke his legs, and soon moved toward his crotch. He stepped back, and the woman stopped—but she returned that evening, eager to discuss our feelings about her gesture. In Chicago, another woman came up to the cage, grabbed his head and kissed him. Gómez-Peña's ex-wife had lawsuit papers delivered to him while we were in the cage at Irvine, and subsequently appeared in a mask and bizarre costume with a video camera and proceeded to tape us for over an hour. While men taunted me, talked dirty, asked me out, and even blew kisses, not one attempted physical contact in any of our performances.

As I presented this "reverse ethnography" around the country, people invariably asked me how I felt inside the cage. I experienced a range of feelings from panic to boredom. I felt exhilarated, and even playful at times. I've also fallen asleep from the hot sun and been irritable because of hunger or cold. I've been ill, and once had to be removed from the cage to avoid vomiting in front of the crowd. The presence of supportive friends was reassuring, but the more aggressive reactions became less and less surprising. The night before we began in Madrid, I lay awake in bed, overcome with fear that some demented Phalangist might pull a gun on us and shoot before we could escape. When nothing of that sort happened, I calmed down and never worried about our safety again. I have to admit that I liked watching people on the other side of the bars. The more we performed, the more I concentrated on the audience, while trying to feign the complete bewilderment of an outsider. Although I loved the intentional nontheatricality of this work, I became increasingly aware of how engaging in certain activities can trigger audience reactions, and acted on that realization to test our spectators. Over the course of the year, I grew fond of the extremists who verbalized their feelings and interacted with us physically, regardless of whether they were hostile or friendly. It seemed to me that they had a certain braveness, even courage, that I don't know I would have in their place. When we came upon Tiny Teesha in Minnesota, I was dumbstruck at first. Not even my own performance had prepared me for the sadness I saw in her eyes, or my own ensuing sense of shame.

One memory in particular came to the forefront of my mind as we traveled with this performance. It involved an encounter I had over a decade ago, when I was finishing college in Rhode Island, where I had studied film theory. I had met an internationally known French ethnographic filmmaker in his sixties at a seminar he was giving, and told him I planned to spend time in France after graduation. A year later, I received a phone call from him while I was in Paris. He had found me with the help of a student from my alma mater. He told me he was going to begin production on a feature and might be able to offer me a job. After having spent part of the summer as a translator-salesgirl at a department store, I was excited by the prospect of film-related work. We arranged to meet to discuss his project.

Even though we were conversing in a language I had not mastered, it didn't take long for me to sense that the filmmaker's interests might be more than professional. I was not exactly prepared to deal with sexual advances from a man who could have been my grandfather. I thought I had protected myself by arranging to meet in a public place, but he soon explained that we had to leave the cafe to meet with the producers for a reading of the script. After fifteen minutes in his car, I began to suspect that there was no meeting planned. We eventually arrived at what looked like an abandoned house in a rural area, without another soul in sight. He proudly announced that this was the house he had grown up in and that he wanted to show it to me. I was by this time in a mild state of shock, furiously trying to figure out where I was and how to get away safely.

The filmmaker proceeded to go into a shed next to the house and remove all his clothes except his underwear. He emerged with a manual lawn mower and went to work on his garden. At one point he ran up to me and exclaimed that he wished he could film me naked there; I did not respond. At another point, he handed me a basket and told me to gather nuts and berries. While my anger mounted, my fears slowly subsided as I realized that he was deeply immersed in his own fantasy world, so self-involved that he hardly needed my participation. I waited for him to finish his playacting, and then told him to take me to the closest train station, which he did, but not without grabbing me and ripping my shirt as I got out of his car.

I got back to my apartment safely. I was not physically harmed, but I was profoundly disturbed by what I had witnessed. The ethnographic filmmaker whose fame rested on his depictions of "traditional" African societies had projected his racist fantasies onto me for his own pleasure. What I thought I was, how I saw myself—that was irrelevant. Never had I seen so clearly what my physical presence could spark in the imagination of an aging colonialist pervert.

The memory of that ethnographic filmmaker's gaze haunted me for years, to the point that I began to wonder if I had become paranoid. But I, having watched behavior only slightly more discreet than his from behind the bars of our cage, can reassure myself that I am not. Those are the moments when I am glad that there are real bars. Those are also the times when, even though I know I can get out of the cage, I can never quite escape.

———

AMERINDIANS: 1) *A mythical people of the Far East, connected in legendary history with Seneca and Amerigo Vespucci.*

Although the term Amerindian suggests that they were the original inhabitants of this continent, the oldest authorities (e.g., Christopher Columbus in his diaries, and more recently, Paul Rivette) regarded them as Asian immigrants, not Americans. Other explanations suggested are *arborindians*, "tree people," and *amerindians*, "brown people." The most that can be said is that *amerindians* may be the name of an indigenous American stock that the ancients knew no more about than ourselves.

AMERINDIANS: 2) One of the many English terms for the people of Guatinau. In their language, the Guatinaui people's word for themselves signifies "outrageously beautiful" or "fiercely independent." They are a jovial and playful race, with a genuine affection for the debris of Western industrialized popular cultural. In former times, however, they committed frequent raids on Spanish ships, disguised as British pirates, whence comes their familiarity with European culture. Contemporary Guatinauis have only recently begun to travel outside their island.

The male and female specimens here on display are representatives of the dominant tribe from their island, having descended from the Mintomani stock. The male weighs seventy-two kilos, measures 1.77 meters, and is approximately thirty-seven years of age. He likes spicy food, burritos, and Diet Coke, and his favorite cigarette brand is Marlboro. His frequent pacing in the cage leads experts to believe that he was a political leader on his island.

The female weights sixty three kilos, measures 1.74 meters, and appears to be in her early thirties. She is fond of sandwiches, pad thai, and herb tea. She is a versatile dancer, and also enjoys showing off her domestic talents by sewing voodoo dolls, serving cocktails, and massaging her male partner. Her facial and body decorations indicate that she has married into the upper caste of her tribe.

Both of the Guatinauis are quite affectionate in the cage, seemingly uninhibited in their physical and sexual habits despite the presence of an audience. Their animist spirituality compels them to engage in periodic gestural prayers, which they do with great enthusiasm. They like to massage and scratch each other, enjoy occasional long embraces, and initiate sexual intercourse on the average of twice a day.

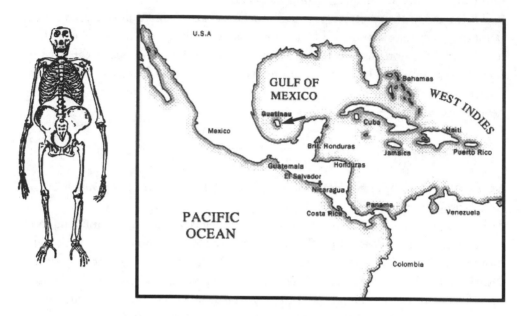

Left: Guatinauis Ancestor.

Anthropologists at the Smithsonian observed (with the help of surveillance cameras) that the Guatinauis enjoy gender role playing together after dark, transforming many of their functional objects in the cage into makeshift sex toys by night. Visitors who get close to them will note that they often seek to fondle strangers while posing for photographs. They are extremely demonstrative with children.

AFTERWORD

Over a year has passed since I wrote this chronicle and in that time, two major events have taken place that have radically altered my understanding of the perceptions and misperceptions of *Two Undiscovered Amerindians*... One pertains to the Latin American reception of the work. The other involves legal and ethical issues relating to the video documentary of the performances, *The Couple in the Cage.*

Throughout our tour of Europe and America, Guillermo and I were questioned by colleagues as to why we did not seek out opportunities to present *Two Undiscovered Amerindians*...in Latin America, to "our own community," so to speak. At first, we responded by saying that we believed that the piece was designed primarily for first world countries, for places in which the practice of the ethnographic display had taken place as part of a colonial project. Several months after we ceased to carry out the piece, however, we received an invitation from the Fundación Banco Patricios to take the cage performance to Buenos Aires. Though we had already decided that the performance had run its course, we could not pass up the chance to test its possibilities in South America. Before heading south, we worried that performing the piece for the Porteños might be too much like preaching to the converted.

Our fears were completely unfounded. Our performance, which took place in the groundfloor vitrine of the cultural center at the busy downtown intersection of Corrientes and Callao avenues, turned out to be more convincing to the Argentines than to any other audience we had had. We received several letters from visitors who felt that our savage souls needed saving, and that colonization would have insured our conversion to the Christian faith. The docents told many audience members that they could attend a panel discussion after the performance, and several older people arrived, asking if a translator would be provided so they could finally converse with us. Several young men spent hours making lurid gestures at me, slipping me their phone numbers and poking fun at Guillermo. A man approached the cage on our first night on display, and hurled acid at Guillermo, burning his stomach and leg. The Foundation security guard who was subsequently assigned to watch out for us confessed his sexual fantasies about me with glee after the performance as I rode with him in an elevator. Another older gentleman told a docent that he was sure that I would perform sexual favors for an additional fee when the performance was over.

Our piece seemed to serve as an ice breaker in an extremely elitist cultural milieu, drawing street vendors, poor children and others who had never been inside the Foundation building in their lives, often to the dismay of the institution's regular patrons. Scores of mestizos and indigenous immigrants to the city from Bolivia, Peru and Argentina's northern regions watched us evening after evening with extraordinary sadness in their eyes. Meanwhile, dozens of Argentine intellectuals sat sipping coffee in the bar directly behind us, often pretending to ignore the scene unfolding before them. The many psychologists and anthropologists who attended were divided as to whether such a piece was too disturbing for the Argentine public, traumatized by the military dictatorship. With the exception of such older generation political artist luminaries as Leon Ferreri and Marta Minujín, most of the local artists and intellectuals we met insisted our work made no sense there because Argentina was "really" European, because there was no racism in their country, and ultimately because American minorities' obsession with identity was parochial and it generated inferior art. Some even admitted that they had been disappointed to discover that we were not "real" American artists, meaning that we were not white. Much in the same way that the Spain we had visited was rabidly rejecting its association with its ex-colonies as it experienced a moment of intense yearning to break with its undemocratic, economically underdeveloped past, Argentina seemed to reject us as a way of asserting its new status as an economically stabilized technocracy aspiring to attain the "American way of life." Only a handful of people we met reminded us that Argentina had conducted its own highly successful extermination campaigns against its indigenous populations around the same time that Americans had conquered the West.

It is still suggested that our performance was an essay in fanciful self-indulgence, but the historical nightmares we allude to have become all too real for comfort. A current legal dispute regarding ownership of the documentary about our performance, *The Couple in the Cage,* has forced us to experience in the flesh the implications of ethical debates about cultural property and appropriation that have pervaded discussions of both documentary filmmaking and art by and about indigenous communities. After two years of conducting historical research and one year of performances, Guillermo and I had accumulated several hours of video documentation which included interviews with audience members that had been conducted under our supervision. In addition, we had compiled an extensive archive of photographs and sketches documenting the history of the practice, and I had written this chronicle to serve in part as a conceptual underpinning of the documentary.

After editing was completed, a dispute arose over whether our efforts were sufficient to establish sole ownership of the documentary. In the absence of a document with a few magic words, it was claimed that the arrangement of pre-existing elements created by Guillermo and myself so radically altered the integrity of the performance as to make it something else altogether. More to our horror, it seemed to us as if the cage performance and documentation of its historical antecedents were being interpreted as raw materials for an exercise in sampling.

Guillermo and I panicked, fearing, as do many artists working in ephemeral forms, that our only means of sustaining the life of our performance would be seriously damaged. The more legal opinions we sought, the more complex the issues involved became. How does one prove that our fiction, which only could exist in the live interactions with others, was a scripted event and that editing could have only reconstituted it? How does one impress upon documentarians that a performance artist's likeness is not raw material but self-consciously constructed art?

Over the past year, I have felt trapped in a frightful chapter of history that had resurfaced before my eyes. There were the circus and freak show manager of yore, claiming that they had "made us" into Guatinauis and that without them we were nothing. There were the anthropologists of the early century insisting that we had performed our identity without knowing, that we had no proper concept of how to record our culture and represent ourselves and therefore needed them to find an order in our madness. And there were the myriad pseudo-liberal documentarians who believed that the "reality" they capture is always spontaneously generated, only to be formed into something meaningful by their magic touch. As performers, we have no legal means to secure ownership of our time-based art form other than to claim its documentation as our property. As experimental artists, we hardly have the means to protect our rights, and face a legal system in which notions of aesthetic value must translate into money in order to make sense to those we contract to represent us. The so-called primitive superstition that photographers steal souls had become terrifyingly real.

As of this writing, the last trace of the Guatinauis is the subject of a pending lawsuit against me. In the age of ongoing copyright wars over rap music, sufficient ambiguities have been created so that an arrangement of pre-existing elements can be construed to prevail. After years of interrogating the implications of the ethnographic gaze, our having to suffer the legal implications of having someone claim to have "discovered" us has been the most painful and ironic lesson of the Guatinaui world tour.

WHO'S DOIN' THE TWIST?
NOTES TOWARD A POLITICS
OF APPROPRIATION

...How are we to understand
the social or psychological bases for this postimperial mode of mimicry,
this ghost dance of white ethnicity?
KOBENA MERCER

DURING A TRIP I made to Germany and France in 1993, I could not avoid taking note of resurgent hatred directed at foreigners in general, and at Muslims in particular. Not a week passed without some news report about Arab, Turkish, and African immigrants being burned out of their dwellings or beaten by neofascists. It seemed as if Europeans reserved a special kind of malevolence for the last non-Christian people to have succeeded in conquering parts of their continent. Sadly, it reminded me of the rising xenophobia in my newly adopted home state of California, a sentiment I interpret as a symptom of the fear that the Southwest might become part of Mexico, as it once was.

In Europe's climate of animosity, derisive comments about the (perceived) stubborn insistence on maintaining traditional connections between identity and appearance were common. More than a few Europeans reminded me of the legal battle involving the young Muslim girls and their *chadors* (veils), which the French state had sought to remove while they were in school. In many more conversations, I noted how even progressive Europeans equated "traditional" appearance with "oppressive" culture and minorities resistant to assimilation. They also insisted on the obverse of this view, saying that if immigrant children no longer *sounded* like their parents, then they were no longer really different. "It's only their hair that let's you know," a German woman told me, speaking of the children of Turkish guest workers. I found no room in these discussions for the idea of a third term, of hybrid identities that result from living between cultures.

The European feminists I encountered were no exception. I heard all too many horror stories about Muslim treatment of women that often began with comments about *chadors* and led to assertions that "traditional" men didn't allow their women to be feminists. At the same time, I also learned that the latest craze for middle-class German women trying to "get in touch with their bodies" was belly-dancing classes, which were even more popular than the salsa workshops that had sprung up like weeds all over northern Europe. No one spoke of the simultaneous embrace of a culture and rejection of the people who originate it as a contradictory behavior with a colonial history. German intellectuals at a film conference I attended on that trip argued that their interest in black culture was not part of a colonial legacy but rather a by-product of their being victims of the American culture industry, thus positing themselves as colonized. Rap performed by white youths, herbal medicine and hair care, nose piercing and world-beat fashion, all gestures of cross-cultural appropriation and identity displacement, were among the latest defining markers of the rebellious northern European. No one wanted to consider how European countercultural groups attempting to redefine, transform, and broaden contemporary societies, depended on reified notions of difference to delimit their transgressiveness.

I didn't have to cross the Atlantic to witness such acts of cultural transvestism, or the resistance of white artists, intellectuals, and global cultural consumers to interrogate the power relations implicit in these exchanges. On the contrary, I was sensitive to this phenomenon because of the emotionally charged debates about cultural appropriation in America. Less than a year after my European visit, during a public lecture I gave at a northeastern university, I made a brief comment about a female veteran of the 1960s New York avant-garde, noting how references she had made to African fertility goddess sculptures as a liberating influence in her search for erotic female imagery were part of a tradition of appropriation I saw as linked to colonialism. I explained that I thought she had conflated the identity imputed to the fetishes by Euro-Americans (i.e., that they were African, therefore erotic, therefore transgressive) with the significance of the objects within their own context.

Afterwards, several of my white colleagues pulled me over quite nervously to ask what was wrong with such borrowing. They assured me that the artist in question wasn't racist, and confessed that they too absorbed visual influences from non-Western cultures. "Are you trying to tell me I have to take all the stuff I brought back from my trip down the Nile out of my studio?" exclaimed one of them. My attempts to distinguish between moral judgments and the politics of cultural exchange were futile, so I opted to drop the issue rather than be ostracized, once again, for appearing to behave like a politically correct hardliner.

No other multiculturalism-related topic I know of has been the source of more defensiveness and explosive reactions from white people than that of cultural appropriation. As I look back on a decade of multicultural debates in the American art world and academia, the memories of that rancor alone are enough to make me persist in asking why whites are so invested in either avoiding the issue of cultural appropriation or refuting racialized approaches. I can no longer keep count of the times I have seen artists and critics of color shunned for raising the issue at public events, or how often colleagues have been blacklisted when they have advocated affirmative action policies as protective measures against excessive appropriation. Could it be that the backlash has generated an intellectual climate in which such vehemence is acceptable from people who might have bitten their tongues in other times?

Between the liberal cries of reverse racism and censorship, and the post-structuralist accusations of essentialism, one might be coaxed into believing that people of color actually had the same kind of control and access that the dominant society and mainstream cultural institutions wield. These hyperbolic accusations, gay Asian-Canadian cultural activist Richard Fung points out, give the false impression that individuals and communities can engage in censorship, which in reality is the sole prerogative of the state, and also perpetrate age-old notions of nonwhites as barbaric philistines.[1] The invectives against political correctness mask what motivates white attraction to cultures and peoples designated as Other, and diverts our attention from looking at how "difference" acts as an antidote to a perceived absence of spirituality, vitality, or erotic pleasure in the dominant culture.

"While some fusions may be celebrated as exchange, a larger proportion is the result of domination," writes Fung after working for a year on the advisory committee to the Canada Council for Racial Equality in the Arts. In his article, "Working through Cultural Appropriation," Fung goes to great lengths to map out a contextually bound system of interpretation to evaluate acts of exchange.[2] He makes crucial distinctions between the needs and priorities of different groups, stressing that it is particular *genealogies* of racial and ethnic subaltern groups that makes their concern for cultural preservation a logical priority. He notes the need to investigate the pervasiveness of misrepresentation in relation to a group, the degree of commercialization of the culture, and the actual possibilities of self-representation. Also, Fung differentiates between distinct modes of cultural production, suggesting that the specific natures of each might entail individualized regulatory policies. The opinions of his committee never became policy. Of the twelve recommendations made to redress racism within Canada's cultural bureaucracy, the only one dealing with cultural appropriation became the centerpiece of a protracted nationwide media attack on multiculturalism, despite the fact that the Canada Council had rejected it. So violent was the reaction to the very idea of regulating access to subaltern cultural property that the valuable efforts of activists were completely lost in the shuffle.

Black British cultural critic Kobena Mercer characterizes these encounters as moments of "acceleration of interculturation," calling them skirmishes played out around the semiotic economy of the ethnic signifier.[3] Mercer's theorization is particularly relevant to me because of his view that the problem is political (i.e., a struggle for power) and economic (i.e., a question of attribution of value to formally similar but distinct operations and entities). Mercer argues that we need to look at the network of social relations and histories that invest the act of appropriation with different values for different groups to make appropriate theories and aesthetic judgments about them. By doing so, he adroitly moves us past the two rationalizations that underpin multicultural backlashers' more frequent arguments—the liberal notion of cultural appropriation as an act of "free will," and the post-structuralist approaches that abstract individual acts of appropriation from the social systems that imbue them with specific meanings. With the help of his analyses, and those of Fung, bell hooks and others, I will attempt to walk through some of the current skirmishes to make sense of the dynamic that unfolds around me daily.

Writing and talking about cultural appropriation, I reposition myself in a some-what precarious way within a society that seeks to deny how segregated it is; I go from being a "minority" critic dutifully explaining Otherness to one who addresses whites as agents in an ongoing dynamic of racialization. This shift in terms disrupts the commonly held assumption that desire for the Other is in itself a way of elimi-nating racial inequality. Furthermore, to speak of whiteness as a way of being in the world still disturbs many of those for whom a racialized discourse is in itself a minority discourse, a mode of marginalization. Dominant cultural and white avant-garde defenses are cast in terms of aesthetic freedom (*But why can't I use what I want as an artist?*) and transgression of bourgeois banality (*But I cross boundaries and there-fore I rebel too*). What is more fundamentally at stake than freedom, I would argue, is power—the power to choose, the power to determine value, and the right of the more powerful to consume without guilt. That sense of entitlement to choose, change, and redefine one's identity is fundamental to understanding the history of how white America has formed ideas about itself, and how those ideas are linked first to a colonial enterprise, and, in the postwar period, to the operations of indus-trialized mass culture.

American history from the late nineteenth and early twentieth century is rife with examples of how black and Native American cultural expression was regulated by a white power structure and removed form its sources to serve as entertainment for whites.[4] Many Native American dances, for example, were outlawed on reserva-tions while they were regularly performed for whites at fairs and circuses. This legacy makes the act of preserving culture and invoking boundaries less a matter of essentialist romanticism than cultural survival. At the same time, absorption and mimicry of Native American, Mexican, and African American cultural forms and philosophies have been absolutely central to the formation and transformation of white Americanness. During the Boston Tea Party, for example, colonials dressed like Native Americans to attack British ships.[5] After the transfer of the northern half of Mexico to the United States, German and Scottish settlers in Texas turned the world of the Mexican *vaquero* into what is now considered quintessentially American—cowboy culture. During the same period, easterners who headed west in search of fortune often changed their last names to Spanish ones to slip in among the *Californios*.[6] Class is woven into this pattern as the transfers of appearance move from the subaltern to the privileged.

There is a long history within American feminism of these sorts of gestures, dating back to the links made by early suffragists between political disenfranchisement of black slaves and white women. During the early stages of the women's movement of the 1960s, it was commonplace for some white feminists to appropriate the terminology of slavery to speak of bourgeois marriage. More recently, many white feminists have chosen to ally themselves, politically and theoretically, with the struggles of women of color in the United States and the Third World. As Chandra Talpade Mohanty eloquently explains in "Under Western Eyes: Third World Women and Feminism," many of these gestures, however well intentioned, too often rely on (with no actual reference), a paradigmatic "Third-World woman" as well as on the universality of the category of women to be politically effective.[7] Resistance from feminists of color has come in response to the awareness that such alliances too often function as a simple means of validating white feminism as morally superior due to its apparent antiracism.

Privileged women in Latin America have also relied throughout history on subaltern cultures for signs they could appropriate as markers of their transgressiveness. One of my favorite examples is that of the *tapadas* of the sixteenth-century viceroyalty of Peru. They were libertine *criollas* who used their shawls as *chador*-like veils, covering all but one eye to hide themselves and thus be freer and less easy to identify in public places. This practice had originated in Spain, where after the expulsion of the Moors in 1492, Islamic veils were banned as *Morisca* slaves turned to shawls to cover their heads and faces. Catholic women quickly perceived in the use of this body covering the advantage of its allowing them more social mobility and privacy. They took on the practice with such gusto and success that the Spanish crown outlawed it thereafter. In South America in the 1580s, the Council on the Indies saw in *tapadas* potential damage to the empire, noting that their sexual behavior could not be controlled and that even men were using shawls to engage in homoerotic "sin and sacrilege." Despite frequent attempts to outlaw it, the practice continued into the eighteenth century, when Enlightenment ideas redirected privileged women's desire for more liberty to cerebral rather than sensual pursuits.[8]

The dynamics of appropriation that evolved with colonialism intensified with the introduction of industrialized mass culture in the postwar period. In *Subculture and the Meaning of Style*, Dick Hebdige notes that in First-World youth cultures one can discern the phantom history of race relations since the war.[9] To this I would add that mass culture cyclically projects the image of an atomistic racial utopia to (white) middle-class consumers, promising individualized, and often eroticized, modes of cultural appropriation and consumption that substitute for equitable exchange or simply contain interaction among ethnic groups. It has been widely argued that white youth in the 1950s danced to "jungle music" and "mambo" to express their rebellion against the repressed atmosphere of the McCarthy era. Though some might claim that their enthusiasm for the music prefigured integrationist ideals of the 1960s, the music industry quickly made whites into the star figures of what began as black cultural movements, thereby strengthening mass-cultural dominance and revalorizing its symbolic capital by means of commodification. The modality of this cultural practice has shifted somewhat in recent years due to the emergence of world-beat culture, which presents a more equitable facade, and also to the growth of black-dominated areas of the American entertainment industry, where some people of color exert a degree of control over their representation. Yet, our projection of racial diversity as desirable, and our sophisticated consumer's attraction to commodified otherness have done little to stop increasing the polarization of wealth along racial lines. In fact, they parallel the intensification of xenophobia and nativism in government policy throughout the nations of the First World.

The postmodernist celebration of appropriation dovetails with a certain kind of thinking about art that extends the notion of creativity to include the recontextualizing of objects and signs. The more Eurocentric versions of this school of thought distinguish between dominant cultural acts of appropriation as creative transformation, and subaltern manipulation of imposed forms as "derivative" activity that distance them from a preferably natural state. The white avant-garde's and the dominant culture's appropriations are interpreted as implicit critiques of a modernist glorification of originality, and of ideologies that conflate nature and culture, while the subaltern version is seen as evidence of self-hatred. In "Black Style/Hair Politics" Mercer provides a detailed analysis of the defects in the reasoning that identifies such practices as hair-straightening as assimilationist. At the same time, he acknowledges the significance of cultural nationalist negation of Eurocentrically imposed aesthetics and standards as a necessary and strategic moment in a process of decolonization.[10] The Eurocentric approach to appropriation does not account for the conditions of colonized societies and other contexts where national autonomy, national culture, and/or subaltern identity are fragile, imperiled, or symbolically effaced by external forces. Attempts to establish protectionist measures in order, for example, to allow national cinemas to develop in such contexts are hardly examples of reactionary essentialism—they are prerequisites to survival and are ways of combating the American habit of dumping its entertainment industry waste on poorer neighbors. These regulatory efforts do not oppose, but complement, the strategies of recycling, creolizing, parodying, and otherwise transforming the imposed symbolic systems that are integral to the history of, for example, most Latin American and Caribbean countries.

Contemporary cultural debate in the United States has tended to depoliticize the act of appropriation by abstracting it from its historical context, as well as from its agents. Too often, the focus of analysis is either on the individual acts of appropriation by artists and identity-benders or the large-scale exchanges of goods within the domain of global capitalism, without a questioning of the ways these practices intersect. Formalist analyses can make different operations appear to be similar, but only the most extreme forms of relativism would allow us to equate the operations of institutions, corporations, governments, and affluent consumers with the survival strategies of marginalized communities. Appropriation is a process that cannot be reduced to what happens once something identifiable is removed from the place it previously occupied. Cultural appropriation is as much a political act as it is a formal operation or linguistic game. It involves *taking* something, often from someone, and it is rarely an isolated gesture. Seen from a semiotic perspective, the act may be interpreted as a dramatic illustration of the arbitrary relationships between identities and bodies, or between signifiers and referents. Seen within the historical context of historical relationships among the different sectors of societies in the Americas, however, that act of taking is marked by a legacy of violence, and of forced adaptation to imposed symbolic orders and the loss of the colonized's right to name things as their own. While it is true that no culture is fixed and that exchange among cultures has taken place throughout history, not to recognize historical imbalances and their influence is *the* strategical evasion that enables the already empowered to naturalize their advantage. As bell hooks points out in her essay "Eating the Other," members of ethnic minority groups that have endured a history of having their cultural production regulated by and capitalized on by whites deploy essentialist arguments as a defense against excessive commodification.[11]

Underlying hooks's, Mercer's, and Fung's arguments is the insistence that not all exchanges of cultural symbols are the same, and that an effective critical vocabulary to address the issue must be able to take the specificities of each situation into account. Methods that proceed from facile generalizations, abstractions, and theoretical paradigms may provide quick results, but abstractions and theoretical paradigms obfuscate the issue. The current moves within gender studies to present passing and drag as psychosymbolically interdependent modes of appropriation might be reviewed in light of the ongoing insistence among white scholars on forging equivalence among different forms of marginality by abstracting examples from their specific contexts. To insist on the equivalence between textual acquisition of information and experiential knowledge, they buttress their arguments not only with diatribes against essentialism, but also an endless artillery of decontextualized citations from subaltern writers. Perhaps the best-known manifestation of this debate involves the writings of bell hooks and white lesbian theorist Judith Butler about Jennie Livingston's film about black and Latino voguers, *Paris is Burning*. I cannot here recapitulate Butler's and hooks's arguments in their entirety, but I will try to gloss the pertinent points, referring to hooks's article "Is Paris Burning?" and Butler's "Gender is Burning."[12]

Reacting to the euphoria in the mainstream media over Livingston's film, hooks took up issues that had been downplayed by white critics; mainly that the drag queens in the film drew their notion of femininity from white suprematist ideals of female beauty, that the film deploys the voyeuristic gaze of the conventional ethnographic documentary, and that its status as a cross-over hit was indicative of its success in exploiting the established colonialist and voyeurist convention of taking the white tourist into the dark underworld. Throughout her piece, hooks stresses that the film is an industrialized form of mass entertainment, which is extremely significant. Crucial to understanding and determining the value and meaning of cultural appropriation is the nature of the genre worked in and the power relations it sustains among artist, subjects, and audience.[13] Commercial cinema's sheer money-making potential sets it apart from many other art practices and invites an analysis of its economic relations. Ethnographic cinema, in light of its historical connection to colonialist adventurism, and decades of debate about the ethics of representing documentary subjects, is a genre that demands a special degree of scrutiny.

Throughout her rebuttal, Butler blurs these distinctions. She declines to address the position of the film in the mass-cultural marketplace, preferring instead to take on an auteurist, psychoanalytic reading that focuses on the relationship between the director and her subject. Even so, Butler makes no mention of the fact that, in 1991, several of Livingston's subjects filed suit against her and the film's distributor for unlawful use of their images. With ease, Butler glosses over substantial differences between the genres of literature and documentary film, moving from the contemporary *Paris Is Burning* to early-twentieth-century novels by Willa Cather and Nella Larsen to support her theoretical claims. Butler's mode of analysis abstracts the issue appropriation from its context, thereby eliding the ghosts of history that might temper her claims of transgression.

Butler's response relies heavily on diminishing the validity of hooks's terms as essentialist, inaccurate, and heterosexist, but I also detect a deconstructionist distaste for social and historical forces, which, if mentioned at all in her analysis, are compressed to the point of triteness (i.e., "the painful and fatal mime that is passing for white"). Butler claims that hooks assumes that the drag queens are imitating women, and is therefore leaning toward female essentialism.[14] Why, Butler asks, should drag be necessarily seen as negative imitations of women? But why should hooks's views be read as part of a history of white feminist critiques of drag as misogynist when her comments are about the reactionary quality of the version of femininity being appropriated? In her digression on drag and misogyny, Butler allows race to drop out momentarily—not acknowledging that hooks's actually refers to the drag queens' embrace of white suprematist notions of female beauty, ideals that are distinguishable from any historical or essentialist category of women and/or women's experience. In not noting this distinction, Butler reverts to the earlier stages of feminist thought that she initially criticizes for positing the primacy of sexual difference as determinant.

As if to "out-race" the race expert, Butler then suggests that hooks isn't sensitive enough to ethnic diversity among the voguers because she neglects to mention that there were Latinos as well as blacks. She herself, however, does not make a critical distinction between the *racial* category of black, which covers all the voguers, and *ethnic* categories of African American and Latino, which divide them. hooks makes no *racial* distinction because there is none to make. Furthermore, while Butler makes efforts to undermine hooks's assertions about racial dynamics in film, she never acknowledges that the sexual history of the Caribbean (the origin of *Paris Is Burning*'s Latinos) is rife with evidence of exploitation of gay and heterosexual men *and* women of color by gay and bisexual whites, heterosexual *criollos,* and tourists. To suggest, as Butler does, that the possibility of a white lesbian director's gender-bending desire for a black transvestite in and of itself subverts ethnographic convention because it introduces ambiguity does not engage with a history of racial exploitation that crosses genders and sexualities. It also overlooks another key chapter in the history of sexual relations between whites and blacks, in which, during slavery and segregation, white women "called the shots" in their actual and invented relationships with black men and "cried rape" as a means of exerting control. Livingston's alleged feminization of her black subject may subvert gender identity for Butler, but it also recalls a long history of white women's power to subjugate black men and thus keep the racial order of things in check.

To allow such a possibility of subversion to hinge on the exaggerated camera movement in one scene that was probably executed by a camera operator rather than the director further destabilizes Butler's critique of hooks's argument about the film's colonial gaze. If subversion occurs because of ambiguity, for whom does it occur? Are we to believe that anything about the life conditions of the voguers is subverted by a camera movement or directorial desire? What kind of subversion or ambiguity, then, is it? Did ambiguity prevent the film from playing into the prevailing racial and economic dynamics of a sexual economy in which "cruising the margins" is an international pastime for filmmakers, tourists, and consumers? hooks's stress on the economic and power relations in the film, and her suggestion that Livingston gained wealth and professional prominence through her capturing that culture on film, are side-stepped by Butler in favor of a reading that transforms every sign of oppression into a symbol of transgression.

In her attempt to show that Livingston's ethnography was a critical parody of convention because the voguers' "houses" constituted radical appropriations of family structures, Butler makes ambiguous assertions that are reminiscent of early anthropological writings. It is unclear at moments whether she is crediting Livingston-the-author for an adaptation of heterosexual kinship structures, or if she is recognizing that the "families" predated the film. Though Butler asserts that the balls catalyze the creation of alternative families, she uses their existence to support her claims of the film's subversion of ethnographic convention. Do the subjects then subvert the filmmaker's ethnographic look, or does the director undermine notions of family by choosing a nonconventional one as her subject? Finally, Butler's concern for the ethnic specificity of the Latino voguers does not motivate her sufficiently to learn that "nontraditional" extended and otherwise re-invented families are a historical constant in Latin American societies, particularly at the lower end of the social and economic scale. Butler's suggestion that the presentation of nontraditional kinship structure as family undermines convention sidesteps ethnography's historical purpose, which was to record and classify "other" kinship systems and thereby distinguish the western family from them. Their difference did not *subvert* the norm, but rather served as proof of it as a superior evolutionary stage. To suppose that voguers reinvented the white American middle-class family also implies that subaltern lives are purposely organized to subvert white heterosexual American norms, which is hardly the case, though whites may read them as such. To assume so, as Butler would seem to do, is surprisingly, if not alarmingly, ethnocentric.

In cultural milieus throughout the country, progressive intellectuals and artists have resorted to sophisticated forms of evasion rather than deal with the anxiety that confronting whiteness can generate. Operations within cultural bureaucracies are somewhat different from the assertions of individuals, but often lead to similar goals. Mainstream museums and curators have become expert at adopting the rhetoric of multiculturalism without having to implement fundamental changes in their institutions. For example, an African American colleague recently received a rejection letter from a prestigious California museum explaining that the exhibit about black masculinity she sought to present there "did not fully take into account artists and attitudes represented in Los Angeles's African American community," a sector that has never been paid attention to by the museum before invoking its name served their purposes. Two years before, another staff member at the same museum had told a Puerto Rican artist from New York that giving him a show might be taken as a slight by the local Latino community, which is largely Mexican, although no Latino show had ever taken place there.

White resistance to reckoning with the politics and economics of appropriation is not the only obstacle to furthering more productive discussion of cultural politics. Subaltern attempts to redress inequities and misrepresentations are still rife with inconsistencies. Protectionist measures are frequently couched in the moralistic language of guilt and blame, or they depend on static notions of authenticity to determine group membership and valorize certain forms of expression. The recent establishment of the Indian Arts and Crafts Act, for example, designed to protect indigenous artists, relies on federal laws governing tribal affiliation that are contested by many Native Americans. At times, the subaltern intervention is not systematic but suspiciously arbitrary, aimed at targets that are too weak to be of significant consequence. The action launched in 1992 by a prison warden's association against New York's Department of Cultural Affairs and a single white artist for having allegedly reinforced negative stereotypes about Latinos in a public mural on a jailhouse wall is a clear example of this. That same association had never considered addressing the systematically racist depiction of Latinos on television, for example, while the National Council on La Raza makes it the focus of one of their annual reports. Another problem is that defensive subaltern reactions often posit all relationships between cultures as binary and hierarchical, implicitly eliminating the critical tools necessary to understand the current interactions among laterally related subaltern groups in contemporary urban areas.

These deficiencies cannot become rationales for dropping these arguments altogether. To dismiss *any* subaltern defensiveness about appropriation as essentialist propagates the notion that people of color are less able to reason. It is all too easy to throw one's hands up and say that culture penetrates all the borders we might erect, so that we might as well capitulate to the logic of desire and global capital. This response has turned into yet another way of evading the more political dimensions of multiculturalism. Such responses do not distinguish between the historical moment of cultural nationalism in the debates about the aesthetics of ethnic minorities, on the one hand, and activist use of essentialist rhetoric to raise the issues of power and access to cultural institutions, on the other. Hence, the protests launched by Chicana

New Line Cinema protest, 1992.
PHOTO BY CYNTHIA WIGGINS.

actresses in 1992 against a film production about the Mexican artist Frida Kahlo, who was to be portrayed by an Italian American actress, was played in the Los Angeles press as an attack on the first amendment rights of the director, Luis Valdez, rather than as an outcry against the reinforcement of Latino invisibility in Hollywood.

These skirmishes over cultural appropriation have sensitized me to the ways that "passing" operates in the post–Civil Rights era, and how the liberal integrationist atmosphere in which I was educated sustained white privilege by enforcing silence about its hegemony. The socialization I and many other affirmative action babies received to identify racism as the property only of ignorant, reactionary people, preferably from the past, functioned to deflect our attention from how whiteness operated in the present. What bell hooks calls the liberal ideology of universal subjectivity (i.e., that we are all just people) made us partners in a silent pact that permitted "good" people of color to circulate among whites as long as racism was not mentioned as part of the immediate present. Whereas "passing" in the pre–Civil Rights era has been mythologized as having resulted from blacks teaching their offspring to dissimulate, we must also take into account how whites continue to reward token people of color with social acceptance as "honorary whites" for not crossing the conversational marker on race. To raise the specter of racism in the here and now, to suggest that despite their political beliefs and sexual preferences, white people operate within, and benefit from, white supremacist social structures is still tantamount to a declaration of war.

Given the current climate, cultural activists of color will continue to be lambasted for attempting to control access to images and ideas through notions of cultural property. This is seen as interfering with freedom of expression and curatorial prerogative. Liberals and postmodernists alike also resent being told that interracial or intercultural desire, whether it goes by the name of "slumming," border crossing, or appropriation, in and of itself does not disrupt historically entrenched inequities. Nonetheless, it is precisely because mass-cultural and avant-garde assimilation of ethnic signifiers has not brought about significant improvement in the conditions of life in subaltern communities that people of color continue to advocate political measures to redress inequities.

I have raised the issue of subaltern cultural protectionism, fully conscious of the fact that in the past decade, scores of artists and critics of color (myself among them) have implicitly and explicitly chipped away at the essentialist aesthetics of cultural nationalism, openly appropriating influences and ideas that could be considered "white," and self-consciously infiltrating traditionally white cultural institutions and academic disciplines. In light of the virulent backlash against multiculturalism in recent years, I find it absolutely crucial to distinguish between philosophically supporting essentialist arguments to the letter, and understanding their spirit and objective politically. Too often, however, the postcolonial celebration of hybridity has been interpreted as the sign that no further concern about the politics of representation and cultural exchange is needed. With ease, we lapse back into the integrationist rhetoric of the 1960s, and conflate hybridity with parity. Still, the critiques of appropriation cannot be reduced to an attempt to ignore the existence of hybridity or to prevent cultural exchange. What is at stake in the defensive reactions to appropriation is the call to cease fetishizing the gesture of crossing as inherently transgressive, so that we can develop a language that accounts for who is crossing, and that can analyze the significance of each act. Unless we have an interpretive vocabulary that can distinguish among the expropriative gestures of the subaltern, the coercive strategies that colonizers levy against the colonized, and dominant cultural appropriative acts of commodification of marginalized cultures, we run the perpetual risk of treating appropriation as if the act itself had some existence prior to its manifestations in a world that remains, despite globalism, the information highway, and civil rights movements, pitifully undemocratic in the distribution of cultural goods and wealth.

ANDRES SERRANO
SHOOTS THE KLAN:
AN INTERVIEW

IT WAS *Piss Christ,* Andres Serrano's photograph of a crucifix immersed in his own urine, together with Robert Mapplethorpe's homoerotic images, that in 1989 set off the far Right's attack against art. In a short period of time, Serrano was transformed from a relatively successful but reclusive New York artist and member of the collective Group Material into a celebrity/pariah under perpetual scrutiny.

He has received death threats and hate mail and has lost grants on the one hand, and on the other has enjoyed dozens of laudatory articles and a sizable hike in his prices. Furthermore, the fuss caused by Christian fundamentalists has hardly dimmed Serrano's fascination with religious iconography. His apartment, nestled in a semi-industrial area near downtown Brooklyn, is full of antique ecclesiastical furniture. It would give the impression of a Mediterranean antechoir were there not also numerous skulls, artworks, and other unusual knick-knacks.

The combination of indirect approach to issues, cool conceptual technique, and emotionally charged focus on symbols that resonate outside the vocabulary of the art world has been Serrano's trademark since he began to produce mature work in the early 1980s. In his first pieces, he concentrated largely on reworking Catholic iconography in highly stylized tableaux. Later he moved into more abstract images that also touched on social and religious taboos, using bodily fluids such as milk, menstrual blood, and semen. *Piss Christ* emerged out of a transition between these periods and was originally part of a series in which Serrano photographed several statues, which had varied connotations, immersed in different fluids. Nonetheless, just as the artist has come to stand for the biggest controversy to rock the art world in the 1980s, so has one photograph come to stand for his entire oeuvre.

Many other artists whose funding and freedom of expression were threatened by

This essay first appeared in *High Performance* in 1991.

the National Endowment for the Arts (NEA) controversy have since made their "censorship" the subject of their work. Serrano, however, has avoided focusing on the far Right's attacks as much as possible, and has ostensibly ignored them in his recent work.

In November 1990, Serrano opened a new chapter of his career with *Nomads*, an arresting exhibition of twenty Cibachrome portraits, thirteen of homeless people in New York, most of whom are African American, and seven of members of the Atlanta, Georgia, chapter of the Ku Klux Klan. Presenting us with an encounter of extremes, Serrano uncovers disturbing paradoxes. The homeless become symbols of the outcome of life for people of color in a racist society, while the Klansmen stand as the symbols of racial hatred; but they are both outcasts, both marginal in relation to the presumed audience. Even the most liberal "other-loving" spectator or collector would have to contend with the impossibility of assuming a racially or socially neutral position in relation to these subjects.

These images confront us with the moral and political dilemmas stemming from racial tensions in this country. Yet Serrano's style, though frontal, is far from declaratory. His pictures are emotive and elliptical, puzzling, frightening, and beautiful at the same time.

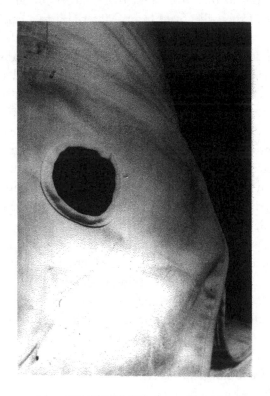

"Klanswoman (Grand Klaliff II)," Cibachrome by Andres Serrano, 1990.
PHOTO COURTESY OF THE PAULA COOPER GALLERY, NEW YORK.

COCO FUSCO: *Your use of Catholic symbolism stands out in part because you are operating in a predominantly Protestant context. An attraction to the sensuality and the carnality that you bring out in your Catholic iconography can develop, since the Protestant symbolism looks rather pale by comparison. How would it affect your work to be exhibited in a Catholic context?*

ANDRES SERRANO: I have always felt that my work is religious, not sacrilegious. I would say that there are many individuals in the Church who appreciate it and who do not have a problem with it. The best place for *Piss Christ* is in a church. In fact, I recently had a show in Marseilles in an actual church that also functions as an exhibition space, and the work looked great there. I think if the Vatican is smart, some-day they'll collect my art.

CF: *Does your interest in Catholicism have to do more with an attraction to the iconography or is it about wanting to make a social or political comment about what the Church represents?*

AS: Look at my apartment. I am drawn to the symbols of the Church. I like the aesthetics of the Church. I like Church furniture. I like going to Church for aesthetic reasons, rather than spiritual ones. In my work, I explore my own Catholic obsessions. An artist is nothing without his or her obsessions, and I have mine. One of the things that always bothered me was the fundamentalist labeling of my work as "anti-Christian bigotry." As a former Catholic and as someone who even today is not opposed to being called a Christian, I felt I had every right to use the symbols of the Church and resented being told not to.

CF: *At the same time you have expressed concern about the Church's position on many contemporary issues.*

AS: I am drawn to Christ but I have real problems with the Catholic Church. I don't go out of my way to be critical of the Church in my work, because I think that I make icons worthy of the Church. Oftentimes we love the thing we hate, and vice versa. Unfortunately, the church's position on most contemporary issues makes it hard to take them seriously.

CF: *So do you see yourself carrying on a tradition of religious art?*

AS: Absolutely. I am not a heretic. I like to believe that rather than destroy icons, I make new ones.

CF: *Your most recent portraits of the homeless and the Klan do not appear to have anything to do with Catholicism. Does this represent a break from your past interests, or will you return to them?*

AS: I leave the option open. When I was photographing the Imperial Wizard and saw him put on his green robe, I said to his secretary that it looked like a religious robe, and she said, "To some Klan members, they are." Some people have compared the Klan images to ecclesiastical figures.

CF: *Many critics who have written about you have attempted to situate your work in the context of art that deals with ethnicity. I would say that your work is better understood as a reflection on culture as institution and symbol, and the power invested in certain icons. Do you see interpretations of your work as problematic?*

AS: Any critic can have his or her own interpretation. I have always felt that I am the sum total of my parts. One of the things that I am happy about in my life as an artist is that I am not considered a Hispanic artist. I am just an artist. That is the way it should be. My work is intensely personal. I don't think that because I am Hispanic I should therefore do Hispanic work. Are cum shots Hispanic? What about close-ups of menstrual pads? Is it Hispanic to photograph the Klan? People have to find ways of explaining the work. Sometimes I don't reach out enough, so they have to fill in the void.

CF: *It is extremely difficult to categorize art by Latinos on the East Coast. The population here is so varied—from the largely middle-class South American emigres, to first and second generation Puerto Ricans, mostly from working-class backgrounds, to Cuban exiles and the newest arrivals, undocumented Mexicans. Little, if any, of the work resembles Chicano art from the Southwest.*

AS: It could be that the New York art world is so cosmopolitan and so international that artists doing this sort of work tend to want to be here rather than on the West Coast. I went to San Francisco last year to give a lecture, a few months after the controversy. The minute I got off the train reporters appeared who wanted to talk to me and all sorts of interviews were set up. People seemed to imply that I was doing something for the race. I was told that no Hispanic artist had gotten this much coverage in over ten years. It was as if they were thanking me. In Boulder, Colorado, I recently gave a presentation to a Chicano class. A student asked me if I would ever want to take pictures of Hispanics, for the race, once again. I said I wasn't sure, but that the best thing I could do for the race, or any race for that matter, is to do my work.

I usually refer to myself as Hispanic. When I was a kid, we were all Spanish. As we grew older, the terms changed and we became Hispanic. The students I met in Boulder were very politicized and used the term Latino or Chicano. I hadn't realized there existed that separation between those who are bothered by the term Hispanic and those who are not.

CF: *Your approach to issues is consistently indirect, including your stance toward ethnicity, which you suggest could be a partial explanation of a work, but not a complete one. Your work has achieved politically volatile results from what you claim is not an overtly political practice. Many artists are cautious about talking about themselves as political artists because it damages their commercial potential and implies an agitprop stance some take to be too limiting and simplistic. Yet, the conceptual art tradition you intersect with has political implications. What then is the relationship of your work to political issues?*

AS: Being born, especially being born a person of color, is a political act in itself.

Everything you do from that point on is political without having to be called political. My work has social implications; it functions in a social arena. In relation to the controversy over *Piss Christ*, I think the work was politicized by forces outside it, and as a result, some people expect to see something recognizably "political" in my work. I am still trying to do my work as I see fit, which I see coming from a very personal point of view with broader implications.

CF: *Many of the performance artists whose work has been part of the NEA censorship controversy have made art and activist interventions in response to having lost grants. You have not. Your answer to having been taken up in this controversy appears to be at least in terms of your work, to ignore it. In doing so, you diminish the importance of that judgment. Is this one more indirect move of yours, one more way of stepping around the obvious?*
AS: As far as I am concerned, I wasn't going to let Jesse Helms or any other politician dictate what direction my work should take. If I didn't directly respond to it, it was my way of ignoring them and continuing on my merry way.

CF: *Your most recent exhibition of portraits of Ku Klux Klan members and homeless people seems to take portraits of these groups as an entity, implicitly referring to each other. Whoever views the portraits of these two very different groups of people must momentarily evade a moral judgment, although most art gallery visitors make judgments about these groups of people all the time. In everything I read in which you talk about your encounters with the Klan, you also seemed to avoid making a moral judgment about the people you were taking pictures of. What does it mean to you to throw morality into question in this way?*
AS: The idea of showing the Klan and the homeless pictures together was exciting like the tension between the two. They are about extreme poverty and extreme prejudice. I like the way you put it that the average gallery goer is probably somewhere in the middle, and he has to reconcile his feelings for one group with his feelings for the other. The homeless by themselves could have worked well, people would have like them, they would have been fine. But then if the Klan pictures had been shown by themselves the first time, it would have been problematic not to have something to balance them.

CF: *I couldn't help wondering about the implications of having an affluent art collector purchase a photograph of the Klan Wizard to hang in his or her living room. Someone who might never associate with a Klan member or admit to being a Klan supporter would end up wanting to consume an image of one. You were bringing them into a relationship with an image of something they might otherwise reject.*
AS: What you just described is exactly what I also imagined in terms of the portraits of the homeless. Collectors would purchase work about people who they would probably never have a relationship with, but are safe for them to admire from a distance. I wondered if there would be any kind of conflict for the collectors. Someone pointed out to

me that it wasn't pictures of Klansmen or homeless people that were being collected—they are Serranos, so the subject matter is secondary.

CF: *I don't think that any other postmodern photographer calls on the viewer to engage with subjects as abject or as socially marginalized as yours. Your work demands that the form expand in order to explore its own moral/ethical implications. You can find sublime beauty in these pictures, but they also evoke a sense of horror.*
AS: I am pulling at the form. My intent as an artist is to monumentalize or aestheticize the mundane. But it is also important that I identify with my subjects. The Klan people and the homeless are outcasts. I have always felt like an underdog; I root for the underdog.

CF: *How did you decide to go to Atlanta to photograph the Klan?*
AS: After making the homeless portraits, I still wanted to continue doing portraits. They had to be unusual subjects for me to be interested in them. I thought that masked portraits would be very unusual and immediately thought that the Klan would be a natural. I was in Atlanta giving a lecture. I had four or five names, and I pursued them until I made more contacts and continued from there.

CF: *So it started as a formal decision—you weren't thinking about who it was that you were photographing?*
AS: I was aware of that dimension as well, and that is why I was attracted to it. Being who I am racially and culturally, it was a challenge. If I had just been a white photographer taking pictures of the Klan it wouldn't have been very interesting for me.

CF: *It seems that the way you photograph your subjects changes with these portraits. The images in the Nomads and Klan series evoke a humanist sentiment that none of your previous work does. You seem to be expressing a desire to connect on a subjective level with your subjects. Why did that happen?*
AS: One of the things that the controversy made me aware of was that I have always been a loner. There have been times in my life where I have been fairly antisocial. I have never been part of the system. I have never voted in my life. Whenever possible, I operate outside the system. Now, I realize that I can no longer function as a human being in a vacuum. All of a sudden people were reaching out to me—in critical or supportive ways—but in either case I was bombarded by human contact , which was very strange for me. It made me change. I began to allow people to enter my life and work.

CF: *So your response to a controversy that made you a public figure was to connect with people more in your work?*
AS: One of the things about the controversy was that it actually hurt. It confused me. It caused me a great deal of grief. Maybe I am now trying to reach out to people and

in some way connect with them in what I hope is a more positive light. That doesn't mean that I am compromising my work in any way. Like I always say, I like to give people what they want and what they don't want. Besides, I know I can take the heat.

CF: *I don't mean to suggest that you are moving into sentimentalized portraiture. I do think that you've chosen your subjects strategically, as representatives of—*
AS: Of undesirables.

CF: *They are undesirable, but they are also people who in and of themselves are symbols. That seems to connect them with your previous work, which is so much about iconography and symbol. A homeless person stands for the homeless, for economic and racial inequalities, and for capitalism's lack of morality. A Klan member with a mask on stands for the entire Klan, and for white supremacy, racism, and the South.*
AS: In dealing with these people, particularly with the Klanspeople, I realized that they became more powerful as symbols than they actually were as human beings. I saw them as human beings first, and then they put on their robes and became symbols. The homeless too are symbols. I see this as my dilemma as well. In a way, I have become a symbol. But I am just a human being—and it is hard for human beings to be symbols.

CF: *They represent two polar opposites of a spectrum of symbols that have to do with racism. The overwhelming majority of the homeless people in your photographs and in New York are black, and the Klan stands for white supremacy. What did you want to express in relation to race in these pictures?*
AS: I am trying to connect with my own feelings. I am somewhat ambivalent about most things and sometimes even confused. I have never been able to fit. I have never been able to see myself as fitting into one category, and I have never been able to limit my contact with people to one group of people. I have always prided myself as someone who got along with people who didn't get along with each other. I am not talking about groups of people. I am talking about individuals. I just extended to a larger arena.

CF: *How did the homeless people deal with you? What were their concerns when you first approached them?*
AS: They were surprised that I would offer them money. After that surprise most accepted the offer. I asked about fifty people. Only two people said no.

CF: *Did any of them come to the show?*
AS: Yes, not to the opening, but several of them went to the show. In fact, the homeless man who opens the door to the Citibank on 14th Street and First Avenue proudly told someone I know, "Oh yes, I have some pictures up at Stux Gallery."

CF: *Your interest in the late-nineteenth-century photographer Edward Curtis and in his portraits of Native Americans is often mentioned. You've said his work influenced the choices you made in taking pictures of the homeless. What is it about his work that led you to take pictures of homeless people?*

AS: His pictures are very heroic. I don't care about the controversy as to whether or not they fabricate a false reality. I like the way the people look, and I get a sense of who they are, and I get a sense of their dignity. I think that is really important. Growing up in the 1950s, the only Indians I ever saw were on TV, and usually they were savages being massacred by soldiers. Curtis felt he was photographing a vanishing race. I didn't think I was photographing a vanishing race, but rather a class of people who are on the verge of extinction as individuals. The homeless problem will never go away. These people may or may not survive the next winter. Being the fameless and nameless people whom we don't even ordinarily look at made me want to monumentalize them even more.

CF: *Your artwork combines strong statements about institutions like the Catholic Church, and about symbols that relate to politically charged groups such as the Klan and the homeless. At the same time, your use of photography suggests a particular stance toward the medium and its power. What exactly is your relationship to photography as a medium?*

AS: I am an artist first and a photographer second. My "medium" is the world of ideas that I seek to present in a visually cohesive fashion. I think of myself as a conceptualist with a camera. In other words, I like to take pictures in my head that may or may not have anything to do with photography.

My use of the medium—photography—is in some ways traditional. At the same time it is very unconventional. The photography critic Andy Grundberg pointed out that I am not that technical, that I don't care about printing. I feel as though I am anti-photography because I have no interest in the medium except as a means to an end. I am interested only in the final image. At the same time, my role as an artist leads me to want to pursue subjects that generate the tensions we talked about. I think my technique is a comment on my subjects and on photography. I say things, but I say them indirectly. At the same time, I try to make my images as direct as possible.

CF: *Do you think your audiences understand your work?*

AS: Judging from what I have read, people are getting the point—even the politicians.

CF: *But you wouldn't want to reduce the work to its shock value for right-wing politicians?*

AS: No, I think that's the dilemma for them. My work does more than just shock. It also pleases—and that really fucks with their heads. My work has often been spoken of in terms of the sacred and the profane. My feeling is that you can't have one without the other. You need both.

PART II

ARTISTS AND THEIR WORK

VERNACULAR MEMORIES: PEPÓN OSORIO

P EPÓN OSORIO'S COLORFUL and brashly resplendent art installations are inspired by Puerto Rican popular culture in New York. Drawing on distinctly Latin American traditions in which material culture, given or imposed, is transformed through exaggerated embellishment, Osorio brings out the social and political implications of domestic decoration within both the colonial context of Puerto Rico and the Latino immigrant experience in New York. Many of his works start with furniture or household decorations (such as cabinets, couches, clocks, trophies, chandeliers, beds, and houseplants), or with extensions of private space (such as a bicycle, coffins from a funeral parlor, or a car windshield). The artist then piles on these objects hundreds of mass-produced toys and miniatures: tiny plastic dolls, ribbons, toy cars, plastic cigars, plastic flies, decals, American and Puerto Rican souvenirs. Creating inanimate equivalents of such parodic and politically charged Caribbean practices as the *carnaval,* Osorio reduces the "original" objects to the skeletons of new creations, allowing the fabulously adorned surfaces to become the focus of attention.

For this reason, Osorio's work has been characterized by some critics as kitsch, either in the sense of sentimental decorativeness or glorified bad taste. Others have attempted to interpret his work as evidence of a neocolonial derivative of the Baroque. His work has prompted critical allusions to such radically dissimilar sources as Francisco Oller, Caravaggio, *tchotchkes* and Parties R Us stores.[1] The current five-year retrospective of Osorio's work at New York's Museo del Barrio, called "Con To' Los Hierros" (or, loosely translated, "Give it all you've got"),[2] provides an occasion not only to reflect on his varied and controversial work but to reconsider our understanding of kitsch in general.

Nearly every Latin American culture has one or many terms to describe what in

This essay first appeared in *Art in America* in 1991.

a Euro-American context is called kitsch.3 All of these terms are linked by their common reference to practices found in urban postindustrial culture, to consumers who transform the ready-made materials of mass culture and to objects that evoke nostalgia and sentimentality. Nonetheless, the pejorative connotations usually attached to the term "kitsch" reflect the class assumptions and cultural biases that govern art's reception. Appreciation of Osorio's oeuvre usually stops at the surface; viewers revel in or rail against its sumptuousness and presume a nonreflexive recapitulation of a "naive" vernacular cultural practice.

Within a culture like that of the United States, informed by minimalist notions of elegance and a puritanical disdain for decoration, it is all too easy for even a highly calculated use of kitsch to be perceived as unselfconscious. The pleasure involved in the high-cultural appreciation of kitsch traditionally depends on an ironic distance and generally imputes naïveté to the original user or producer. Yet, Latin American hosts a variety of popular and high-art traditions in which kitsch is deployed self-consciously as a gesture of cultural resistance. Osorio underscores the colonial subject's awareness of being surveyed from outside or above by stressing his culture's tendency to respond with visually excessive spectacle.

Osorio subverts through reinterpretation. His familiarity with and affection for his own culture plus his ability to tease out latent meanings from everyday life allow him to use kitsch in a critical way that simultaneously indulges in sentimentality and reveals its political and satirical edge. His three strategies are the use of the miniature, which deflates the ineffable or transcendent qualities of the thing being remade; parody, in the form of grotesque or excessive exaggeration; and a use of multiples and industrially produced objects that become visual signs for the many meanings that can be ascribed to any one thing. These practices form a visual analogy to parodic literary traditions and Puerto Rican vernacular culture and run counter to folkloric or indigenist views of Latin American art, stressing instead a postmodernist tendency toward appropriation, pastiche, and the collision of "high" and popular culture. Moreover, Osorio's work shows how these transformative practices have been adapted to the Puerto Rican immigrant experience of cultural displacement and political marginalization.

Osorio draws on both the concrete objects and the shared experiences that form the history of Puerto Rican migration to the United States. Key moments in this history—departure, the plane rides, setting up house, the travails of the single-parent households run largely by women, the division of families between New York and the island—become the starting point for the creation of images and installations, often produced for use in performances with his collaborator and wife, the dancer and choreographer Merián Soto. For these installations, furniture and walls are often covered with brightly patterned fabrics, velvets, lace—even fake grass and foliage—in addition to many small toys and souvenirs. Leaves, rugs, and seats become surfaces for Osorio's handwritten testimonials, literal inscriptions of the self onto prefabricated objects. In one work, Osorio has written autobiographical stories word by word, in white paint, on the silk leaves of several artificial trees. Making things one's own is for him equivalent to making them new.

Significantly, Osorio's use of art as an arena for investigating his cultural identity as a Puerto Rican began as recently as 1984, nearly a decade after his arrival in New York. In fact, this new direction marked a clean break with his previous work, which consisted of abstract paintings based on what he calls "universalist" principles. Osorio's interest in Puerto Rican vernacular culture was precipitated by his encounters with the Nuyorican community in the United States and by his sense of geographic dislocation from the island. His shift from the universal to the culturally specific, however, also took place within the context of the resurgence of multicultural debates in the United States and the intensified demand for art reflective of the experiences of people of color. The combination of these factors heightened Osorio's awareness of the difference between his own cultural identity and that of the Euro-American mainstream from which he considers himself excluded.

Osorio's aesthetic sensibility combines an acute awareness of Puerto Rico's colonial history with personal memories from his childhood on the island, where he

Installation detail from "El Velorio: AIDS in the Latino Community,"
by Pepón Osorio, 1991.
PHOTO BY FRANK GIMPAYA.

was born in 1955. He recalls a communal predisposition toward seeing "more as better," and he cites the early influence of his mother, Maria Luisa Encarnación, and his "second mother," Juana Hernández, who cared for him as a child. Central to Osorio's vision of the past are his own memories from when he was a small child: decorating elaborate cakes baked by his mother for local festivities, staring with fascination at Juana's costume jewelry, wearing suits adorned with ribbons and pom-poms for important occasions.

Arriving in New York in the mid-1970s, Osorio attended Lehman College and earned a degree in sociology. For five years he was employed in the child abuse prevention unit of the Human Resources Administration, working primarily with the Latino community. Although he exhibited art work intermittently during this period, Osorio's experiences as a social worker laid the groundwork for his collaborative efforts with activist organizations and members of the Puerto Rican community. Several pieces in "Con To' Los Hierros" resulted from Osorio's dialogues with nurses, undertakers, upholsterers, Vietnam vets, and others.

Scattered throughout the exhibition are other reminders of Osorio's experiences as a black Puerto Rican, particularly the racism he has felt in his own community and in American society at large. The clusters of plastic babies and ballerina dolls on *El Chandelier* (1985) and along the headboard of *La Cama* (The Bed, 1987) show white dolls in the minority—the world as Osorio claims he would like to see it. (In fact, as Kellie Jones points out in her catalogue essay, Osorio's proportions are a more accurate representation of the world population.) The faces of the twelve plastic wall clocks in *El Tiempo Dirá* (Time Will Tell, 1990) are covered by old photographs of black Puerto Ricans, implying that the country has chosen to forget or suppress the African dimension of its history and in so doing has created a kind of time bomb that ticks away, waiting to explode.

Osorio's installation of the show suggests that the domestic sphere of the Puerto Rican household in exile serves multiple functions; it is a kind of liberated space for self-expression. Individually decorated domestic objects become receptacles of personal and collective histories, invocations of community, and marks of personal achievement in the face of adversity. One of Osorio's most heartfelt combinations of personal and collective history is *La Cama*, an homage to Juana Hernández and Merián Soto.

A four-poster bed sits in the middle of a pink room with gilded patterns on the walls and imprinted on the linoleum. Along the baseboard of the room is scrawled Osorio's recollection of a dream in which he approached Juana on her deathbed and introduced her to Merián; Juana responded in a mixture of Spanish and an African-sounding language, invoking Oshun, the goddess of love in Santería. Adorned with photographs of Osorio and Soto as children, the bed symbolizes their union and Juana's spiritual presence. The coverlet is festooned with *capias* donated by dozens of members of the Puerto Rican community. These commemorative ribbon arrangements, an island tradition, are usually prepared for weddings, baby showers, and other festive occasions. Here the *capias* celebrate matrimonial and familial bonds, and affirm, in a situation of exile, an intensified cultural identity.

Osorio makes the experiences of dislocation and disenfranchisement intelligible by transforming familiar, functional objects into unique and singularly valuable ones. Just as religious kitsch transforms the transcendent into the apprehensible, Osorio domesticates the idea of his homeland. In *El Chandelier*, a hanging lamp becomes an expression of the immigrant's attempt to overcome a hostile outside world by embellishing the hearth. Inspired by glimpses of ornate chandeliers inside New York City's *Loisaida* housing projects apartments, Osorio decorated his light fixture with tassels, fake pearls, plastic palm trees, grass, dominoes, water guns, miniature bowling pins, toy cars, and (again) black and white dolls; also present are miniature Afro-Caribbean syncretic saints, such as San Lázaro/Babalú-Ayé, patron of the blind and the sick. Osorio's home shrines are invested or even over-charged with redemptive powers.

Osorio is quick to note that Puerto Rico in the present and his reconstruction of it in the language of immigrant popular culture are radically dissimilar. Osorio's Puerto Rico is a phantasmic re-creation of the place he left in 1975. The materials used in his work (and in Nuyorican culture as well) refer largely to lifestyles and trends of the 1950s and 1960s, when the majority of islanders now living in New York migrated. The earliest work in the show, *La Bicicleta* (The Bicycle, 1985), is a nostalgic tribute to the vendors, knife grinders, and others who always decorated their means of trans-port, giving each vehicle a personal style. Hanging from the ceiling, Osorio's bicycle is covered with ribbons, flowers, plastic swans, Kewpie dolls, and beads, all of which transform it into a shrine.

Several of the works in the exhibition were used as parts of stage sets designed by Osorio for performances created in collaboration with Merián Soto. In "Broken Hearts" (1990), photographs and film clips of Puerto Rican women and children of divided families were intermittently projected behind the performers, while voice-over recollections and news reports provided data on the traffic between New York and Puerto Rico since the U.S.-sponsored Operation Bootstrap in the 1940s com-pelled many Puerto Ricans to emigrate. Dance vignettes captured the anxiety of arrival, the shock of learning of the existence of a long-departed father, and the macho posing that leads to a street fight. Finally, a couple's miming of lovemaking led to a comic and touching climax.

Osorio's set design for "Broken Hearts" (partially reconstructed for the retro-spective) extended into the audience, where spectators sat on lush and colorfully decorated seats. The centerpiece of the set was a purple velvet couch that, according to its inscription, was owned by the female character whose suicide precedes and sets the tone for the performance. Here entitled *A Mis Adorables Hijas* (To My Darling Daughters, 1990), the couch has a mournful apology handwritten on it, explaining in Spanish that the woman no longer felt she had the energy or spirit to withstand the difficulties she faced. The purple velvet redoubles the message, associating the couch with San Lázaro/Babalú-Ayé (who is identified with the color purple), whose lesion-covered body is a symbol of physical suffering. Once again, an article of furniture, a symbol of domestic comfort, becomes a surface for inscribing the self and even affirming one's presence after death.

In the exhibition's final full-scale installation, *El Velorio* (The Wake, 1991), created especially for El Museo del Barrio, Osorio explored the transformative powers of Puerto Rican cultural practices. In creating this memorial to Latinos who have died of AIDS, Osorio managed to communicate the ambiguous sentiments of a community faced not only with rising death tolls but also with the social and political implications of the epidemic. The room was designed as a funeral parlor, with several coffins, two body bags, numerous flower arrangements, and couches and chairs for mourners. Upon entering, one was struck by the chilliness of the room, which made it seem more like a morgue than a funeral parlor. Near the entrance was a carpet inscribed with a text comparing the AIDS crisis to past cholera epidemics in Puerto Rico, making the distinction that this time people are unwilling to talk about their pain.

Other texts—on the carpet, on the walls, and on the body bags—presented the sentiments of surviving friends and relatives who must confront the pain of loss, as well as the knowledge of the homosexuality or drug use of their dead friends or family members. While, clearly, not all those Latinos with AIDS are gay or IV drug users, Osorio suggests that the difficulty of reckoning with the existence of homosexuality and of drug abuse explains to some extent the long-delayed political response to AIDS by Latino communities. Some of the texts convey the fear of being "discovered" by suspicious neighbors and the realization that even economic security cannot protect middle-class families from AIDS. Most of the texts were written by Osorio, based on comments he overheard or was told. One text is a direct quotation from Mildred Pierson, an African American activist whose gay son died of AIDS and who was Osorio's principal collaborator in conceptualizing this work.

To illustrate how the AIDS crisis has cut across social groups in the Latino community, Osorio included coffins representing varying economic statuses, one with a flag draped over it, some open, some closed. (In researching the installation, Osorio learned from an undertaker that early in the AIDS epidemic, many people, out of fear, insisted on sealed coffins; education and experience have subsequently worn down such superstitions.) Two body bags, one at each front corner of the room, acted as eloquent reminders of those forgotten by community and family—and of the extreme rejection, by some, of people with AIDS. Some of the open coffins had photographs of faces and bodies printed on clear acetate over the interior cushions; this created the eerie impression that one was being confronted by gazes of the dead.

The reference to cholera was not the only connection to the past in the installation. At each side of the room was a book stand with a reproduction of the painting

El Velorio (Child's Wake, 1893), by Francisco Oller, the Courbet-influenced realist who is often considered Puerto Rico's greatest artist. Osorio's work was thus given a historical context, but Oller's painting contrasted startlingly with Osorio's installation. Oller's wake takes place in a home filled with people, some crying, some carousing. The painting hums with activity and even evokes a certain joyousness: Since the death represented is that of a child, this would traditionally have been interpreted as the birth of an angel. Osorio's quiet, frigid funeral parlor, on the other hand, with its many containers for the dead, was literally waiting for the bodies to fill it.

Perhaps the most apt metaphor for Osorio's method is a recent work consisting of a glass-windowed cabinet in which souvenirs of New York City are joined with Puerto Rican symbols—including a Statue of Liberty with a Puerto Rican flag on her head. The piece is entitled *100% Boricua* (1991), doubly ironic in its use of Puerto Rico's indigenous name to refer to New York. Across glossy tourist images of the city, Osorio has scrawled phrases referring to the high incidence of police brutality against Latinos. In this way, Osorio symbolically claims New York as Puerto Rican territory. On the eve of quincentenary celebrations that threaten to obfuscate a history of colonial violence extending to the present, Osorio reminds us that although more than one empire has impinged upon Puerto Rico over the last 500 years, he and the people so lovingly recalled in his art are striking back—*con to' los hierros*.

UNCANNY DISSONANCE:
THE WORK OF
LORNA SIMPSON

ELLIPTICAL AND MINIMAL, Lorna Simpson's pieces elicit a powerful call to viewers to unpack densely laden layers of meaning imbedded in them. The sheer volume of critical response to her photo/text works is in itself testimony to their evocative power. In an ironic doubling of the paradox at the heart of her work, the more Simpson points to the inadequacies of language, written and photographic, to represent the experience of black women, the more interpretations emerge that struggle to overcome those inadequacies by writing about her art.

Simpson's focus on the construction of meaning and value, and how they are generated out of the relationship among the artist, viewer, and object, places her work within the realm of philosophical questioning that has been central to conceptual art for decades. Using juxtapositions of text and image to unseat the photograph's apparent iconic stability (referent = image = text/caption), Simpson situates her practice within postmodernism's exploration of photography's social functions and political implications. Within that field of inquiry, she centers her work on how racial and sexual identity are shaped. That endeavor takes on a specific resonance in a society whose current fixation on cultural and ethnic difference, and on Simpson's identity as a black woman artist, is a symptom of a historical incapacity to accommodate precisely what she represents. Simpson's images—her art and her self—make a simple resolution to the question of difference impossible. She is not proposing or presenting us with an "alternative" set of images to counter past invisibility or stereotyping; rather, she empties photographic images of their specificity and embeddedness in the world to create a scenario in which the object refers back to the act of looking, the position of the looker, and the cultural baggage that determines what we understand about what we see.

This essay first appeared in the catalog for the Lorna Simpson exhibition at Colgate University in 1991. It subsequently appeared in *Third Text* in 1993.

Cultural critic Michele Wallace writes in *Invisibility Blues* that black women face the contradiction of being all-too-present as fetishized objects of the mass media and the entertainment and cultural industries while glaringly absent from the production of knowledge about those images. Unlike white women, who occupy the place of complementarity vis-à-vis white men in the white patriarchal structure, or black men, who are positioned as "other," black women are relegated to the doubly negated status of being "the other of the other." As Simpson began to examine the implications of that condition, she quite appropriately moved from social documentary photography, which so often seeks to redeem subjects of a marginalized social world, to a studio set-up in which she could produce images without furthering the illusion of a sense of place. Standing out against neutral backgrounds, her people and objects create the feeling of being in a dreamscape, not beyond language, but outside any singular, lived experience.

Traveling through this imaginary space, Simpson continually makes the point that her images do not give answers. With their turned heads, faces cut off at the nose, and neutral costumes, Simpson 's images of body parts appear to be fetishlike symbols of something or someone unfathomable or unrepresentable. Her images do not "identify" the women in them to an unknown viewer; they do not give "insight" into character, as conventional portraiture was designed to provide; and they do not illustrate a communal black experience as some might seek to find. The words and phrases Simpson chooses are always presented in ways that emphasize their polysemous potential and thus postpone closure. Images and texts bounce back and forth off each other, multiplying possible meanings that often allude to social conditions affecting black people, but are never reducible to purely descriptive significance. Experiencing that "incompleteness" can provoke anxiety and frustration, and in fact, early on in her career, Simpson was criticized by a white feminist critic who interpreted her work as "enforcing black women's invisibility," or rather, I would argue, for reflecting the audience's own limitations back at them.

Less morally inflected readings might account for how Simpson's style engenders a desire to take the word game another step. Michele Wallace interprets black women's literary production of the 1970s and 1980s in ways that are applicable to Simpson's image/text interplays. Arguing that no existing language can easily reflect or describe the location of women of color, Wallace sees black women writers' tendencies to create ambiguities and internal contradictions, stress multiplicity and word play, and undermine objectivity as modes of "radical negation" that demonstrate efforts to reformulate the "problem" of black female subjectivity.[1] Key to Wallace's insights is the understanding that not offering a secure, stable answer is a conscious and creative position in itself. Like many other black artists of the postnationalist generation, Simpson is not seeking to represent a proto-photographic "black condition" so much as to reflect on the construction of race through identification with things that connote blackness. Probing the deep structure of a system that forges differences and generates social dilemmas then, Simpson reframes race as a question of the "already seen " by foregrounding the gaps between perception and intellection, and between language and experience.

Several cultural theorists including Wallace have analyzed art forms that underscore the social function of language in ways similar to Simpson's, but they have stressed the linguistic and literary production over the visual. In *Writing Degree Zero*, Roland Barthes describes the "zero degree" character of modern poetry as an existential geology in which nouns are presented as absolute quantities accompanied by all possible associations. This aesthetic procedure, Barthes argues, reverses the "natural" knowledge of things, turning each poetic word into a Pandora's box.[2] Importantly, Barthes in his analysis stresses nouns, which are always signs of "thingness" as well as ciphers denoting concrete entities; these linguistic equations are perhaps most closely linked to conventional photographic constructions of meaning. In similar

figured the worst

figured on all the times there was no camera

he was disfigured

figured there would be no reaction

figured legality had nothing to do with it

figured she was suspect

figured he was suspect

figured someone had been there because the door was open

"Figure," by Lorna Simpson, 1991.
PHOTO COURTESY OF THE SIMON WATSON GALLERY, NEW YORK.

fashion, Simpson isolates individual figures and objects not to identify them, but to enable their abstracted singularity to generate a variety of meanings.

In a piece entitled *Figure* (1991), Simpson opens up the term, and a solitary image, precisely to subvert a "natural" sense of knowledge about the focus of her photograph. Her emblematic black woman stands in a rather nondescript dark dress with her back to the camera, relaxed with hands at her side. She is a figure, devoid of psychology or personality, much in the same way that this art historical term reduces the human body to a formal cipher. In the bottom left and right corners of the image are eight texts employing the term as a verb (to figure) and adjective (disfigured). In each case, the use of the term suggests subjectivity, conjecture, and ambiguity— the power to attribute meaning and the inevitable margin of error. Having been brought to the perception that "figure" can mean so many things and still be wrong (or at least never unequivocally right), we turn back to the figure at the center of the photograph and wonder what, if anything, she means. Poised at the "zero degree," viewer, artist, and subject stand full of possibilities, yet at the same time deracinated from any one of them.

Analogies have also already been drawn between literary critic Henry Louis Gates's theories of African American "signifyin'" and Simpson's image word plays.3 Designed to reverse one's status, "signifyin's" object is to transform an ostensible meaning from bad to good, negative to positive, and so on. Gates explains that this rhetorical strategy, known as the slave's trope, developed out of a dynamic in which the slave attempted to symbolically overturn his or her status through a carnival-esque destabilization of meaning. Using repetition and revision—of image and text—to create a situation in which the viewer arrives at a reading through conjec-ture, Simpson retraces a practice that Gates posits as quintessential to African American vernacular culture. Her pieces underscore language's slipperiness as they slide across the range of meanings in an image or word. The result is a kind of reversal in which a once privileged denotative reading of a photograph or word is destabilized through continual juxtaposition.

A perfect example of this is Simpson's *Untitled* (1989), a piece in which two photographs of a black woman's neck are set in circular frames with a vertical row of words between them. Most of the words allude to circular shapes with varying degrees of confinement implied by them: "ring," "lasso," "halo," "areola," "noose," "collar," and so forth. In the middle of the list is the word "eye," and at the bottom appears the phrase, "feel the ground sliding from under you." What might have been perceived as a "nice idea"—that is a black woman's portrait—becomes implicated through the play of word and image in a power struggle over meaning in which the eye of the photographer, camera, and viewer all participate. To begin with, the repetition of two identical images thrusts their ability to singularly represent anything into the process of reception. The frame of the photographs, which reminds one of the circular aperture of the camera, is here linked with other modes of social control, often carried out on women's bodies. Their connectedness is brought out through a synonymic listing of terms whose meanings we begin to intertwine as we read down the list. As Simpson deploys language to approximate and retreat from meanings, we reach a point when the "ground," or portrait, slips out from under us.

Although she usually centers her images on the black female body, Simpson also at times abstracts the notion of the body's representativity by bringing certain highly charged elements and objects into her visual configurations. Significantly, these additions are highly coded symbols of racial identity, or more specifically, of one's identification with "blackness." Several of Simpson's pieces focus on hairstyles, denaturalizing the connection between hair and body by separating braid from head. The curly-hair braid, conjuring Afrocentric hairdos and mythical associations of hair and femininity, is here also associated with a range of social forces, linguistic constructs, and power relations.

Memory Knots (1989), for example, contrasts five months of the calendar's seemingly innocent linear ordering of time with the recalcitrance and density of memory. The liberalized connection between the recalcitrance of the mind and of hair, with the image of the knot, creates the possibility of another level of interpretation, in which the hair becomes a symbol of black women's resistance to established modes of representation. Simpson creates several possible stories within stories as she highlights the power struggle behind strategies for extracting and organizing data. Those methods of ordering information grow increasingly insistent and sinister, beginning with "narrative response" and ending with "lie detector." Sandwiched between these texts are images of knotted braids, connecting femininity with enigma and recalling psychoanalysis's original task of employing language and power to "interpret" women's problems. Something as seemingly evident as hair—a physical attribute that is often read as a telltale sign of identity—Simpson manages to render as a sign, making the difficulty of attaining trouble-free communication seem boundless.

Flipside (1991) returns to the issues of identity, blackness, and hairstyle, but eliminates the braid. Instead, two photographs—one of the back of a black woman's head, the other of the back side of an African mask—are joined by a text underneath that reads, "the neighbors were suspicious of her hairstyle." Ambiguity and juxtaposition of elements here enable us to tease out several possible interpretations. The woman's naturally kinky hair might in some contexts connote rebelliousness, or pose a threat simply as a sign of blackness. But Simpson will not allow us to take any connection between hairstyle and blackness for granted. Ironically, the African mask is shaped in a manner reminiscent of Euro-American flip hairdos of the 1960s, which became a trademark style of many black women entertainers of that period. The mask, a symbol for many of Africa and African aesthetics, is here recoded to also recall a European hairstyle appropriated by black women. Finally, that an African mask could suggest straightened hair puts into question any essentialist interpretation of its identity. As Simpson explained in our interview, she is less interested in passing judgment on black representations or in rejecting negative images and stereotypes than she is in exploring their evocative potential by reformulating them.

The pun suggested by *Flipside*'s presentation of the back of the mask is carried over into many of Simpson's latest works, where African masks are continually reversed to show their inside. While the artist stressed in our interview that she chose to reverse the masks to recodify their meaning by unseating their conventional reception as beautiful objects, I would argue that this reversal also invites spectators to see themselves as the masks' potential wearers. Placing this relationship at the heart of the experience of viewing, Simpson calls upon us to reflect on our relationship to this icon of Africanness at a critical juncture in black American thought when the pros and cons of Afrocentrism are debated daily. The diasporic dilemma—of being only able to apprehend one's relationship to origin symbolically only through self-conscious recollection and reconstruction—shines out of that seemingly unassuming image. Simpson ironically juxtaposes that dilemma with the painful realities of black male life in America in *The Service* (1991). Three reversed masks against four texts evoke the tragic conditions of many black men whose lack of economic possibilities compels them to serve in the military, or to meet violent death leading to funeral services. Alluding to key disparate elements that define black experiences, Simpson illustrates how their complex interplay might generate an ambivalent relationship to identity.

Simpson is well aware that even though she does not place herself inside her frame, her own image as a black woman artist is central to the nature of the reception of her art, at times transforming it into a power struggle to define (and reach a conclusion about) not only her work but herself. That awareness delimits her conceptual terrain—namely, the tenuous area in which the language of classification, interpretation, and even praise can turn easily into alienating epithet and confining cliché. Never purely formalist or linguistically reductive, Simpson filters her social statements about the lives and souls of black folks through the mournful tone of her work, which continuously alludes to mortality, tragedy, confinement, and domination. Still, instead of positing direct answers, her challenge to herself and to her viewer is to pry open all the mechanisms of understanding that a photographic image might invite one to take for granted—and then leave them open, in order to feel that ensuing discomfort. As she turns the denotative dimensions of the photograph and the written word inside out, Simpson explores the ensuing interstices and achieves uncanny dissonances, showing us, as she puts it, "how language doesn't jibe with my experience."

ESSENTIAL DIFFERENCES: PHOTOGRAPHS OF MEXICAN WOMEN

The place of otherness is fixed in the West
as a subversion of Western metaphysics and is finally appropriated
by the West as its limit-text, anti-West.
HOMI K. BHABHA, "THE OTHER QUESTION"[1]

AFTER A DECADE of multicultural debates, the gap between "the Other" and its many potential referents still constitutes an arena of semiotic confusion. Now that consciousness of cultural specificity has been somewhat institutionalized within art criticism, elision of the Others has given way not to immediate understanding but to the myriad difficulties of reception and contextualization. In exhibitions, conferences, and writings that address issues of cultural and ethnic difference, artists and their work are often grouped together in ways that presume the interchangeability of their differences of race, class, culture, and media. What is an apparently benevolent gesture of paying attention, for example, to women of color often carries within it a reductive equation of distinct aesthetic sensibilities, making it seem as if cultural and ethnic difference from a white, Euro-American norm were the determining factor of any work positioned outside that framework.

If we take the implications of recognizing difference seriously, then we must understand that the designation of and even the very concern with Otherness are culturally relative. Still, within the art world a strong impulse persists to erase the distance between an artist's representation of his or her own cultural identity and a self-conscious aesthetic inquiry into the social and psychological construction of difference from a dominant culture. The multicultural paradigm as we now know it demands that its Others (which constitutes most of the world) conform to recognizable standards of difference that rarely question the power relations that define those distinctions. To my mind this constitutes multiculturalism's most fundamental flaw.

Nonetheless, not even the power of this Western cultural imperative to designate the cultural Other as its antithesis can transform reality into convenient dualisms. The gap that continues to exist between the fixed theoretical paradigm (Western self/non-

This essay first appeared in *Afterimage* in 1991.

Western other, etc.) and the contradictory and categorically distinct cultural terrains to which it is applied bears comparison to what Homi K. Bhabha has called, in reference to colonial discourse, the "syntax of deferral." He writes of the "slippage between the Western sign and its colonial significance which emerges as a map of misreading that embarrasses the righteousness of recordation and its certainty of good government.[1] In art-historical discourse this could be translated as follows: the slippage between the Euro-American designation of difference and its signification in Other contexts opens a space for misreading that defies any attempt to maintain the legitimacy of the mainstream terminology.

As important as recognizing the contextuality of cultural and ethnic difference is a critical awareness of the very concept's contextuality. It is Euro-American postmodernism's stress on difference, together with the growth of racial and ethnic "minorities" in the First World, that have propelled the question of the Other to the forefront of First-World cultural debates. But the contemporary demographics and colonial histories of the northern and southern halves of the Americas have contributed to radically distinct interpretations of Otherness. In Mexico, for example, the term "the other" conjures a different set of signifieds. It refers not so much to the Third-World "foreigner-outsider" as to the indigenous peoples that existed there prior to the Conquest and the cultures that form the symbolic foundation of contemporary national identity. The term also refers to the external Other— i.e., Mexico's northern neighbor—a construct that "legitimates" the myth of Mexican cultural homogeneity that has been levied throughout the twentieth century as a defense against the invasion of American consumer and entertainment culture. The Mexican dynamic, then, between cultural difference and national identity diverges widely from that of North America.

In raising these problems, I do not mean to suggest that Mexican artists working outside the geographic boundaries of Europe and North America operate without any awareness of Euro-American concerns. Dependency on "foreign" legitimation and markets in the visual arts has had a profound effect on Mexican cultural production of the last decade. Many artists, recognizing the appeal of difference, have perfected an aesthetic practice of recycling, for export, recognizable Mexican signs. In a humorous critique of this phenomenon, the Proceso Pentágono collective held a performance/garage sale in Mexico City in the fall of 1990, in which reproductions of works by Frida Kahlo were sold as "raw material for a New Mexican Art."

Nonetheless, the issue of cultural identity has its own complicated history within Mexico and its own discursive history within Mexican photography. While the sign of *la mexicanidad* (Mexicanness) plays a central role in photographic imagemaking, no consensus exists as to the referent. Furthermore, the coexistence of the radically disparate social and cultural realities that characterizes postmodern Mexico further destabilizes any fixed relation between identity and image or between cultural identity and Otherness. To get a sense of the range of representations that articulate the interplay among identity, difference, and Otherness in Mexican photographic representation, I will compare Graciela Iturbide's series on the Juchitecas with work by two of her contemporaries, Mexican photographers Lourdes Grobet and Yolanda Andrade.[2]

All three of these artists choose elements of Mexican "popular" culture (which does not equate, but at times overlaps, with mass culture) as their focus. Like the majority of photographers in Mexico, they are members of the largely white intellectual sector of a country that is overwhelmingly racially and culturally mestizo, where the existence of dozens of ethnic groups and racial hybrids makes it difficult to reduce "difference" to a binary system. Due in part to gross economic disparities among social groups, and perhaps also to the lack of participation in cultural debates by indigenous peoples, class distinctions mark progressive discourses more than distinctions of race, ethnicity, or gender do.

This does not mean that racism and sexism are nonexistent or that they are not articulated in photography. What it does mean is that the experiences of race and gender are less likely to be separated from those of culture and class than they are in North America. Cultural discourses on identity are largely absorbed by a nationalist problematic; that is, what it means to be Mexican. It has even been argued that culture has become a terrain for the imaginary resolution of difference; for example, between largely urban, middle-class artists and audiences and the sometimes rural, "popular" masses that are at the center of Mexican photography. Instead of separating their solidarity with these Other women from other issues and turning female representation into a distinct project, Iturbide, Grobet, and Andrade integrate their sense of gender identification into these larger social and aesthetic concerns. Furthermore, extensive critical discourse on racial and sexual difference in photography, or for that matter in other visual arts, is generally elided, in part because there is no institutional infrastructure, no network of galleries, art schools, and specialized publications to support such work. A confluence of factors, then, attracts these Mexican photographers to *lo popular* and *lo mexicano*. However much the object of their search may have been adapted to contemporary realities, the project itself remains profoundly marked by the nationalist romanticism that emerged in the wake of the Mexican revolution.

Dominated at the onset by the style of photographer Manuel Alvarez Bravo and cinematographer Gabriel Figueroa, a school of image making assumed hegemonic prevalence in Mexico by midcentury, to the point of becoming a stereotype. We know that Mexico—rural, timeless, brimming with natural beauty and supernatural belief, brought to us in glorious black and white. Its protagonists are the reticent *campesino* and the mysterious *indigena*, fantastic survivors of the past. I do not mean to suggest that rural, non-"Western" Mexico does not exist, but rather that its diminishing social presence in the postmodern age makes its symbolic weight all too apparent. For an increasingly urbanized middle class, these figures offer psychological resolution to its existential dilemma; to be truly Mexican and save oneself from the decadence and *malinchismo*[3] associated with modernity, one need only identify with them. During the golden age of Mexican cinema, superstar Maria Felix donned indigenous costumes in more than one of her films as a sign of rebellion against the patriarchal mores of the middle class. In contemporary Mexico, where the airwaves are saturated with images of blond and beautiful American Others and local peroxide-induced simulations, a nationalist vision of a better, purer Mexico is marshaled by sectors of the Left and the Right. Mexican cultural identity develops within the dynamic of attraction to and rejection of these two images of Otherness—the rural, indigenous past, and the present and future threat of "gringoization."

Several critiques of cultural nationalism have developed in Mexico in recent years. Social anthropologist Roger Bartra, in his book *La jaula de melancolia* (The Cage of Melancholy), argues that regardless of the prior or present existence of a real rural Mexico, the lyrical fiction operates as the collective fantasy of a country in the process of modernization.[4] Others have noted that the official celebration of Mexico's indigenous peoples has always gone hand in hand with their exploitation. Cultural critic Carlos Monsiváis suggests that the influence of the conceptual art of the 1970s has made it difficult not to perceive how that nationalist myth has been constructed and how certain schools of Mexican art have perpetuated it. This awareness of the symbolic dimension of the supposedly mimetic representations of Mexican culture, he claims, together with the rapid growth of urban popular culture and the increasing Americanization of everyday life in the 1970s and 1980s, has made it untenable for the majority of Mexicans to equate the myth with any actual sense of cultural identity.[5]

Whatever criticisms may exist in Mexico, images of rural, indigenous life still exercise tremendous influence on the North American imagination. They stand for the radical Otherness many here seek as an antidote to overdevelopment. They camouflage the more conflict-ridden encounters with real-live Mexican Americans. For some they confirm that somewhere there exists a world unspoiled by American corporations and soldiers. For others they assure that air-conditioning, beauty products, and VCRs do make for a better life. These readings almost inevitably ascribe truths about "Mexicanness" to the images in question or fault the photographer who does not satisfy the desire for images that verify a "real" Mexico. Eugenia Parry Janis, for example, in the book *Women Photographers,* claims that Iturbide's work is "too theatrical…[and] strives too much after surrealist effects…Iturbide's women associate comfortably with monsters in a way that likens them to monsters themselves, heroines of tooth and claw."[6]

It is worth noting that, far from monstrous, the iguanas whose use Janis addresses are considered a delicacy in Mexico; that they are also used for medicinal purposes; and that vestiges of pre-Colombian lizard worship still exist in Juchitán. Janis deploys a common ethnocentric strategy: in using a morally inflected aesthetic judgment, she betrays her reluctance to engage with these culturally different representations. At the same time, I would stress that her irritation is provoked by the awareness that the culturally different reality she seeks in these photographs has been rendered mythical and, I might add, without any apparent dissimulation. While I do not think that all American critics would agree with Janis, I would suggest that the apparently "documentary" style of these photographs hides this process of mythification and in so doing facilitates their entry into a North American repertoire of cultural "difference." And in this sense, intentionally or unintentionally, cultural nationalism in Mexico dovetails with the North American positivist quest for work that transparently reveals the essential Otherness of "non-Western" culture.

All this contributes to how we take in Iturbide's series on Juchitán. The photographs are unquestionably of extraordinary quality. I am struck by the combination of candor and dignity in the women's faces, in contrast to the deferential demeanor of the men. The women literally and figuratively fill the frames; they are central to nearly every picture, every ritual, and every life-sustaining activity. The pride with which they carry their stocky figures, their elaborate braids, and even the wrinkles of old age bespeaks codes of attractiveness and sensuality that have little to do with Western standards of female beauty. Only Magnolia, the transvestite, seems to be concerned with Western aesthetic conventions. Inside their homes the women make altars for themselves and their loved ones. Their public sphere activity appears to exist to further comradery among themselves, and their friendships are represented as just as important to them as are their relationships with their male partners—if not more so. These women seem to radiate spiritual integrity.

It is practically impossible not to notice the aesthetic influence of Alvarez Bravo in this work—Iturbide filters those visual poetics through a feminine sensibility and an impressive ability to divest her subjects of any shyness and to engage their gaze. So strong is her identification with her subjects that many photos give the impression of having been requested or staged by the women themselves. Yet, were it not for the synthetic fabrics used for some of the clothing, one might wonder in what time period these Juchitecas live. Modernity is barely hinted at in this hermetic world, free of conflict. There is hardly a sign of industry or technology in these pictures, not even a wristwatch. One shot of a car window with children peering in, their faces pressed to the glass, lets you know how unusual it is to find cars in Juchitán.

What many may not be able to glean from the photographs is that Juchitán is in the state of Oaxaca, the region of Mexico with the largest, most varied indigenous population, the lowest standard of living, the highest rates of illiteracy, malnutrition, and unemployment, and the highest rate of emigration to the capital and to "el Norte." None of these factors appears to have affected the subjects of these photographs. I do not mean to suggest that they should, but their absence further underscores the editorial processes that transform these photographic "documents" into mythical symbols of Mexican cultural identity. Furthermore, Juchitán's women have acquired near-mythic status in Mexico as a vestige of an ancient Mesoamerican matriarchal society. For many female members of the urban intelligentsia, Juchitán is a pre-Colombian protofeminist paradise on earth, and evidence for the claim that sexism is a European perversion of Mexico's "natural" order, an argument not infrequently heard in populist, progressive sectors.

I cannot speak to Iturbide's intentions; I am more interested in how these photographs function in relation to each other to create a sense of "another" place, and what relationship they establish with the viewer outsider. The Juchitán series is one of many in which Iturbide concentrates on locales. An individual photograph in the series

"Los Pollos," from *Juchitán de las Mujeres* by Graciela Iturbide, 1986.

may be appreciated and even analyzed formally, but the work's primary significance is in the "story" that is formed by the sequence, in which the inhabitants determine the difference or distinctiveness of the place. That Iturbide has returned to Juchitán for extended periods of time over several years suggests an intent to forge a relationship with her subjects that would preclude objectifying or sensationalizing them.

Iturbide shares the practices of immersion in a particular environment or community and narrative construction of meaning with her contemporary Lourdes Grobet. Iturbide chose the real but symbolically overdetermined terrain of Juchitán to create a kind of blueprint for a Mexican feminist imaginary. Grobet has concentrated in the last decade on prime examples of the stylized expressiveness of popular culture— *La Lucha Libre* (Mexican wrestling) and El Laboratorio de Teatro Campesino e Indigena de Tabasco, an experimental theater troupe of peasant and indigenous actors that often adapts and presents Western works in indigenous languages. Grobet makes no attempt to mask the fact that these practices are part of modern Mexico; but it is significant that these activities are visible evidence of the simultaneous persistence and transformation of pre-Colombian culture. Here *lo popular* reflects the transformative processes of modernization—what was once part of everyday life remains, but becomes a specialized profession.

Grobet's images of women constitute a definitive presence in these series. She captures the actresses from Tabasco in moments of intense concentration and

"La Venus," by Lourdes Grobet, 1983.

reflection, displaying the costumes and body paints they were required to design from natural materials as part of their training. Moving from the protected environment of the theater lab to the urban sprawl of the city, Grobet traces multiple manifestations of these theatricalized renderings of "Mexicanness." Her photographs recall Octavio Paz's characterization of Mexicans in *El laberinto de la soledad* (The Labyrinth of Solitude, 1950), as perpetual mask bearers, people who wear one self but hide another—but her subjects all focus on projecting their notions of cultural identity, however syncretic. It is difficult to say whether the *conchera* (dancer) with her synthetic costume, a mainstay of street culture in the *zócalo* (city center) of the capital, is more or less "realistically Mexican" than the mestiza intellectual who watches. One might ask which is more traditional or theatrical, the intellectual's poncho, the mask made by an indigenous actress, or the *conchera's* glittery garb.

Grobet's interest in the theatricality of urban popular culture has also led her to the wrestling ring, where she has produced the most extensive documentation in Mexico of this extremely popular sport. Her work on the female wrestlers, *luchadoras*, is unique. Their involvement in a sport like the *lucha libre* often surprises viewers, and aware of this, Grobet represents them affirmatively, underscoring the powerful female presence in working-class social and economic activity. At the same time that she champions the female wrestlers' physical prowess, Grobet seeks out ways to reveal their vulnerability and sense of femininity, defying the butch stereotype of the *marimacho* (an overly masculine female). Her attraction to the drama of the ring does not prevent her from delving into the *lucharoras'* private lives to reveal their triple burden as nighttime wrestlers, daytime workers, and full-time mothers. In absolute complicity with her subjects, she photographs only those wrestlers who wear masks, even outside the ring; she maintains the mystery of their identity that is part of their cachet in the ring, while her subjects continue their theatrical posturing for the camera outside the ring. For Grobet, the "difference" that makes one Mexican is found in these dramatic acts; her subjects perform, paint themselves, display themselves, and mime fighting in a seemingly endless whirl of activity. In her work *la mexicana* moves from earthy icon to ludic dissimulator with a heart.

"Aztecas Punk," by Yolanda Andrade, 1985.

Yolanda Andrade's subjects also perform and display, but their resources come from the ready-made world of urban mass culture, their references are more eclectic, and it's more difficult to discern the traces of the past in them. The series of photographs in her book *Los velos transparentes, las transparencias veladas* (Transparent Veils, Veiled Transparencies) forms an asphalt landscape strewn with the result of urban performances: Youngsters with painted faces create their version of punk; androgynous figures with plastic masks hide their real faces in order to project a constructed self-image. Nonetheless, live people are only a small part of a world filled with inanimate human figures. Statues, portraits, mannequins, life-sized figures of saints, and paper skeletons act like extensions of the quintessential Mexican mask, mediators that also remind one of the space between the identity and projected self-image of an individual or of the culture. A number of those projections are feminine but are clearly separate from the representation of female subjects; vehemently anti-essentialist, Andrade explores the transmutability of femininity in the urban public spaces of Mexico City.

The act of embellishment, of creative appropriation and reworking of already existent materials, in Andrade's photographs becomes an expression of how her culture recontextualizes and absorbs "difference" as part of its own self-image. Many of the objects and figures in these images are reproductions of European and North American artworks and artifacts that take on different meanings in this Other space. Andrade seeks the most ironic, if not unmediated, juxtapositions and presents them as ciphers, evidence of people's responses to living in colliding worlds. Simply by setting these objects apart, placing them at the center of her lens, she transforms them into contemporary versions of ancient monuments; the pictures are elliptical documents, she seems to say, of what people are constantly leaving behind as traces of themselves.

We never know whom these things belong to. Andrade positions her viewer as a flaneur who catches glimpses of an uncanny cityscape, but never gets beyond the surface. The street experience she recapitulates in her engagement with the viewer is one of defamiliarization, of following a series of related images without ever knowing the provenance of things. Out of this encounter one cultivates an attitude of distant affection rather than intimate connection. Grobet and Iturbide, on the other hand, go to great pains to connect artifact with maker, identity with person, and people with their place. They both retain an interest in preserving unity, in creating an identification with their subjects, in erasing that "difference," so to speak. Grobet looks for the actions that demonstrate how her characters constantly remake themselves. Iturbide evokes a rhetoric of essence; her Juchitecas seem to transmit what they are simply by being there.

It may be more difficult to assimilate Grobet's and Andrade's work into an American viewing context—the issue of cultural identity is far more submerged, and Andrade's hybridized world filled with cultural debris may be a bit too much like our own. Iturbide's Juchitán, on the other hand, is recognizably and comfortingly different—a closed universe of serenity held up for our contemplation. Furthermore, although all three identify their work as progressive, oppositional cultural practice, none of them calls photographic discourse into question by putting it at the center of her inquiry. While they address differences within the same culture, they do so without foregrounding the issue of ethnic or cultural Otherness, either their own or that of their subjects, as we in this part of the world might. The reduction of the meaning or use value of their work in terms of that problematic occurs in their reception here, not there. To interpret their work as transparently applicable to our cultural debates misconstrues the very constitution of identity and the function of noncommercial photography in a context other than our own.7

RICAN/STRUCTIONS: JUAN SÁNCHEZ

RECENTLY, THE ART WORLD has displayed an inordinate sense of satisfaction with its own belated discovery of the Other. Given this particular theoretical fashion, it is perhaps not surprising that the work of Juan Sánchez should suddenly be of general interest. In the past, Sánchez's work has frequently been dismissed as too narrowly political, but today it seems to reverberate with new meanings for different audiences. Those in search of a more culturally and racially diverse canon can find in Sánchez an American-born painter of black and Puerto Rican descent. Those in search of an antidote to the ethical bankruptcy of Euro-American postmodernism can find paintings imbued with religious symbolism and social consciousness. Those in search of a convergence of political radicalism and aesthetic innovation can find in Sánchez an artist committed to the integration of the two avant-gardes.

As satisfying as it might be to regard Sánchez as yet another newly arrived Other, it is nonetheless crucial to avoid conflating the art world's rather recent acceptance of his work with his own emergence as an artist. Indeed, Sánchez's retrospective at Exit Art in the summer of 1989 was less a coming out than the culmination of an extraordinarily productive decade in which he has been active as an artist, curator, writer, and political organizer. Well before issues of ethnicity began to restructure mainstream aesthetic debate in this country, Sánchez focused his own efforts on an investigation of difference and cultural identity. Drawing energy from his own ethnically diverse background, Sánchez has consistently endeavored to develop forms of cultural resistance, specifically resistance to the neocolonial destruction of Puerto Rican culture on the island and to the disempowering marginalization of Puerto Ricans in the United States.

In her catalogue essay for the Exit Art exhibition, critic Lucy Lippard calls

This essay first appeared in *Art in America* in 1990.

Sánchez a healer, an artist who takes elements of his culture, fragmented by colonial and neocolonial powers, and reworks them in a restorative manner.[1] She suggests that by absorbing and reformulating sources from the island, from the barrio, and from the Anglo mainstream, Sánchez forges a bond with his various audiences. Sánchez himself describers his artistic efforts as "reconstruction" (or, borrowing from salsa musician Ray Barretto, "Rican/struction"), a process that involves creating a common language, forging an identity, and reacquainting himself with the world he calls "home."

After years of self-directed research into his own heritage, Sánchez now moves with relative ease between the universe created by his art education in New York and the visual world of the Nuyorican neighborhoods of Brooklyn, where he now lives. Sánchez always tries to make his art accessible to a wide range of responses. Though intent on communicating specific information about the condition of his Puerto Rican homeland and his people, he has not forsaken pleasure or sensuousness. His expressionistic use of color, alluding to the tropical landscape through a highly emotive palette, provides one of the levels at which even a distant, uninformed observer can be drawn into the work. While his commitment to the cause of Puerto Rican independence and to rendering his vision in terms that are intelligible to his own culture are clear, I believe that in an important way his acts of mending are purely symbolic.

Sánchez has frequently voiced his support for the Puerto Rican *independentistas*, proponents of Puerto Rican nationalism who have been especially active in the United States since the mid-1970s. While many Puerto Ricans have rallied to the defense of *independentistas* harassed by the FBI and abused by the U.S. judiciary system, the goal of actual political independence remains a source of controversy, not consensus, among them. Sánchez is well aware of this, as he is cognizant that his own distance from Puerto Rico and the atmosphere of cultural apartheid that surrounds him in the United States redouble his need to shape a sense of cultural identity as a displaced Puerto Rican. He is also conscious of how part of the neocolonial experience of political and cultural oppression is the internalized alienation from one's own culture, a process that forces one to see that culture and to see oneself as Other.

Sánchez's sense of the vernacular Puerto Rican culture is intensified by the symbolic and geographical space that separates mainstream (white) U.S. culture from that of the island. Raised in Brooklyn by parents who crafted popular religious artifacts, Sánchez was encouraged from an early age to pursue his interest in art. He studied commercial art at the High School of Art and Design in Manhattan before entering Cooper Union in 1973 (as one of only two Latino students, at that time, in the School of Art). From the start, Sánchez based his subject matter on his political convictions. He was deeply influenced by the Young Lords, a militant political group dedicated to advancing the rights of Puerto Ricans in the United States and on the island; the Young Lords began in Chicago and opened a branch in Harlem in 1969. Sánchez's first student works were idealized portraits of Young Lords in a style heavily influenced by his early training in commercial design. Many of these early works incorporated actual posters or photographs that were affixed to the canvas.

While his own activism was later to take many different forms, in the early 1970s the awakening of his political commitment and the development of his subject matter were inextricably linked. Sánchez was encouraged by teachers such as Hans Haacke (at Cooper Union) and Leon Golub (at Rutgers) and by fellow artists at the then-emerging Taller Boricua, a Puerto Rican artists' collective. With these influences, Sánchez's progressive rhetoric and technique became more reflexive. By the time he had completed his MFA at Rutgers, Sánchez had developed his characteristic mixed-media format. Using typically large-scale rectangular canvases, Sánchez combines photos, newspaper clippings, and found objects with paint. Often the objects include religious paraphernalia bought from barrio *botánicas* (neighborhood shops that sell herbs, amulets, and other objects for Afro-Caribbean *Santería*). Sánchez also frequently inscribes texts over and around the images. Sometimes the texts are his own; sometimes they are quotations from Puerto Rican authors or political leaders.

The surfaces of Sánchez's paintings are virtual palimpsests of scratched graffitilike text, evoking the anonymous scribbling on crowded urban walls or the hand-torn edges of public posters. At first, Sánchez's collage paintings may suggest an expressionistic social vision close to that of Leon Golub or Sue Coe, but his broad abstract forms, his bright acid palette, and his sense of a communal, epic history are more akin to the wall paintings of the Mexican muralists. At the same time, the centered formats (often triptychs) of Sánchez's work simulate the domestic altar arrangements found in many Puerto Rican homes, arrangements that incorporate religious calendars, photos, and prayer cards of favorite saints.

Due in part to the lack of knowledge in the United States about Puerto Rican political and popular culture, and in part to his outspoken support of the Puerto Rican independence movement, Sánchez has been perceived as a one-dimensional "political artist," one who simply illustrates his commitment in his art. But Sánchez's work is never about only one level of political experience. Even in his paintings that are focused on explicitly political themes, the ostensible subject matter is often psychologically inflected, refracted through religious and mythical symbolism, and represented ambivalently. In other words, his approach to the political issue of independence is dialogical, always connecting that issue to other symbologies or discourses. In his work, Sánchez makes clear that the interaction of these various symbolic orders shapes a sense of Puerto Rican identity, not as something fixed or established, but rather as something in the process of becoming.

In his well-known painting *Mixed Statement* (1984), Sánchez once again employs a triptych, altarlike format, this time to confront the issue of political martyrdom.

The work consists of three brightly colored panels in each of which are black rectangular areas that contain similar photos of a Puerto Rican man, his head swathed in a Puerto Rican flag. Each black panel also contains handwritten text, news clippings, petroglyphs, or other symbols. A handwritten statement in Spanish at the top of the central panel describes how crosses were erected to two martyrs of the independence movement. This text is flanked by torn halves of a Puerto Rican flag. At the bottom of this panel is an American dollar obscured by a hand-painted cross. Traces of spray paint in the lower corners evoke urban graffiti and offset a tattered reproduction of a painting of the Last Supper and a bright red handprint, the mark of the death squads that have preyed upon the *independentistas*.

The painting pays tribute to *independentista* Angel Rodriguez, who, in 1979, was arrested in Tallahassee, Florida, as an alleged terrorist and who shortly thereafter died in prison under suspicious circumstances. Rodriguez's nationalist objectives are expressed in quotations from other *independentistas* and in the news clippings affixed to Sánchez's canvas. But if Sánchez's painting is honorific, it is not unambivalently celebratory. The three Puerto Rican flags Sánchez has painted are either ripped in half or incomplete, hinting at similar rifts in the political rhetoric of Puerto Rican nationalism. Sánchez seems to suggest, for instance, that just as the Puerto Rican flag obscures the man's face in the three photos, the meaningful lessons of Rodriguez's life and death are obscured by a process of martyrly mythification.[2] Sánchez's inclusion of the image of Christ at the Last Supper underscores this reading. Despite his own fervent support of the *independentistas*, Sánchez registers sadness and regret that a religiopolitical discourse validating (and even encouraging) self-sacrifice for the cause has taken the upper hand in the political battle for Puerto Rican independence.

Never losing sight of the material reality of Puerto Rico's neocolonial status, Sánchez nevertheless chooses to represent the struggle symbolically, never as itself alone. The movement is always linked to the mythical, religious, and cultural sites of resistance from Puerto Rican history that together form a world view. On a symbolic level, Sánchez sees the quest for political independence as the struggle of a colonized entity in search of its identity. To reduce his message to a rallying cry against an outside oppressor is to overlook his work's essential polyvocality.

To call a visual artist's work polyvocal might seem inappropriate, but Sánchez's pieces are charged with many voices and covered with many words in Spanish and English. Drawing heavily on the forms of oral culture, particularly Puerto Rican *plena* songs, as well as radical poetry and *oraciones*, Sánchez pays homage to the way those storytelling practices serve as testimonials in a resistance culture. Further evidence of how such traditions have nurtured him is his sensitive use of documentary-style photographic portraits, images that ennoble his subjects rather than fetishize them. It is important to Sánchez to reframe and recombine these shards of subjective resilience (in both texts and photos) in order to pose them as another side of history, a counterhistory. Reading against the grain of the dominant culture, without turning his subjects into icons, Sánchez restores to them their spiritual integrity.

In his work, Sánchez refers regularly to nationalist heroes and to contemporary protests, placing the present independence struggle within a history of anticolonial activity and radical cultural practices. Against the destructive forces of colonialism and imperialism, Sánchez always emphasizes the regenerative powers of spiritual and communal bonds. One of the most crucial vehicles for reconnecting traditional bonds is the reinvigoration of historical myths and symbologies. The Puerto Rican visual tradition employed by Sánchez ranges from petroglyphs of the indigenous Taino culture of prehistoric times to Afro-Caribbean Santería figures, religious sculptors, religious sculptures that are still used today and that appear in his work as signposts of survival, Sánchez's sense of faith is not precisely grounded in one religion but is more generally invested in a belief in the power of several religions and mythic systems. The symbols that most often represent his faith—maternal figures and the signs of Afro-indigenous Puerto Rican culture—are for Sánchez the stalwart bearers of his country's cultural, historical, and religious traditions.

One of his favorite mythical symbols is Caguana, the incarnation of Mother Earth in Taino legend. For Puerto Ricans, Caguana is the most primal sign of origin, of renewal, and of the oppressed, expropriated island itself. In Sánchez's *Luchar Past and Present* (1982), the matriarchal deity is drawn as a sarcophaguslike figure, broken in two, her bottom half displaying images of a march in New York protesting the arrest of *independentista* María Haydée Torres. Above Caguana's image is a text by Sánchez recounting a legendary confrontation between Tainos and Spaniards, the moment when the Indians tested the Europeans and discovered they were not gods. The presence of this legend as background, with the two halves of Caguana as a framing device, creates a sense of historical continuity in the Puerto Rican struggle for self-identity.

In another work, *Cultural, Racial, Genocidal Policy* (1983), a remarkable and angry response to the forced sterilization of Puerto Rican women, Caguana's head is split in two and the halves flank a central panel on which an image of Christ is also torn in half. The split figure suggests the way in which Puerto Rican culture is never allowed to be whole, but is always riven, broken, damaged by outside forces—in this case, the U.S.-planned program of sterilization to control population.[3] Caguana resurfaces restored in *Mujer Eterna: Free Spirit Forever* (1988), one of Sánchez's many homages to his mother, Carmen María Colon, who died in 1987. In *Mujer Eterna*, the schematic head of Caguana supports an upper panel with an altarlike array of snapshots of Sánchez's mother as a young woman. Here Caguana acts as a guarantor of links between the living and the dead.

Each of Sánchez's works is a panorama of images, beliefs, practices, and symbols with which he constructs a common language for a nation fragmented by neocolonialism and the population divisions that result from forced exile. Sánchez is a bricoleur who has set out to repair his fractured culture. Examining the discontinuities and contradictions within his people's quest for identity, Sánchez recognizes that

"Cultural, Racial, Genocidal Policy," by Juan Sánchez, 1983.
PHOTO COURTESY OF EXIT ART AND GUARIQUEN, INC.

any unity will have to allow for the variety of and disparity among influences that make up Puerto Rican history. He is unabashed in the display of affection for his subjects, presenting a poignant, almost reverential, view of his world. His purpose is largely but not exclusively celebratory: Commenting as a black Puerto Rican, Sánchez accuses us of one of the less obvious effects of colonialism, his own people's racist denial of their African and indigenous roots. Another effect of colonialism that he deplores is the shallow, commodified version of nationalism or ethnic pride that Puerto Ricans are allowed.

Sánchez realizes that it is only recently, with the latest surge of interest in non-European cultures, that the Euro-American art world has developed an informed critical reaction to the intercultural, interdisciplinary practices he has engaged in for year. The times when his appropriations from Puerto Rican vernacular culture might have been perceived as an unselfconscious or illegitimate mode of aesthetic inquiry are, after all, not long gone. And the economic reality of an art market that more readily accepts an Anglo artist's political engagement than that of a "minority" artist has changed little, despite increased critical attention to the work of nonwhite artists.

Until now, it has been the directness and consistency of Sánchez's political message that has had the greatest appeal for a North American audience unfamiliar with the popular cultural references that frame it. But a deeper understanding of his work demands a bilingual, bicultural viewer for whom the abundant and varied Puerto Rican and Nuyorican signs resonate. The full impact of Sánchez's work depends on familiarity with its complex symbols and references, and on an allowance for difference. To regard his work as a strange emanation from another culture is to fail to comprehend that Sánchez is not working out of a distant locale. Instead, Sánchez moves among different cultural spaces. In this respect, his situation is not unlike that of another bicultural artist, the late Ana Mendieta. Her work also dealt with displaced Latino culture by redirecting the artistic language of exile toward healing rather than conflict. As a healer himself, Sánchez addresses in his art the fissures among American cultures, seeking to bind up the painful psychic space that the artist/writer Guillermo Gómez-Peña has called "the infected wound."

TRACES OF ANA MENDIETA
1988 – 1993

F OR MANY, ANA MENDIETA is the victim in an infamous and unsolved death that resulted from a fall from a thirty-fourth-story window in the home of her husband, the minimalist sculptor Carl Andre. In the downtown New York art world of the 1970s and early 1980s, she was one of the first Latin American woman artists, and the only Cuban, to achieve indisputable prominence on the art world's terms, without compromising her own. For the Cubans, she was among the first exiles to renew bonds with her homeland and express in her art the pain of rupture that is so much a part of Cuban history. For me and every other Cuban American, Ana opened up a way of looking at our own existence. Any of us who choose to confront the manifold dimensions of the exile and the colonial and neocolonial violence that create our fractured identities as New World Hispanics will retrace her footsteps.

She was born in 1948 into a wealthy, politically connected Havana family and lived a comfortable early childhood, but the conflicts that determined the future of her class after the Revolution were soon to shape Ana's life. Heeding the anticommunist claims of the Cuban Catholic Church, Ana's parents sent her and her older sister Raquel to the United States in 1961 through Operation Peter Pan, a CIA-backed project designed to encourage emigration and family divisions. Upon arrival in the United States, the girls were placed in a camp with adolescent delinquents. After this transitional period, they were shuttled from one Iowa foster home to another. By the time they were reunited with their mother, who arrived in Iowa in 1967, their father had been imprisoned for his CIA connections and would not be released for another decade.

Ana began her life as a foreigner in relative isolation, without the imaginary and often sclerotized vision of a homeland that an exile community usually provides.

This essay first appeared in *Poliester* in 1993. An earlier version of this article, entitled "For Ana Mendieta," appeared in *The Portable Lower East Side* in 1988.

She faced on her own the racism and cultural ignorance of a homogeneous American environment, and later in her career, would sensitize her art world colleagues to their own forms of prejudice. One of the first important choices she made as a young adult was to study visual arts, reaching graduate school at the University of Iowa multimedia and video art program in the early 1970s. At that time, the program was extremely receptive to anti-gallery, anti-art-as-commodity currents on the rise in New York, which doubtlessly contributed to Ana's creative trajectory. American critics and colleagues have been quick to point out that Ana combined these developments in performance, body art, and site-specific sculpture with feminist concerns, and some have even mentioned Ana's interest in her "roots."

Ana's understanding of Afro-Cuban ritual and music and of Latin American history was the result of self-conscious research more than osmosis. Going to the heart of Cuban popular culture, Ana uncovered a history of cultural adaptation and response to the disruption and dislocation of the New World colonial experience, as well as the murmurs of preexistent, precolonial forms. Appropriating from Santería, the synthesis of Yoruba religion and Catholicism, what she called its "healing imagery," Ana drew on rituals and symbols that affirm social bonds, connect the practitioner to the past, and seek to overcome limits of time, place, and mortality. Santería is essentially performative, integrating process and objects, and singling out the transformative power in the act of making meaning out of natural materials and human gestures. In her *Silueta* series, which she worked on throughout the 1970s, Ana hewed her own figure into various landscapes in Iowa and Mexico, expressing her desire to establish her place in the world by retracing an elemental connection with nature. Using gunpowder and firecrackers, she would burn signs of herself into sand and soil; using mud and feathers, she would blend herself into the landscape; using blood mixed with tempera, she would metaphorize her pain.

Moving to New York in the late 1970s, Ana established ties with the feminist and Third World subcultures of the art scene. She also joined the Cuban Americans involved in El Diálogo, a series of talks held during the Carter administration's rapprochement with Cuba which led to the release of dozens of political prisoners, including Ana's father, and the possibility for many exiles to visit Cuba. (It also included negotiations for new emigration policies, which were to backfire with the 1980 Mariel exodus and later be terminated as a result of Radio Martí.) After nineteen years, Ana returned to Cuba, taking a group of artist friends with her. Already accustomed to transforming her sentiment into symbol, Ana proposed to execute an artwork in Cuba, and went back again in 1981 to carve her figures into the caves of Jaruco, just outside Havana. She herself became a symbol of friendly reunion, appearing on Cuban television and in magazines at a time when there was still hope of more amicable relations with the United States.

When she arrived in Cuba, Ana's work had already begun to change. The Rupestrian sculptures made in Cuba are part of a transition to a graphic style in which the female form is refracted through mythological and precolonial symbolism. Titling her works in Taino, the language of one of Cuba's indigenous peoples, Ana created works that self-consciously blurred the lines between art and archeological artifact, between "prehistoric" cave painting, iconic glyph, and sculpture.

Ana left her mark not only in Jaruco, but in Cuba's artistic community. She arrived at a time when a young generation of visual artists were undertaking a critical revision of history and cultural practice. She encouraged them to take risks, to experiment with forms and techniques they had had little access to during the cultural isolation that marked Cuban artistic life in the 1970s. To the young Cuban artist José Bedia, who had been developing his own hybrid aesthetics out of archeology and Afro-Cuban ritual, Ana was a kindred spirit. For Marta María Pérez, whose work

"Arbol de la Vida," by Ana Mendieta, 1977.
PHOTO COURTESY OF GALERIE LELONG AND THE ESTATE OF ANA MENDIETA.

includes photographs which document her pregnancy and the popular myths that enshroud it, Ana's work no doubt served as an important point of reference. To Gustavo Pérez Monzón, who was working with young children not far from where Ana carved her Rupestrian sculptures, her engagement with nature offered an alternative model of artistic activity to him as a creator and educator. For painter and insatiable art/media consumer Flavio Garciandía, discussion with Ana on Cuban popular culture and cultural identity undoubtedly helped him to refine his use of kitsch.

Ana's perceptive insistence on distinguishing art from her activities likened her to the young generation of Cuban artists who gained prominence in the 1980s. Acutely aware of how she and her work could be used for someone else's reductive polemic, she was not about to relinquish aesthetic complexity or political commitment. Yet, while working in Cuba seemed logical to Ana, settling there was impossible and, in any case, displacement had already become her *modus operandi*.

Like many Cubans educated before, outside, or even within the Revolution, Ana had to make a self-conscious choice to go beyond a neocolonial rejection of "popular" culture and nostalgic, simplistic attachment to folklore. Artist, lay archeologist, and shaman, she excavated links that would reinscribe her self-expression into the world from which she had been cast out. Her intensity of vision and artistic integrity forced her to delve beneath surface layers of the religious and nationalist symbol and stricture that are so much a part of Latin cultural history. As a result, she surprised many of those whose paternalism generated more limited expectations, and stunned others, including family members who to this day refuse to release her complete oeuvre for public viewing.

Ana's unique and haunting poetics speak to the experience of many in the Americas whose histories have been shaped by forced migration, enslavement, expropriation, and loss, and whose expressions have borne out the salutary power of myth, the persistence of belief, and the resilience of the spirit. She sensed that postrevolutionary generations of Cubans, whether at home or in exile, would have to undergo a long and painful process of rethinking ourselves and dismantling imposed histories in order to rediscover our America, its voice, and its art.

Although Ana's return to Cuba has become a paradigm followed by dozens of Cuban Americans, there can as yet be no official recognition, either in Cuba or in the United States, of the significance of these other efforts. On the contrary, while Ana's work is celebrated by many as a symbolic union of exile with homeland, her followers are dismissed as interference by official chroniclers of both sides of the great divide. Those chroniclers who favor Cuba deny the importance of any exile's work in relation to Cuban art, while those who favor Miami stress Ana's alleged disillusionment with the Revolution near the end of her life.

Despite the growing interest among Cuban American artists in making contact with those on the island, no exile since Ana Mendieta has been able to exhibit in Cuba or participate in a cultural event such as the Havana Biennial. Attention has instead been directed elsewhere, away from Cuban-to-Cuban dialogue, at a kind of exchange that does not disrupt age-old schisms. Hence, over the last five years, the flow of cultural exchange has been directed largely at launching work by Cuban nationals into the mainstream art world of the United States. This has been accompanied by consistent efforts to draw well-known American artists and intellectuals with leftist sympathies to the island; it should not be forgotten it was at Ana's stubborn insistence, over a decade ago, that many of those same people took interest in the burgeoning art scene on that tiny island. This was quite a feat, considering the insularity and ethnocentrism of the New York art world at that time.

Ana Mendieta's life and art have also rendered symbols in the now more self-consciously multicultural America, but of an entirely different order. The trial of her husband, Carl Andre, who was accused and then acquitted of having killed her, divided the New York art world along ethnic, gender, and economic lines that are still existent today. Scores of (mostly white) feminists artists have claimed affinities to Ana, and have invoked her name as a metaphor for female victimization, transforming her into a contemporary New York version of Frida Kahlo. Most recently, when the Women's Action Coalition staged a protest at the opening of the SoHo branch of the Guggenheim Museum, the activists threw photocopied images of Ana's work atop sculptures by Carl Andre, and paraded signs with the rhetorical question. "Where is Ana Mendieta?" There are more than a few of Ana's colleagues who, remembering her struggles to gain recognition in that same milieu, find the current appropriation of her image painful and even exploitative.

Despite all these attempts to make convenient use of her image, Ana's spirit survives. Her work continues to intrigue and inspire many, and her life and her death continue to haunt us all. I am sometimes moved to believe that the power of that spirit should be proof to us all that Ana could not have wanted to die. Then I think of all the Cuban artists from the island who in the past three years have chosen Mexico as a neutral terrain on which to continue their work, and remember that Ana Mendieta spent a crucial period of her artistic development in Mexico in the mid-1970s. "Plugging into Mexico," she once said, "was like going back to the source, being able to get some magic just by being there." It was during that period that she would engage in a communion with the earth, a process that would eventually take her to the caves of Jaruco, to the sacred ceiba tree in Miami, and onward. It seems hardly coincidental that Cubans from all sides, however inadvertently, continue to retrace her path.

THE AMERICAN BLUES OF
CATALINA PARRA

I REMEMBER A CONVERSATION I had with a cultural critic when I visited
Chile in the summer of 1989. Some years earlier, he had published a book about
Don Francisco, the master of ceremonies of the weekly variety show, *Sábado
Gigante,* that had become the country's most popular television program. The
critic had based his analysis on the idea that the absence of political life under
Pinochet had generated a need for mass media-induced illusions of well-being.
He was consequently surprised to find that *Sábado Gigante* had gone on to become
the highest rated program on Spanish-speaking television in the United States.
It might make sense, I suggested, to speculate on the possibility that political life
in the United States might not be that different—or at least that the function of
the media was very much the same.

Catalina Parra arrived in the United States in 1980 after formative experiences in
Germany and Chile that had left her with an acute sensitivity to the illusory qualities
of the mass media. She has since made art out of the "informational" materials of print
journalism, seeing them as the base of contemporary popular or, better said, mass culture. At the heart of her work lie recurring dualities that speak to her hybrid condition
as a migrant artist and to her double-edged sensibility, which is both coolly analytical
and expressively libertarian.

On the one hand, Parra's focus on the mass media bespeaks her recognition of its
materiality and real power; on the other, her technique foregrounds how unreal, or
better yet, how uncanny these media are in their continual production of illusions
about security and hegemony. The artist/subject projected in her work is constantly
attempting to decipher information that is never familiar enough to be taken at face
value; in a sense, this highlights the experience of displacement within which one must

This essay first appeared in the catalog for the Catalina Parra exhibition at INTAR Gallery in 1991.

regularly come to terms with the foreignness of the new location. At the same time, the force and focus of Parra's work come from where she is, not where she came from. Making art becomes a way of rooting herself firmly in a North American present. Yet, even as I take note of her positioning herself in the here and now of New York, I could also characterize this same disposition as an example of a transferred Latin American tradition of the artist as social critic and visionary spokesperson of his or her times. For Parra, these apparently conflicting aspects of her sensibility are not a source of conflict. "What are Chileans?" she asked in our interview. "We are a *revoltillo* (a scrambled mixture)…I am a citizen of the world society, and am a part of New York with all its chaos."

As adapted as her focus is to this context, Parra's work still bears the traces of other influences. The issue of popular culture's relation to high art is at the root of the creative endeavors of other members of her family as well. Her father, the Chilean poet Nicanor Parra, is Latin America's foremost exponent of colloquial poetry, drawing on aphorisms and other vernacular expressions. Her aunt, Violeta Parra, led the revival of indigenous music in Chile, and her songs became anthems of the Latin American New Song movement of the 1970s, which fused troubadour and other folk traditions with politically charged lyrics. Yet, it is the moment of separation from the familiar that marks her emergence as an artist in her own right. The four years she spent in Germany from 1968–1972 constitute this watershed period. In Germany, Parra developed an interest in photomontage and in the American and British Pop Art that was gaining ground at that time. Apart from her German experience, Parra also frequently cites her attraction to Brazilian concrete poetry, with its stress on the visual impact of language, and the process orientation of the Fluxus movement.

All of these influences fed into the development of Parra's style, which is, on the one hand, distanced and analytic, and on the other, intimate and charged with emotion. After returning to Chile just prior to the CIA-backed coup that ousted Salvador Allende and ushered in General Augusto Pinochet, she became part of a group of artists and writers that critic Nelly Richard calls the "avanzada." Developing a consciously rarified aesthetic language with which to further a critique of the regime and get past the censors, they introduced the use of nonartistic materials, as well as conceptually infused body art and performance to Chilean cultural circles. The loosely associated group also published several magazines—Parra served as a designer of one of them, entitled *Manuscritos*—that brought post-structuralist theory to bear on the anecdotal and populist modes of art criticism that were dominant during that period.

It was also during that period that Parra reinterpreted the Imbunche myth she first came across in novelist José Donoso's *The Obscene Bird of the Night*. This indigenous legend of people whose orifices were sewn up by witches became the basis from which to create extended visual allegories about censorship and violence in Pinochet's Chile. Hand-stitching together her symbolically charged materials—gauze, plastic bags, animal hides, maps, texts, and media images—Parra derived an approach that expressed indirectly what could not be publicly addressed in a more obvious manner. She has frequently noted that the military was baffled by her recondite allusions to wounds, hospitals, body bags, and disappearances, and that even in Chile, the Imbunche myth was so little known as to have passed unnoticed until she chose to make it new.

From what was at first, then, a means of creating metaphors about repression, Parra has evolved over the last decade into a commentary on the suppressed, subliminal significance of the mainstream media in the United States. Her mixed-media works do not replicate or parody advertising and journalism, as does much of contemporary media-based art. Rather, Parra concentrates on the process of coming to terms with information that connotes something other than what it denotes. In this sense, her work differs fundamentally from the Baudrillardian slant of postmodern art that implies that "real" communication in this society has already been replaced by

"American Blues," by Catalina Parra, 1990.

endless simulation. Parra's hand-sewn collages of actual newspaper and magazine text and image posit critical interpretation and constant vigilance as concrete political action. Art making becomes the individual response to the endless bombardment of pseudo-information.

The works in *American Blues*, then, evolve out of this long process of fusing political, geographic, and aesthetic influences. The puns and double meanings that join the expressionistic and the technical begin with the title, since "blues" can suggest depression, mournful music, and the proofs a printer provides before sending a publication to press. Parra's view, we are to understand, is both an indignant cry and a calculated blueprint of the collective unconscious. Four panels are divided into two sections of ten images, all of which were made in the last year and a half. Individual works are separated by vertical red strips, perhaps a punlike reference to the red tape one encounters in deciphering corporate-speak. The first section of hand-sewn images is framed by Chemical Bank ads that in their original state read *The Human Touch/ The Financial Edge.* Parra eliminates so many of the letters from "financial" as to leave us with "final edge" as the only logical reading, heightening the sense of pending doom. The second media patchwork in the set is framed by the ad's accompanying image of coins. Inside both are jigsaw puzzles of images that refer to environmental issues, animal rights, political protests, hostages, the homeless, and the military— a panorama of domestic and foreign problems that corporate finance is responsible for, however indirectly. *"Let's Talk Dirty,"* says one of the first images, as if to call corporate America on the carpet.

The second set of media patchworks forms a more direct and topical comment on the Persian Gulf crisis. According to Parra, she began working on these just prior to the Iraqi invasion of Kuwait, at which time she was already able to predict the American military response by simply sifting through the media. "Advertising was already talking about the war," she insists. Combining automobile and Wall Street corporate ads, Parra once again underscores the connection between big business, banking, and the military-industrial complex. The phrase that repeatedly frames the first half of these panels— *"Exceptional Performance Doesn't Just Happen"*—flies in the face of government attempts to create the impression that the U.S.-Iraq conflict arose overnight in response to the invasion of Kuwait. The other half of the panels consists of another corporate ad with a pen posed at the top of a sheet of paper, suggesting both the act of signing and thus assuming responsibility, and also its opposite—writing it off, so to speak.

Parra stitches her images for the first set onto the symbolically reflective surfaces of automobile windows and the "blank" page below the pen. Bush and Hussein stare each other down, while the repeated appearance of a tiger heal pokes fun at America's need for a "paper tiger" during its time of recession. Other panels connect U.S. militarism with the Middle East colonial past and problematic postcolonial division by Britain and France, as well as with America's image of itself as an Indiana Jones–like cowboy, and of the Third World as an extended backyard for American tourism.

The final set of works in this exhibition forms a singularly appropriate coda to *American Blues.* These four pieces are collaborations with Parra's father, Nicanor, whose poems provide the text. Each one of the four comments on the current and confused state of affairs, aptly turning recognizable, even clichéd phrases on their heads to express the paradoxes of contemporary politics and the difficulty of finding a new vocabulary with which to give events a name in the waning years of the Cold War. What was once "The people (or the Left) united will never be defeated" becomes "The Left and the Right united will never be defeated," sarcastically appraising the decline of progressive political sectors. *"Well/and so now who/will liberate us/from our liberators?"* evokes both the Chilean situation of a dictator being usurped by a political leader and party that was instrumental in bringing him to power, and the larger issue of the former socialist block's new status vis-à-vis the capitalist West. Parodying the syllogistic form, the statement "White House/America's House/Lunatics' House" hardly needs commentary. And finally *"New Man/New Hunger,"* which in Spanish (Nuevo Hombre/Nuevo Hambre) forms a more evident play on words, succinctly captures the destitute state of much of Latin America two decades after the heyday of Che Guevara's radical dream of creating a new society with a new man. Interestingly, these phrases act almost as verbal resolutions to the visual diagrams that precede them. Once again, the individual creative act, here in the dignified form of poetry, is not only a way of fighting back, but of closing this Pandora's box of imagery.

Looking at Catalina Parra's works, I am repeatedly struck by its unusual insistence that a terrible reality exists beyond the mediated world of images that literally makes it up. Her stress on the cold-blooded instrumental reason of those in power redoubles the sense of urgency evoked by those images of violence. And if the hand-stitching gives it a feeling of domestic intimacy, so does her sticking to actual newspaper pages—the latter perhaps even more. Set on the walls for us at a comfortable reading level, that pages transport us instantly back to our own breakfast tables and office desks, where we peruse those same pages every morning. The choice between being passively drawn into the media's manifold illusions and taking that same "information" on is ours to make. Parra offers us an example. As we read her *America Blues*, we are catching her in the act.

A BLACK AVANT-GARDE?
NOTES ON BLACK AUDIO FILM
COLLECTIVE AND SANKOFA

O NE OF THE CRUCIAL THINGS *about media education in Britain is that you're involved in very Eurocentric theories, and if you have any sort of black consciousness you begin to wonder where there might be room for your experience within these theories. In Roland Barthes'* Mythologies, *one of the key texts for students of semiology, the only reference to anybody black is to the soldier on the cover of* Paris Match. *The very superficial critique of colonialism found in such texts really isn't enough.*

As we began to think about images and about our politics, we realized that the history of independent film and black images was pretty dry, politically speaking. And political films were also really dry stylistically, mostly straight documentary. And there is always the problem that there hasn't been much space for black filmmakers in Britain. In terms of political film also, there wasn't much room for pleasure. MARTINA ATTILLE, SANKOFA

In the winter of 1986, two films from the British workshops opened at downtown London's Metro Cinema.[1] One was a multilayered dramatic feature, and the other a nonnarrative, impressionistic documentary—formats usually considered to be too difficult for the theatrical market. While it was highly unusual for low budget "experimental" films to find their way to commercial venues, what made these runs even more unusual was that the films, *The Passion of Remembrance (1986)* and *Handsworth Songs (1986),* were produced by the London-based black workshops Sankofa and Black Audio Film Collective. Those theatrical screenings were firsts for local black film collectives and are one of the many signs that the black workshops are effecting radical changes in British independent cinema.[2]

Sankofa and Black Audio's intervention in British media institutions seems to

This essay appeared in the 1988 monograph *Young, British, and Black.* An earlier version of the essay, entitled "Black Filmmaking in Britain's Workshop Sector," appeared in *Afterimage* in 1988.

have touched several raw nerves. Their insistence on shifting the terms of avant-garde film theory and practice to include an ongoing engagement with the politics of race sets them apart from long-standing traditions of documentary realism in British and black film cultures. Black Audio's *Handsworth Songs* is a collage of reflections on the race riots that shook Thatcherite England in the 1980s and the inadequacy of all institutional explanations of them—particularly those of the mass media. The filmmakers weave archival footage with reportage, interior monologue, and evocative music to create a gracefully orchestrated panoply of signs and sounds that evoke black British experiences. Sankofa's *The Passion of Remembrance* is the story of Maggie Baptiste, a young woman grappling with the problematic legacy of a black radicalism that foreclosed discussion of sexual politics, and with the differences between her vision of the world and that of her family and friends. Public and private memory reverberate through interconnected stories that take different forms: dramatic narrative, allegorical monologues, and film within film.

Critical attention to *Handsworth* and *Passion* has outstripped the response to other workshop films of the same scale. The films are at the center of polemical debates in the mainstream and black popular press that often do little more than bespeak critical assumptions about which filmic strategies are "appropriate" for blacks. At its best, institutional recognition takes the form of the John Grierson Award, which Black Audio received in 1987 for *Handsworth Songs;* the more common version, however, is the constant scrutiny to which the entire Black workshop sector is subjected.[3] All the black workshops contend that they must conform much more consistently and closely to the laws that regulate them than must their white counterparts.

As filmmakers and media activists, Sankofa and Black Audio question black representation in British media, from mainstream television to such bastions of liberal enlightenment as the British Film Institute (BFI) and academic film journals such as *Screen* and *Framework*. They are interrogating "radical" film theory's cursory treatment of race-related issues, and subverting the all-too-familiar division of independent film labor between first-world avant-garde and Third-Worldist activism. Sankofa and Black Audio are also concerned with mainstream images of black identity, preconceived notions of black entertainment, and the terminology and mythologies they inherit from the 1960s-based cultural nationalism that remains allied with a realist tradition. Sankofa's reflections on the psychosexual dynamics and differences within black British communities, and Black Audio's deconstruction of British colonial and postcolonial historiography, are groundbreaking attempts to render racial identities as effects of social and political formations and processes—to represent black identities as products of diasporic history. While the artists in these workshops are not the first or only black filmmakers in Britain, they are among the first to recast the question of black cultures' relations to modernity as an inextricably aesthetic and political issue.

Although racism is not a problem specific to Britain, the English version has its own immediate history. The existence of the black British workshops and the nature of their production are due to the 1981 Brixton riots and the institutional responses that gave the filmmakers access to funding.[4] The newly established workshops provided the infrastructure that, combined with racially sensitive cultural policies, created conditions for filmmakers to explore and question theoretical issues. Though the chronologies of events that inform *Passion* and *Handsworth Songs* are specific to Britain, institutionalized racism, its attitudes, arguments, and historical trajectories are not. In addition to institutionalized racism, we in America share the legacy of cultural nationalism, its ahistorical logic, anachronistic terms, and the scleroticizing danger of separatism. The U.S. psychosocial dilemma of belonging, which harshly affects people of color, might be offset slightly by melting-pot myths and a longer history of black American presence. But the massive influx of peoples from Latin

Still from *Handsworth Songs*, Black Audio Film Collective, 1986.

America and the Caribbean since World War II (not to mention the abundance of mixed-race Americans) is both evidence of a similar plurality of black cultures here and a symptom of the U.S. neocolonialist projects. The contemporary U.S. situation, then, exceeds any monolithic discourse on race, calling for. strategic recognition and articulation of a multitude of racial differences. The British use of "black" as a political term for all U.K. residents of African, Afro-Caribbean, and Asian origin expresses a common social, political, and economic experience of race that cuts across original cultures, and works against politically divisive moves that would fragment them into more easily controlled ethnic minorities. As mainstream American media attempt to constitute new markets by race (the heralding of the new Hispanic movie-goer with the opening of *La Bamba* is one example) and as critical reflection on media culture hovers around the question of colonialism, treating it at times as if it were a phenomenon that exists "elsewhere," we must continue a systematic, ongoing analysis of the homogenizing tendencies of both the mass media and post-structuralism, as well as the contrived segregation of post- and neocolonial subjects into folklorically infused, ahistorical ethnic groups. Recognizing nationality's problematic relation to the diasporic phenomenon, I will, in this article, examine the work of Black Audio and Sankofa as an instance of the development of a neces-sarily international critical study of race and representation.

Given the two black workshops' stress on how multiple histories shape their presence/present, it is appropriate to begin by outlining events that led to their prac-tice. Sankofa's and Black Audio's members are first-generation immigrants, largely from West Indian families that arrived in Britain in the 1950s and 1960s. The combination of an expanding post–World War II economy in England, changing immigration laws, and chronic economic hardship in newly independent colonies resulted in rapid growth of the British-based, black population into the mid-1970s, when economic decline and stringent immigration policies began to close the doors. Most of the first generation of, black British subjects reached adolescence in the 1970s, with little hope for decent employment, a minimal political voice, and virtually no access to media. This atmosphere of despair and foreboding was sensitively portrayed by black British independent pioneer Horace Ove in his first feature, *Pressure* (1975), focusing on the frustrations of black youth, and later addressed by Menelik Shabazz in his 1982 feature, *Burning An Illusion*.

Britain, in the last years of the Labor government before Margaret Thatcher, saw the rise of neofascist groups and racially motivated attacks against Afro-Caribbean and Asian peoples, coupled with changes in policing tactics now aimed at containing the black population. Public gatherings within the black community, such as carnivals, were increasingly perceived and represented as sites of criminality.[5] The Brixton riots of 1981 were not the first violent response by blacks to their situation, but the ensuing spread of civil disturbances throughout the country generated enough fear and media coverage to prevent the explosive situation from being ignored by the government. Despite statistics indicating that the Brixton riots resulted in the arrests of more whites than blacks, the mass media and adjunct power mechanisms had already succeeded in constructing a new Black Threat, with a new black, male youth as its archetypal protagonist.

The independents and the Association of Cinematograph, Television and Allied Technicians (ACTT) directed many of their efforts toward the establishment of Channel 4 as a commissioning resource and television outlet for British films.[6]

Channel 4's charter affirms its commitment to multicultural programming. Those interest groups' lobbying, together with support from Channel 4 and the BFI, also led to the Workshop Declaration of 1981, giving nonprofit media-production units with at least four salaried members the right to be franchised and eligible for production and operating monies as nonprofit companies. Workshops are expected to engage in ongoing interaction with their local communities through educational programs and training, and at the same time produce innovative media that cannot be found in the commercial sector.

Nineteen eighty-one was also a crucial year for the Greater London Council (GLC), as the beginning of its governing Labor party's six-year effort at social engineering through politically progressive cultural policy.[7] This project ended in 1986 with Thatcher's abolishing the council. A race relations unit and Ethnic Minorities Committee were instituted largely in response to the 1981 riots and sociological studies that followed. Within the Ethnic Minorities Committee was the Black Arts Division, which, under the supervision of Parminder Vir, slated monies for black cultural activity, particularly those areas such as film and video that had previously been inaccessible due to high costs. The future members of Sankofa and Black Audio had, at this time, just completed their academic and technical training—Sankofa's members were primarily from arts- and communications-theory backgrounds, and Black Audio's members had studied sociology.[8] Funding from organizations such as the GLC and local borough councils financed their first works and made them eligible for workshop status.

By the time Sankofa and Black Audio began to work jointly, a race-relations industry had developed not only in nonprofit cultural institutions, but in academia as well. The ensuing theoretical debates on colonialism and postcolonialism, in which Black Audio and Sankofa actively participate, draw extensively on the work of Homi Bhabha, Stuart Hall, and Paul Gilroy.[9] Bhabha's writings combine a Lacanian perspective on the linguistic construction of subjectivity, with Fanon's investigations of racism as a complex psychic effect of colonial history.[10] These ideas provide a theoretical framework from which to investigate the unconscious dimensions of the colonial legacy, to understand racism as a dialectical encounter in which victim and oppressor internalize aspects of the other, at both the level of the individual and the social.

Passion's concern with sexual conservatism in contemporary black communities and *Handsworth's* poignant resurrection of the 1950s immigrants' innocent faith in the "motherland" resonate with these psychological dilemmas in an expressive manner that transcends didactic illustration. They suggest alternatives to predominant forms of representation that posit the colonized as helpless victim (the liberal view) or as salvageable only through a return to an original precolonial identity (the underlying assumption of cultural nationalism). By bringing out their historical inextricability, they also undermine the liberal assumption that racism is an aberration from democratic ideals of the nation-state. In other words, the development of capitalism and the rise of the British Empire were based on colonial exploitation and racism; the colonial fantasy, as Bhabha puts it, is nationalism's unconscious, its dialectical negation. Black Audio's stunning reassemblage of archival images from the British colonial pantheon—*Expeditions* (1983)—is a critical reinterpretation of the fantasies that give rise to both the imperial project and its documentation.

Also influential to Sankofa's and black Audio's aesthetics are the writings of Paul Gilroy and Stuart Hall. The two social theorists bring Foucaultian methods of institutional critique to the issue of race and the constitution of the black subject. In their analyses of racism's many mechanisms and manifestations, they are acutely sensitive to the significance of the media and image production as means of transmitting ideas about nationality and nationalist prejudice.[11] Gilroy's interpretations of black British culture (particularly music) as a synthesis of modern, technologically influenced aesthetics and black oral traditions theorize cultural dynamics in the black diaspora, significantly shifting the terms of contemporary debates on postmodern eclecticism. While Hall employs Gramscian theories of hegemony to comprehend the complex power relations between institutions and the "resistance" of specific groups, he is particularly sensitive to the danger of imputing radicalism to all forms of popular expression, tempering widespread tendencies of cultural nationalism to project resistance as a leitmotif onto all popular history. In *Passion*, the character Maggie's search for new ways of approaching past and present desires evokes the condition these writers address. Like them, she seeks a more nuanced political vocabulary to approach a range of subjective and collective concerns.

Before *Passion* and *Handsworth Songs*, however, came the two workshops' earlier, more esoteric endeavors: Black Audio's *Expeditions* and Sankofa's *Territories* (1985). *Expeditions* is a two-part tape/slide show, subheaded *Signs of Empire* and *Images of Nationality*, in which archeological metaphors organize an aestheticized, ideologically charged inquiry. Drawing on images from high colonial portraiture, ethnographic photography, and contemporary reportage, Black Audio uses them as raw materials in a choreographed audiovisual performance. Over images of the past are inscribed philosophical phrases of the present. Between images of present conflict are "expeditions" that open onto a past seen through the representational genres that elide the violence of the orders with which they collude. From this new angle, maps become measurements of both distance and domination, and placid portraits take on a sinister cast. As a majestic male voice claiming that blacks "don't know who they are or what they are," repeats over and over, it becomes a stutterlike symbol for the speaker's own incapacity to comprehend the Other's identity. Ambient sounds and manipulated voices resonate forcefully, unearthing the deep structural meanings that bind the signs together. *Expeditions* is an antirealist document; instead, its makers struggle with every possible formal means of achieving a vision both poetically allusive and lucidly interpretive.

Sankofa's *Territories* also uses formal experimentation as a means of decentering thematic and structural traditions. Their first collectively produced film was made after founding member Isaac Julien's video documentary, *Who Killed Colin Roach?* (1983), about the mysterious death of a black male youth—a case similar to that of American graffitist Michael Stewart. It is a self-conscious return to the most visible Afro-Caribbean stereotype—the carnival—examining its places and displacements within British society. Charting the intensification of policing practices over three decades, *Territories* represents carnival as a barometer of institutional attitudes. Interconnected with these political and historical developments is a critique of ethnographic representations of carnival, which reify it as a sign of "original culture," masking its evolving sociopolitical significance. The two strategies bespeak the colonialist presupposition that carnival, as an architect of black expression, is by nature eruptive (savage) and erotic (dangerously pleasurable and potentially explosive), and therefore calls for order imposed from without. The film's second half, a surreal collage of gay couples dancing over riots, bobbies, and burning flags, is a formal rendering of that very threat of chaos, a site of excess that mocks attempts at discursive and institutional control. The film, however, not unlike the carnivalesque, is somewhat limited by its own idiom, falling back on an all-too-familiar avant-garde conflation of all forms of realism and narrative to add strength to its counternarrative's assertions.

This issue, however, was not central to the film's critical reception in Britain. Like *Expeditions, Territories* was deemed by many to be too intellectual and inaccessible. According to the filmmakers, the doubts about both works often came from white media producers who had surfaced after a decade of immersion in structuralist stylistics with a zealous new concern for "the popular." Also participating were proponents of the "positive image" thesis, who argue that positive representation of black characters is the answer to racist misrepresentation. They faulted the two workshops for, in a sense, missing the point. The ironic result of this sort of social engineering is that, despite its sensitivity to media and its attempts to create new spaces, it imposes limitations that eschew any psychological complexity. As Julian Henriques puts it in his article, "Realism and the New Language,

> The danger of this type of approach is that it denies the role of art altogether. Rather than appreciating works of art as the products of various traditions and techniques with their own distinct language, art and the media are reduced to a brand of political rhetoric.[12]

What is at stake in all these arguments, and what explains Sankofa's and Black Audio's notoriety, is that their works implicitly disrupt assumptions about what kinds of films the workshops should make and about what constitutes a "proper" reflection of the underrepresented communities from which they speak. As BFI Ethnic Affairs Advisor Jim Pines put it, the overriding assumption of the debates is that black filmmaking is a form of social work, or rather that aesthetically self-conscious film practice is too highbrow and superfluous.[13]

Clearly, there are also economic imperatives operating here. As many more established British independents gain international acclaim, arguments in support of a more commercially viable product gain momentum. For the burgeoning collectives, the production costs of dramatic narrative are prohibitive. But the problem for the workshops remains that the combined effect of the arguments is to restrict the space they need to develop a critical voice and vision, to experiment with a variety of ready-made materials and discourses in order to "tell stories of our experiences in a way that takes into account the rhythm and mood of that experience.[14]

Still from *The Passion of Remembrance*, Sankofa Film and Video, 1986.

Confronting the positive image as a problem rather than a given and defining relations to trends beyond the traditional parameters of "black communities" are issues that figure prominently in *The Passion of Remembrance*. Its dialogues are filled with questions about the images of black identity that surround the characters and inform their behavior. The allegorical black radical woman rebukes the allegorical radical black man for the latent sexism in his Black Power ideology; Maggie and her family evaluate the black couples on a prime-time TV game show; she and her brother attack one another's visions of political struggle; Maggie faces her peers' accusations that her interest in sexuality and sympathy for gay rights are not really black concerns. Contradictions between self-image and prescribed images, between desired ones and painful ones, are repeated in the film's different generic sites, or levels. In the dramatic narrative devoted to the Baptiste family, identity conflicts are articulated as generational and cultural. The immigrant father's skills are no longer applicable in the labor market. As if to protect himself, he holds on to an outdated image of both England and the West Indies, while his son's grass-roots radicalism fossilizes into romantic nostalgia. When Maggie and her friend get ready for a night on the town, the conflicts between the men's world view and Maggie's are beautifully underscored by vivid intercutting of calypso and pop music. Indeed, what stands out most in *Passion* is the soundtrack, rich in music, poetic excerpts, and charged verbal exchange. At times, the filmmakers rely a bit too heavily on dialogue to carry the film's ideas, rather than exploiting the possibilities of its visual material. But even if *Passion* suffers at moments from a lack of formal cohesiveness, its intellectual strength comes from its insistence on the multiplicity of elements and images that shape black consciousness.

Perspicacity of this sort appeared to be beyond the capacities of mainstream documentation of the 1985 Handsworth and Broadwater Farm riots.[15] In response to this conceptual lacuna came Black Audio's first film, *Handsworth Songs,* which shatters the reductivism of previous media coverage. Countering the desire of the nameless journalist for a riot "story" is the film's most often quoted line, "There are no stories in the riots, only the ghosts of other stories." In the place of monological explication are delicately interwoven visual fragments from the past and present, evoking larger histories and myths. Among the images are familiar scenes from previous riots, such as the attack of nearly a dozen policemen on one fleeing, dreadlocked youth from the Brixton uprisings. With the shots of news clips, they remind us that by the time of the 1985 riots, an established and limited visual vocabulary about blacks in Britain was in place. These references to a "riot" iconography form the synchronic dimension of Black Audio's poetic analysis of the representation of "racial" events.

The film uses archival cutaways to reveal an uneasy relationship between camera and subject. At one point, an Asian woman turns, after having been followed by the camera, and swings her handbag at the lens; at another, the camera swoops dizzily into a school yard, holding for several seconds on children's faces, nearly distorting them. This dreamlike movement is repeated in the filmed installations of family portraits, wedding pictures, and nursery school scenes, which, combined with clips from dances and other festivities, become images of the "happy past" that are a precious part of the black immigrants' collective memory. Juxtaposed against the violence and frustrations of the present, these "happy memories" brim over with pathos, but they are also set against other images from the past which betray their innocence. Newsreel images highlight the earnestness and timidity of the immigrants, while voiceovers belie the hostile attitudes expressed at their arrival. The film depicts how a

Black Threat was perceived to be transforming the needs of British industry into the desires of an unwanted foreign mass. These judgmental voices are confronted by newer ones, which offer no direct explanations or responses. Refining the style they developed in *Expeditions,* the filmmakers achieve such an integration of image and sound that the voices seem as if they arise from within the scenes. We hear poems, letters, an eyewitness account (by her daughter) of Cynthia Jarrett's death, introspective reflections, which together create a voiceover marked by lyrical intimacy rather than omnipresence. That sense of intimacy shines throughout both, *The Passion of Remembrance* and *Handsworth Songs.* Rarely do such formally self-conscious projects express comparable sympathetic bonds with their characters, maintaining a delicate balance between a critique of liberal humanism and a compassion for the spiritual integrity of their subjects.

Some British critics have attempted to identify specific avant-garde influences in Sankofa's and Black Audio's works, citing Sergei Eisenstein and Jean-Luc Godard as predecessors. While these assertions have undoubtedly helped to legitimate the filmmakers in the eyes of some, Sankofa's and Black Audio's direct concern with current media trends and with rethinking black aesthetics compels us to look elsewhere. The two groups, while well schooled in Eurocentric avant-garde cinema, are surrounded by and acutely aware of "popular" media forms. They can draw on the experiences of a cultural environment in which musical performance can function as a laboratory or experimenting with ready-made technologically (re)produced materials.[16] They also produce films in an environment where television is the archetypical viewing experience. The fast-paced editing and nonnarrative structures found in advertising and music video—not to mention the effect of frequently flipping channels—have already sensitized television audiences to "unconventional" representation, upsetting the hegemony of the classic realist text.

The filmmakers are also concerned with how to develop an aesthetic from diasporic experiences common to black peoples. This involves rethinking the relationship between a common language and a people, between ideas of history and nation. Paul Gilroy has pointed out that modern concepts of national identity and culture have invoked a German philosophical tradition which associates a "true" people with a place.[17] Access to historical identity as a people with a common voice is bound to the ideas of a single written language and of place. Yet centuries of capitalist and colonial development have literally displaced black populations. Their cultures have evolved through synthesis with others as much as through preservation and resistance, forging an ongoing dialectic of linguistic and cultural transmutation. While I am wary of labeling this process a kind of proto-postmodernism, I cannot avoid noting the formal resemblances. What seems more important than ascribing terms to diasporic cultural dynamics is to be aware of the ways in which Black Audio and Sankofa have taken this dynamic into account.

> Our task was to find a structure and a form which would allow us the space to deconstruct the hegemonic voice of the British TV newsreels. That was absolutely crucial if we were to succeed in articulating those spacial and temporal states of belonging and displacement differently. In order to bring emotions, uncertainties, and anxieties alive, we had to poeticize that which was captured through the lenses of the BBC and other newsreel units—by poeticizing every image we were able to succeed in recasting the binary of myth and history, of imagination and experiential states of occasional violence.[18]

Sankofa and Black Audio speak from Britain, with a clear focus on the conditions of racism in a country where their right to full participation in civic society is more obviously complicated by legal questions of citizenship. Given our own immigration dilemmas and the chronic inequities of black American participation in the political process, however, parallels are far from contrived. The black British filmmakers are keenly aware of their spiritual kinship with black American cultures, though their actual connections are primarily textual. They clearly see themselves as heirs to developments that have roots in this country, evidenced by *Handsworths*'s poignant passage devoted to Malcolm X's visit to Birmingham, and Sankofa's acknowledgment that their critique of sexual politics in black communities draws on black American feminist writings of the 1970s and 1980s. The same GLC policymakers who funded their first works also organized black cinema exhibitions, introducing audiences to the cinematic endeavors of Julie Dash and Ayoka Chenzira, Haile Gerima, and Charles Burnett.

Nonetheless, there are certain distinctions between the American and British conditions for black independents. Institutional structures such as the workshops and ACTT grant-aided division, while far from ideal, do not work against notions of shared interests the way that America's individualized, project-specific funding procedures can. Competition with the more monied, auteurist ventures of Britain's more mainstream independents is a far cry from the economic and philosophic chasms that divide marginalized independent experiments from high-budget productions in the United States. But Britain specifically, and Western Europe in general, is involved in a larger postcolonial crisis that has forced them to rethink national and cultural identity; the dilemmas touched on by Black Audio, Sankofa, and others are part of that crisis. Theirs is a poetics of an era in which racial, cultural, and political transitions intersect. It is no surprise then, that their works contain references to sources as varied as Ralph Ellison and Louis Althusser, June Jordan and Jean-Luc Godard, Edward Braithwaite and C. L. R. James. On this very sensitive point, I must insist that this is not a rejection of the goals of black consciousness. This "eclecticism," aimed at theorizing the specificity of race, reflects the mixed cultural, historical, and intellectual heritage that shapes life in the black diaspora. The sad truth is that many blacks must live that biculturalism, while few others seek to do so. If dominant cultures' relation to black cultures is to go beyond tokenism, exoticizing fascination, or racial violence, the complexities and differences which these film artists address must be understood. Sankofa, Black Audio, and many other black media producers in Britain are mapping out new terrains in a struggle for recognition and understanding.

PART III

FUSCO/GÓMEZ-PEÑA PRODUCTIONS

Mexican artist and writer Guillermo Gómez-Peña and I met in 1988 at a conference at New York's Dance Theatre Workshop. At the time, he was a member of the San Diego-based art collective, The Border Art Workshop/Taller de Arte Fronterizo, and I was an independent curator and writer in New York. Several conversations later, we began to collaborate on a variety of projects, which include performances, experimental radio, and installations. Our ongoing dialogue about relationships among Latinos east and west, and north and south, has been carried out via e-mail, satellite, audio and video recordings, as well as over dinner.

BILINGUALISM, BICULTURALISM, AND BORDERS

COCO FUSCO: *Are there any significant antecedents to the art work you have been doing at the U.S.-Mexico border?*

GUILLERMO GÓMEZ-PEÑA: In 1969, at the peak of Chicano nationalism, there was an interdisciplinary group called Toltecas in Aztlán that, without ever explicitly stating it, used the border as a laboratory. They were very interested in using poetry in the community, and in exploring relationships between dance, poetry, and political action. They were the precursors of our current dialogue with Tijuana. And there were some magazines such as *Liz Maiz,* one of the two magazines that started publishing people from both sides of the border. Just before the Border Art Workshop/Taller de Arte Fronterizo (BAW/TAF) was founded, a group of journalists also formed a group aimed at furthering dialogue across the border. They decided that there was a really strong need to link the Spanish media from Los Angeles and San Diego with Tijuana and Mexico City. They generated a number of projects in radio, magazines, and newspapers with the notion of the border as a site of encounters and alternative networks to distribute ideas and images. Before the Border Art Workshop, however, there were no interracial groups. In 1984–1985, the idea of Chicanos, Mexicanos, and Anglos sitting at the same table to work through issues was extremely subversive.

At that time, the U.S.-Mexican border region did not have a developed cultural infrastructure, so we had to create one. We became community organizers and popular politicians in order to speak. We created radio shows and magazines to open spaces and generate binational encounters.

CF: *What are the main influences on your work?*

GG-P: Three major traditions converge in BAW/TAF. One is the Mexican counter-

An earlier version of this interview, entitled "The Border Art Workshop/
Taller de Arte Fronterizo," appeared in *Third Text* in 1989.

culture of the 1970s, the groups of collectives that were interdisciplinary associations of artists working with similar goals. They wanted to bring art to the streets and to redefine the notion of public space. They wanted to utilize the city as a gallery. They also wanted to demystify the sacredness of artistic materials. They started using mimeograph, Xerox, Super-8, Polaroids, cheap audio art, and minimal props in performance, and so on.

Another influence is the Chicano movement: Chicano art, muralism, Chicano theater, Chicano poetry—bilingual Chicano poetry linked to the notion of the artist as an activist. The third influence is the European and Euro-American contemporary art from Fluxus to Happenings, conceptual art, all the way to performance art and video.

CF: *Are you in dialogue with any artists in Mexico?*

GG-P: We feel very strong kinship with the Postarte group in Mexico City. Postarte is an organization of artists, conceptual artists, visual poets, some performance and video artists, and mail artists, who, in the absence of a very strong and developed infrastructure, use the format of art packages, telephone, Xerox, small films, and audio as a way to create a network. We identify with Postarte because they underwent a similar process of redefining what Latin American art was—as we have. We have discussed how, for us, Latin America doesn't end at the Rio Grande. Instead, we see it as a kind of archipelago that includes the Nuyoricans and the Chicanos in the United States. Many of our images and texts find their way into the Postarte network. Every time we send a small audio piece or a text, we find out later on that somewhere in Buenos Aires, São Paulo, or Mexico City, the piece had been recontextualized, but in a different format.

CF: *What are some of the difficulties of evolving as a collective and working as a group?*

GG-P: We have to depart from the basis that we each represent the enemy of others in the group. This implies a complex process of negotiation. We have been making art about this process: about the process of healing, articulating, subverting, reinventing this relationship with the cultural Other.

CF: *What about the Other outside your group? You may be the other to each other, but then there's the rest of the world where that kind of democratic interaction isn't always possible.*

GG-P: I think that the most we can aspire to is to articulate the immediacy of this process, which can enlighten communities elsewhere.

This brings us to the notion of what the border is. What does the border mean? The border for us is an elastic metaphor that we can reposition in order to talk about many issues. For example, for the Mexican, the U.S.-Mexican border is an absolutely necessary border to defend itself from the United States. The border is a wall. The border is an abyss. The Mexican who crosses traditionally falls into this abyss and becomes a traitor. For the Chicano, the border has multiple mythical connotations. The border is the umbilical cord with Mexico: the place to return to, to regenerate.

For the North American, the border becomes a mythical notion of national security. The border is where the Third World begins. The U.S. media conceives of the border as a kind of war zone—a place of conflict, of threat, of invasion. More recently the Mexican press has exoticized the border. It has rediscovered Chicano culture; Chicano Cholo culture and low-rider culture have become exotic.

CF: *They no longer reject Chicano culture from the Mexican side as impure?*

GG-P: Not anymore. Throughout the 1970s, many Mexican artists and intellectuals crossed the border, brought new information, and helped to redefine the notion of what Chicano is for Mexicans. Chicano literature and cinema entered Mexico for the first time. Mexicans started to look at Chicano culture through its art. And that helped to redefine the notion of what a Chicano is. Mexicans have begun to look at the Chicano experience as a viable alternative. There are a number of conferences and exhibitions in Mexico dealing with the Chicano experience.

In this ocean of mythical misconceptions, of half-truths, of exaggerations, of hyperboles, border artists try to find more coherent means of articulating experience. The first stage of the Border Art Workshop was to deconstruct the mythology of the border. We were determined from the outset to overturn the assumption that experimental, outrageous, innovative creative work doesn't speak to community concerns, or that "the community" will be perplexed by it. What we find instead is that the tolerance for otherness, for eccentricity and extreme behavior in Mexican and Chicano communities is incredible.

CF: *When you talk about border artists, are you talking about more people than your group?*

GG-P: The border experience can happen whenever and wherever two or more cultures meet peacefully or violently.

CF: *You could in that case be talking about Mexico City, where you can move from one area that is totally Americanized to another that is completely not. If that is your logic, how far does the border extend?*

GG-P: Tomás Ybarra-Frausto explains this phenomenon as the mutual penetration of Anglo and Latin America. This process of inter-, trans-, and multiculturalization extends to other urban centers on this continent.

CF: *What happens to the group away from San Diego/Tijuana, or what happens to individual members of the group who go to work off site? Do you have to reconceptualize your work in order to put it in another kind of space?*

GG-P: I think that border culture is a minefield of cultural misunderstanding. When we are close to the border, we have more control over the possibilities of cultural misunderstanding than when we are away from it. When we take the work to other parts of the United States, the work is seen as exotic; at worst, it is just seen as political art hanging hypocritically in galleries.

CF: *What about your performances?*

GG-P: My performances are often exoticized. Border Brujo is a performance character I began working on in 1988. He appeared for the first time as a homeless inhabitant of Balboa Park. He has appeared at political events, on the streets, at community centers, and so forth. But Border Brujo is also a frequent visitor to the art world. He appears in alternative spaces, museums, and theaters. He is a confrontational character who, through an experience of the crisis and rupture of language, bilinguality, and tongues, tries to convey a sense of the border experience.

"Border Door," by Richard Lou, 1989.
PHOTO BY JIM ELLIOTT.

CF: *Does it make sense to link the choice to work in a variety of languages, the choice to work in a variety of disciplines, and the choice to work as artists in different media?*

GG-P: The multifaceted nature of the U.S.-Mexico border demands a multidimensional perspective. Every member of the workshop has a particular direction. I am a performance artist and a writer. Sometimes a billboard might be more effective than a performance piece. We have done very effective work recontextualizing imagery and texts. A text that appears on a wall one day may the next day be printed in a Chicano newspaper. And two days later it's going to be part of a Mexican magazine. And a month later it is part of a performance piece, or a film.

CF: *What about bilingualism? Sometimes it is the subject matter of your pieces; sometimes it is the rhetorical strategy in a performance; sometimes it is the political objective.*

GG-P: The notion of bilingualism is very tricky. It can be reactionary or progressive, depending on the context. When North Americans talk about bilinguality, they think that it is the Mexican who has to be bilingual, not themselves. For example, the rapid Mexicanization of the Southwest has provoked a number of reactionary measures—English has been declared the official language of the four major states in the Southwest with the biggest Latino populations, and bilingual education is under attack.

Working in different languages creates different levels of complicity. When we speak in English, we are the Other. Spanish is for us the language of translation and interpretation. When we use it, we explain the condition of the Mexican-American to the monolingual Mexican. Using bilingualism implies a complicity and speaks to the experience of the Chicano as one who understands biculturalism. Those three registers operate simultaneously in the performance. They create three levels of communication with three distinct sectors of the public.

CF: *I want to talk about historical precedents, to make a distinction between the kinds of conceptual games that you are playing and the way in which bilingualism has been dealt with in other Latino writing. A major stumbling block for the formal development of a hybrid Latino literature in the United States has been the dearth of literary bilingual fluency—a biculturalism that would express both languages and both cultures at the same time. The South American and Caribbean intellectual and middle-class professionals who migrated to the United States created works in their first language. Their subject matter may be imbued with nostalgia, but the effect on language is not the focus of the work. Another model is the Nuyorican and Chicano writing that emerged in the 1960s and 1970s— testimonial, autobiographical and/or colloquial in style. Spanish encompasses the private; English stands for the public. Spanish stands for the family; English stands for society. Spanish is nostalgia; English is confrontation and assimilation. One can note the attrition of Spanish, the retention of individual, isolated vocabulary units and of cadence, not of syntax. Spanglish evolves in the context of the street. What becomes eroded is the deep grammatical structure. Now, your group is working on something else. How do you see yourself in relation to these models?*

GG-P: One of the differences that I see is that a border artist is aware of the tricontextuality; the border artist has to exhibit and perform and interact in a Mexican, in a Chicano, and in an Anglo context. If we go to Mexico, we still want to keep the sense of linguistic otherness for Mexicans, because it is very important for us to help Mexicans understand that the Chicano experience is valid and important and necessary. We would perform seventy-five percent in Spanish and twenty-five percent in English—and that twenty-five percent of linguistic otherness that half the audience will understand, more or less, and the other half won't understand, is absolutely necessary. If we are performing in an Anglo context, we would reverse the process. The twenty-five percent in Spanish would be enough to make them uncomfortable, to feel threatened, and to make them feel that they are not receiving the entire experience.

If we are performing in a Chicano context, it's even more complex. In the Chicano context, we have to acknowledge that many Chicanos don't speak Spanish. Or many first generation Mexicans speak very broken English. They're going to get the Caló in between—the transitional parts, the fibers of the text—but some of them are going to feel very alienated in this situation.

Then there is the level of the tongues—of playing with dialectical forms, playing with sounds from Nahuatl, experimenting with the phonetical structures of indigenous languages—that is a level of absolute Otherness, the ultimate margin.

CF: *We've spoken about the integration of languages in your work. Now let's talk about what's different about your conceptual frameworks and the orientation of the different languages. The Cuban writer Edmundo Desnoes has said that he perceives the Anglo use of language as an instrument for acquiring things, as always having an objective. For him, the quintessential space for discursive exchange in an Anglo context would be the mall. On the other hand, he conceives of Spanish as a language in which people realize themselves in the act of speaking. The quintessential space that goes with that language use is the plaza, where everybody meets to exchange language. Earlier on, we were talking about the political dimension of bilingualism, how it means one thing to be bilingual and Anglo, and another to be bilingual and Latino. Is there some way we can begin to talk about this so that it doesn't seem as if any language you use is the same, any space is going to be the same?*

I am not implying that these two languages are completely decontextualized or dehistoricizable entities. I am talking about two languages which are varied in themselves but have different reference points. They have produced different philosophical traditions, literatures, and uses of imagery. How do you see these differences affecting your attempts to communicate in both languages? Where do you see the points of friction or tension in moving from one to another? What are the possibilities, the potentialities, for you in working in both, working in either?

GG-P: There are innumerable misconceptions related to the use of language in the border. I think that these misconceptions generate mistrust from one group to the other. Mexicans have traditionally been seen as extremely oral; Chicanos, having a culture of resistance and not a culture of affirmation like the Mexicans, have developed an extremely minimal, direct, and confrontational way of relating intellectually. Right there you have two modes of utilizing language that generate incredible mistrust. The Mexican is seen as flowery, as talkative; the Mexican perceives the Chicano as rude and as too direct. Another opposition that we find generates a lot of tensions and problems is that California is extremely antiintellectual. It is an outdoors culture, an easygoing culture. There is a basic distrust of cultures that use language as intellectual inquiry and as pleasure—the whole notion of conversation as pleasure, as dialogue, as intellectual inquiry, as social event, as ritual, is very foreign to Californians. When Californians and Mexicans try to sit at the same table, it's very, very difficult to communicate. For the Mexican, the language has extreme connotations of plasticity, of texture, of sensuality, and of communication. For the Californian, it's very pragmatic.

There is another level, which is the level of irony. Spanish language in Mexico is imbued with irony, parody, self-deprecating humor. In California, irony signals insensitivity, harassment, duplicity, hypocrisy. I think the language problem, beyond the merely linguistic, is extremely complex. You can sense that in the literary productions at the two sides of the border. That is one of the reasons the two sides have trouble with the literary production of the other. I think that Mexicans find Chicano literature very simplistic. Chicanos find Mexican literature extremely coded, extremely intellectual. North Americans, with the exception of those who are enamoured with the Latino boom, and who love magic and politics when they go hand in hand, find Mexican literature too wordy and too poetic. I have been told innumerable times by artists and writers from the United States that my language is too poetic and that I need to develop the descriptive and factual aspects of my writing. These are sources of ongoing misunderstanding. I think that the function of language is different. This is expressed very much in the context of the group. Mexicans don't believe that the sole function of language is communication. The pragmatic view is a very foreign notion to us. For us there is a ludic element. There is a mystical element, there is a whole level of imagination; language for the sake of imagining, of inventing, of playing. All these elements that exist in Mexican art and literature are not found on this side of the border, and the border artist has to walk on these bridges very often.

CF: *A significant way for immigrant cultures to deal with the new reality is through reterritorialization—rejection of the new reality and construction of a fictitious past.*

GG-P: That's the Chicano movement. It's very important to make a distinction between the experience of an immigrant, an exile, a frequent traveler, or a person who has grown between two or more countries, and the experience of a "minority." For Chicanos in the Southwest, the process of reterritorialization took place throughout the 1960s and the 1970s. It began as a reclaiming of a territory that was first expressed with the myth of Aztlan. Chicanos are now undergoing a new process of redefinition because of the new Central American immigration. Thousands of new immigrants from Mexico and Central America are arriving in the Chicano neighborhoods by the month. This is radically transforming their environment and their sense of cultural identity.

CF: *Still, the overwhelming majority of Latinos in the U.S. are of Mexican descent.*

GG-P: There is a nonsynchronicity in the moment that many Latinos are living here. The state of identity is multileveled in the Southwest and in the border region. There is no such thing as a permanent, static, homogeneous sense of identity for Chicanos or for Mexican immigrants. In many ways, I can say that I am a Mexican in the process of Chicanization and that I am developing a multiple identity. I am Mexican, but I am also Chicano, and I am also Latin American. When I am in Mexico, Mexicans often note the figures of speech of mine that are *pocho.* When I am in the United States, some Chicano nationalists object to the fact that I wasn't born in a Chicano barrio, and that I don't speak Chicano slang. When I am in Spain, they call me *Sudaca,* and in Germany I'm confused for a Turk. There is a point at which you realize that to defend this monolithic concept of identity—*la Mexicanidad*—in a process of ongoing border crossings and reterritorialization and deterritorialization is absurd. What many people in the border say is that we assume a multiple repertoire of identities. We have transitional identities in the making. We are developing new cultures. Jokingly, we have talked about imaginary identities that make more sense than the ones we are offered as possibilities. We call ourselves trans-Chicanos, or post-Mexicans.

CF: *How do debates on postmodernity in the Latin American context relate to your work?*
GG-P: There are some in the United States who believe that postmodernism doesn't make sense in Latin America, because they see it as part of the European and North American intellectual process. I think that perhaps postmodernism à la New York, à la France, might not make sense in Latin America, but right now there is a very heated debate in Mexico, Brazil, and other Latin American countries about postmodernism. Unlike the European and North American version of postmodernism, which is largely confined to intellectual milieus, in Latin America the focus of the discussion is on a vernacular postmodernism, a kind of popular postmodernity, that is related to the syncretic nature of Latin American culture.

"Superbarrio Visits San Diego/Tijuana 1989."
PHOTO BY MAX AQUILERA-HELLWEG.

Many of the so-called postmodern techniques in art, such as quoting, borrowed imagery, pastiche, juxtapositions of image and text, and recycling of historical imagery, had taken place in Mexican art, even in popular art, way before the term postmodernism was coined. Latin America is such a syncretic, eccentric, disjointed fusion of European, Amerindian, and Afro-Caribbean culture. This fusion has created a kind of multicentric perspective in Latin American culture that allows for narrative, for spiral thinking, for violent juxtapositions, that take place in the world, in society. Artists and writers observe them and later make art or write about them.

García Márquez has said many times that he doesn't invent, he simply reports, he simply chronicles. Many other artists are doing the same. When you walk into a little home in central Mexico and you see a family of peasants who have a TV monitor as an icon of an altar, you have before you an involuntarily postmodern object. When you go to a *conchero* celebration you realize that the *concheros*, the traditional Mexican dancers, are wearing tennis shoes and leather bracelets. In the very same dancer you can see a punk hairdo and Aztec feathers, the juxtaposition of heavy metal and Nahuatl. They are not necessarily doing this as a self-conscious act; they are reflecting the kind of syncretic nature of the culture they are living in. In that culture, the pre-Columbian and the contemporary exist shoulder to shoulder. In this sense we can talk about a vernacular postmodernism throughout Latin America.

CF: *How is this expressed in the border region?*

GG-P: The recently deceased Benjamin Serrano, a Tijuana artist who had been describing the dynamics of Tijuana pop culture since the 1950s. In the late 1950s, he was utilizing pop cultural imagery just as Andy Warhol and Robert Rauschenberg would do later. One of Benjamin's pieces of the early 1960s was a Virgin of Guadalupe with a bottle of Coca-Cola.

Chicano artists in the 1960s began utilizing folk formats such as the *retablo* and the mural; they imbued them with political and pop cultural imagery. The original religious meaning of the object was replaced by a pop cultural critique of the hybrid condition of the Chicano. I see this as a proto-postmodern pastiche.

Low riders, Cholos, Chicanos, heavy *metaleros*, Indian rockers, the heavy *mierdas*, and others are utilizing the imagery of consumer culture in extremely creative and postmodern ways. Then there is the velvet painting of Tijuana, with its own brand of social criticism. When you enter a Tijuana velvet painting store, you see a temple of binational pop culture that, through juxtapositions, creates a social dialogue about the relationship between the two countries. You see Martin Luther King next to Cuahatemoc Cardenas. The Virgin of Guadelupe next to Madonna. Jesus Christ next to Buddha. Cindy Lauper next to *la India Maria*. A low-rider car next to an Aztec pyramid. Many people say they are just responding to the tastes of the tourists. But many velvet painters have a critique of U.S. culture, and of how U.S. pop culture is transforming Tijuana. Some have told me that their velvet canvases are a mirror for the "ugly American" to see themselves reflected and to see what they are doing.

So there is this very rich vernacular, extremely experimental, and crazy aspect of Latin American art that has influenced the BAW/TAF. We have said jokingly that when people come to Tijuana and they want to see the alternative spaces, we take them to the wrestling match. Tijuana is one of the biggest installation art pieces in Mexico. Just walking the streets of Tijuana you can see the incredible historical, racial, linguistic, and cultural processes that are transforming Mexican society.

CF: *How does the Mexican capital look at Tijuana? Is it also considered to be a kind of bastard, being so close to the United States?*

GG-P: Tijuana has a double function in this respect. On the one hand, it is a place where so-called Mexican identity breaks down—challenging the very myth of national identity. The Mexican government has constructed this myth, which is that we have a univocal identity, one that is monolithic and static, and that all Mexicans from Cancun to Tijuana, from Matamoros to Oaxaca behave, act, and think exactly the same. By homogenizing all Mexicans and saying that, for example, Mexicans have a hard time entering into modernity, the Mexican state can offer itself as a redeemer of Mexicans, as the one who is going to guide them by hand into modernity. So in this respect, Tijuana's heterogeneity is really a kind of challenge for the Mexican government.

Many intellectuals and social scientists have seen in Tijuana a very explicit example of how this Mexican identity is just a myth. What actually exists is a pluralistic sense of self—multiple repertoires of identity. Social and ethnic groups from all over Mexico end up in Tijuana looking for a job, running after the El Norte myth, some of them trapped because they cannot cross the border. Here is the pluralism that the Mexican government has tried to hide. Walking down the streets of Tijuana you can find a Lacandon Indian next to a *Norteño,* next to a Mexico City punk, next to a conservative Opus Dei señorita from Guadalajara, next to a prostitute from Guerrero—an incredible mosaic. Tijuana is a strange mirror of the new culture that is emerging in Mexico. Crossing the border—that in itself is involuntary postmodernism. You cross the border and in a matter of seconds you move from Catholicism to Protestantism, from the past to the future, from Spanish to English, from pre-Columbian to high tech, from hedonism to Puritanism. This experience of disjunction, this experience of rupture, is a quintessential contemporary experience. In our work, we ask, what happens when Mexican *corrido* (ballad) meets video? What happens when a little Indian altar meets audio art? What happens when Mexican *carpa* (popular traveling theater) meets multimedia.

CF: *Do you see yourselves as anthropologists studying this phenomenon in your laboratories or are you a part of the phenomenon?*

GG-P: I don't think that we are anthropologists, but we are chroniclers of this phenomenon.

CF: *What has it been like for you to take on writing in English?*

GG-P: To cross the linguistic border implies that you decenter your voice. The border crosser develops two or more voices. This is often the experience of Mexican writers who come to the United States. We develop different speaking selves that speak for different aspects of our identity.

I am very interested in the epic genre because I believe that the Mexican immigrant experience is of an epic nature. The journey is linguistic, cultural, political, and geographical. The journey goes from the past to the future, from the South to the

North, from Spanish to English, from pre-Columbian America to high tech, from folk art to new technology.

One of the things that has happened is that my Spanish hasn't evolved that much since I left Mexico. My relationship with Spanish, literary and colloquial, is part-time. If I had stayed in Mexico and had written only in Spanish all these years, my Spanish would be much more complex. but I don't mind that. I think that what it has lost in possibilities of vocabulary and syntax, it has gained in conceptual strength.

I am very interested in subverting English structures, infecting English with Spanish, and in finding new possibilities of expression within the English language that English-speaking people don't have. I find myself in kinship with nonwhite English-speaking writers from India and the West Indies, Native Americans, and Chicanos.

When I make the choice to work in Spanish, English, Nahuatl, or Caló, I am expressing those transitional zones within my identity that are part of my life as an intellectual and as a border citizen. When I perform in Mexico, Spanish is my calling card. I contain this linguistic spectrum in my experience as voyager, and inevitably it surfaces in my literature.

I am not a writer of books. I have a bittersweet relationship with the Chicano and Mexican literary scenes. They want to incorporate me into their scene but they are having a hard time understanding why a writer would choose film, performance, and visual arts as the context for his literature, rather than a solely literary context. I am working in a country—the United States—that doesn't value the written word very much. I feel that my voice as a poet is less effective, less public, and less transcendental than my voice as a performance or media artist.

CF: *What about the history in Latin America of the figure of the poet as an integral part of each community—Does this tradition have anything to do with your work?*

GG-P: When Border Brujo performs in Mexico, he is that crazy poet, the poet-priest, the town crazy, the one who speaks for the community, and the one who incarnates the pain of the entire community. When he performs in the United States, he's a performance artist.

CF: *There are European traditions of town criers, local poets, bards, and storytellers, which might be seen as equivalent. But they are traditions that are, for the most part, dead. One might say that this tradition is revived somewhat through some performance art, but it is much more rarefied. What about some of the strategies you use in your writing? You often present highly compressed historical narratives, and, in doing so, play with creation myths, and biblical forms. Your personal epic becomes the story of an entire civilization.*

GG-P: One of the characteristics of my Mexican self is my obsession with history, while my Chicano self has one of my eyes looking into the future or the present. Metafiction is a trajectory in Mexican history, and is very prevalent in twentieth-century Mexican literature. We are reinventing the past. We are creating mythical categories that explain our contemporary experience.

In one of my poems, the undocumented worker suddenly finds himself in the mirrors of a mall as the reflection of an Indian warrior. A Mexican maid lost on Broadway becomes aware of her mythical dimension as a *hechicera* (sorceress) from the seventeenth century—or a fallen oligarch in La Jolla or Coronado realizes in his drunkenness that he's related to a Viceroy from Spain or to Porfirio Diaz.

CF: *What I was struck by in your poem Califas was your parody of a nationalist tendency to take the project of cultural recovery very seriously. Instead, here we have people inventing pasts for themselves by looking in a mirror that provides an illusory one.*

GG-P: We have to be delicate about this. I have had many problems with Chicanos precisely because of that. What I am saying in *Califas* and with Border Brujo is that Chicanos have created a metafiction about themselves.

CF: *Haven't Mexicans?*

GG-P: Sure, but I think that the metafiction of Chicanos is even more extreme. There is no reflexivity, no historical coherence and no irony. It is a very serious metafiction that is meant to replace history.

CF: *I can see what you are opposing yourself to —now what do you relate to stylistically?*

GG-P: To a certain extent, I can relate to the Latin American boom writers, but I think that I am the product of a crisis that they never lived. The orderly world that Márquez and Fuentes create doesn't have enough crisis to express my experience. I am a child of the ultimate Mexican crisis, of the financial, ecological, intellectual culture. My experience is one of absolute syncretism.

CF: *Any other influences?*

GG-P: I am interested in performance as a text, a multidimensional text. The kind of formal experimentation taking place in the performance art world, is much more interesting to me than most American fiction. I can also relate to *rasquachismo*, Chicano kitsch street culture, and border vernacular poetry. I think that the freshness of bilingual border poetry is extremely interesting. All the traditions that inform the text are extremely syncretic. Another important area is cinema. My texts are very cinematic.

CF: *Do you consider them visual? Do you work with a montage principle?*

GG-P: The way I construct them is in many ways like constructing a film. The way I edit—the syntax of my texts—is very inspired by the montage of experimental cinema.

NATIONALISM AND LATINOS, NORTH AND SOUTH: A DIALOGUE

GUILLERMO GÓMEZ-PEÑA: *What do you think are the possibilities of dialogue between U.S.-born Latino artists and Latin American artists?*

COCO FUSCO: It is a very complicated situation, and the differences between them are often startling. I have the impression that this dialogue with the South is much more important to Latinos in North America than it is to Latin Americans. Latinos in the United States live daily the problems generated by cultural misunderstanding, making us perhaps more sensitive to the personal and subjective dimension of intercultural issues.

GG-P: *Living in the United States, we confront perpetual cultural misunderstanding. We are obsessed with the question of intercultural communication, precisely because we suffer from a lack of it. It also concerns us because of our deterritorialization. We live outside our cultures of origin, and we find ourselves forced to express ourselves in a language that is not ours. We also feel that our ex-compatriots either exoticize us or flatly do not consider us to be part of their cultural panorama. This hurts us very much, as Mexicans who work outside Mexico, because the interest that North American cultural institutions have recently developed in Latino and Latin American culture is the result of our activism over the past twenty years, not of the apparent generosity of Anglo liberals. Latin Americans should recognize this. The Mexicans favored by this dialogue, for example, do not recognize the importance of work done by Chicanos. They even look down on us, and prefer to deal directly with whites. This, to my mind, is a form of colonialism.*

CF: I would add that Latino artists and intellectuals in the United States are particularly sensitive to this condition of dislocated communication because, in the North, the dominant culture tends to see all Latinos the same, which is really quite stupid. Living inside those communities, we recognize that there are similarities and differences between, these let's say, Chicanos and Cubans, and that these differences

This conversation was first published in *La Jornada Semanal* in 1992.

are often surprising. We are also very conscious of the rhetorical and political strategies the U.S. government has employed in its attempt to transform a series of diverse, primarily Spanish-speaking, cultures into a single race. This had to be done to create an identifiable voting block and a "target market." But, as a result, when many white Americans use the word Latino, they believe that they are dealing with a race, equivalent to Asian or black.

Recognizing this tendency toward homogenization, intellectuals and artists have undertaken a more profound search for connections between our deterritorialized communities and homelands of origin. Yet we often find that, in our countries of origin, there is little interest in our project.

G G - P : *Why do you think so?*

C F : Four or five years ago, when the legendary Latino Boom began, editors at several publications began asking me for articles about Latino culture. I began to deal as a critic with the same complexities of communication among Latinos in the United States that I had grown up with; the political in-fighting between Chicanos and Puerto Ricans, the ideological and class wars between Cubans and Central Americans in Florida, and the pronounced differences of race and class among *criollos,* mestizos, mulattos, blacks, and indigenous Latinos.

G G - P : *So you're saying that Latinos are just as divided as North Americans are?*

C F : We are not only distinguishable by race and class, but also by types of immigration. There are elite emigrations, such as the Cubans who came in the 1960s. There are political refugees from Central and South America. There are working-class emigrations, such as the Mexicans, Puerto Ricans, Dominicans, and Haitians. That working-class emigration has to be divided between the urban and rural. There are also those who emigrated for more existential reasons, as is the case of many middle- and upper-class South Americans in New York. To turn this variety of experiences into a monolith simply doesn't make sense—and in our art and literature, those differences become quite evident.

G G - P : *That myth of unity has existed for decades in different places, for different reasons. Among many Latinos in the United States, there is a tendency toward a kind of facile pan-Latin Americanism, which comes from the need to create a political alliance among different groups to combat dominant Anglo culture. It then, at times, becomes an ultra-romantic vision of what Latinness is, and sometimes lapses into insipid generalizations. According to this vision, food, language, sense of humor, art, and music are all crucial factors of this essential identity. In reality, as we know, another Latin America lives and breathes in the United States, and it is as complex and diverse as Latin America is. In other words, what does a low-rider rapper from East Los Angeles have in common with his neighbor who just arrived from Michoacán or Honduras? And what do they have in common with an exiled Chilean intellectual or a Peruvian who teaches at UCLA? Not much, right?*

C F : Living in New York, it is impossible to forget these differences, since on nearly every block of every barrio, there are ten different Latin American countries represented. I think there are bonds that derive from experiences of disenfranchisement among different Latinos who are part of antiracist movements, and Chicano and Puerto Rican nationalist movements. Those are, for the most part, people who experienced racism and prejudice in their schools and workplaces, and they have little in common with Latin Americans who arrive here as middle-class adults, never having endured those sorts of hardships.

GG-P: *I think that some of those who arrived as adults went to work with Latino and Chicano organizations to understand the experience that you are talking about. Even though there are aesthetic, linguistic, and cultural differences among Latinos in the United States, there is a need to recognize the political power and representativeness of each Latino in each specific struggle for power. Therefore, if I am on a panel at the National Endowment for the Arts, I pay careful attention to projects submitted by Latinos and by other people of color; I consider it my political responsibility.*

For me there is no moral dilemma in recognizing this "burden of representation," especially when I take into consideration the power of the far Right and of anti-Latino attitudes in our context. At the same time, I recognize that there are incredible differences between, for example, the New York–based Cuban American photographer Andres Serrano and the Chicano photographer Harry Gamboa; or between my own work in performance as a Chicano-Mexicano and the work of Puerto Rican performer Merian Soto. Nonetheless, American cultural institutions do not recognize these differences. For them, we are all equally exotic, passionate, Catholic, quarrelsome "bandidos," or savages, so to speak.

CF: With the exception of those who associate themselves with the leftist politics of the 1960s and 1970s, many of the middle- and upper-class Latin American artists and intellectuals in the United States reject the notion of a unified Latin identity. Some of them don't even like to refer to themselves as Latinos. They don't like to use cultural identity as a term or even as a semiotic system with which to analyze their work. They prefer not to get that involved in the treacherous debates over multiculturalism. If they get involved, they often do so with many doubts and fears. They prefer to avoid many Latino cultural institutions, not considering them to be serious, and do not support efforts made on behalf of the Chicano or Puerto Rican community. Many upper-class Latinos in the United States see making connections between politics and culture as regressive, and prefer to identify themselves as generic postmodernists. I live this every day with Latino gallery owners, artists, and intellectuals, who are for the most part *criollos*, who detest identifying themselves as minorities, and who see work produced by American artists of color as inferior, or of bad taste.

These upper-class Latinos come from all over Latin America and are the product of an arts education that promotes a universalist, Eurocentric, and modernist notion of art and culture. For them, popular culture is regionalist and of poor quality, and pertains to other social classes. Of course, they do not want to be identified with the marginal. What is curious is that while they reject that identification, they marginalize themselves, since what the American art market wants from them is cultural specificity produced by exotic Others. These attitudes also exist among many Latin American intellectuals and artists living in Latin America, who would rather deal exclusively and directly with whites. Unfortunately, they do not recognize what has happened to the cultural landscape of the United States in the last decade. When many Latin American colleagues visit me in New York, the last thing they want to do is go look at art made by Chicanos or Caribbeans.

GG-P: *I think there are many differences that contribute to these problems in understanding. Latinos on either side of the border do not share visions of identity, of language, of artistic production, or of nationality. We are a family divided by the border and by history. Now, as we approach 1992, we should look for shared visions and experiences that can establish the basis for the creation of transborder dialogues in the 1990s. We find ourselves faced, for example, with the Free Taco Agreement, which worries Mexicans more than it does Chicanos, since it will probably affect Mexico more than Chicanolandia. But if we're not careful, we could end up with eighty million more Chicanos, or Canochis, which is Chicano backwards. On the other hand, the quincentenary means much more to people in the United States, a country that has not resolved its own identity and that right now is obsessed with multiculturalism. Mexico has been dealing for at least two hundred years with its own debate about concepts of its indigenist and Spanish aspects of identity. It's only recently that the border has become fashionable.*

Mexico was interested, because its destiny was and continues to be debated at the border, with the situation of the maquiladoras, *and with the tragic reality that undocumented people live in that place, the constant violation of human rights there, that affects us all. Who doesn't have a relative or a friend in the United States? For the United States, the border was more interesting as a metaphor, as an intellectual paradigm, as a cultural fashion. I call this the cholo-chic syndrome. It was a complete and total mis-encounter.*

CF: I would add to that that Anglo interest in the border was largely expedient. It gave them a geographic rather than racial or ethnic paradigm to work with, which enabled Anglo artists and intellectuals to equate their work with that of others on the border and gave them access to Chicano cultural organizations and academic departments. It was also an apolitical paradigm that enabled them to elide questions of power, privilege, and access. Who was asking them in the 1980s to take note that only whites cross the border with relative freedom, and that only Americans escape the repressive apparatus of the border patrol? Who was asking about the significance of the fact that all the border books and blockbuster shows were being done by whites? If Chicanos did, the postmodern Anglo *borderólogos* would just write them off as incorrigibly retro nationalists.

GG-P: *Perhaps some positive change has taken place in certain very restricted artistic and intellectual circles. But, in general, the age-old misunderstandings persist between Chicanos and Mexicans. In Mexico, people still operate with a very simplistic vision of Chicanos. People believe that all Chicano artists use nationalist symbols from Mexican official culture, that they are all muralists and activists, and that all of them speak Spanish poorly and voluntarily reject Mexico. But reality is much more complex. In my opinion, the problem is that the Chicano experience reminds Mexico of the traumatic amputation of its northern territory, and that this is a very unpleasant memory. Furthermore, for the Mexican middle class, Chicanos as well as blacks have always been seen as "ugly and dark Americans," perhaps because Chicanos have the same Indian features that the majority of Mexicans have, features that "tarnish the landscape" of a Mexico that wants to see itself as modern.*

Chicanos continue to resent the scorn Mexicans feel towards them because of their Spanish, and that is a really infected wound. Traditionally, it is thought that identity is located in language: If one does not speak Spanish, one is therefore not Mexican. This belief could be extended to all the Latin Americans who look with skepticism on their own diasporic populations, which are slowly losing their mother tongue. In the 1990s, we cannot speak of Latin America as a linguistic community, since it is clear that not all of us speak Spanish. There are British and Portuguese Latin Americas; there are Latin Americas outside Latin America, those being the Chicano world in the Southwest and the Caribbean world of New York. This linguistic community begins to come apart when you cross the border. In the North, different Latinos have different degrees of closeness to the Spanish language. Even though some speak Spanish clumsily, or in a syntactically deformed manner, they don't stop being Latinos. This is not yet understood in Mexico. This is also reflected in the absolute lack of communication between Chicano writers, whose work is mostly in English and Spanglish, and Mexican writers, who are more interested in dialogue with other Latin Americans and with Europeans. They see our literature as a minor art, picturesque in the best of cases.

CF: Do you see possibilities for a transborder artistic dialogue in the 1990s?

GG-P: *Mexico is in a very fragile position with respect to its identity. The Free Trade Agreement will logarithmically multiply the processes of Americanization and Chicanization. In this sense, border culture and Chicano art can serve as bridges between cultures, as translators and interpreters of binational cultural codes, and as warnings about a transcultural future that awaits Mexicans.*

CF: I see some problems in this area. Suspicion in Latin America about identity politics exists because those debates are seen as part of the ideology of the state. It is a cliché to say that Latin America has resolved its problems of identity. What has actually happened is that the state has created ideologies that propose solutions to the problem of identity, but those solutions always occlude the existence of marginalized groups who are not part of the "national project." In this sense, we cannot think that everyone in Cuba, Mexico, or Puerto Rico identifies with the official celebration of *mestizaje*. Things get even more complicated when we take into account that the official notion of *mestizaje* is connected to concepts of nationality and territoriality.

So, to be Mexican, or Cuban, you have to stay in your country. How does that theory explain the condition of the thirty million Mexicans who live in the United States? In the United States, artists and intellectuals of color do not operate with a uniform notion of identity. Our approach comes out of the Civil Rights movement, is contestatory and potentially liberating, and is always in opposition to the racism and patriarchal tendencies of dominant American culture. Our visions of identity are influenced by the black, Chicano, and feminist movements, and take into account paradigms of race, class, and sexuality. They have little to do with the official notion of nationality propagated by the U.S. government. I don't know many artists of color who would state unequivocally that they are proud to be American.

"Allá en El Rancho Grande," *Medal of Honor* series #15, by Alfred Quiroz, 1990.
PHOTO BY PETER TREXLER, COURTESY OF THE ARTIST.

GG-P: *You don't sound very optimistic.*
CF: I'm trying to be realistic. These debates on identity are very popular in the American art world. The significant cultural debates of our historical moment are connected to notions of cultural marginality, sexual identity, race, and multiple identity. The notion of Third Worlds existing within the First World has been debated intensely in the last five years. I know of little that could constitute analogous discussions in contemporary Latin American art. Feminism is still seen as suspect in Latin America, and explorations of ethnicity are often seen as naive and passé. I think that there will not be a really open dialogue until it is understood that those debates on

sexuality, ethnicity, and cultural politics are crucial to defining "identity," American or otherwise, and that they are just as important as the well-worn discourse against cultural imperialism.

GG-P: *You can't demand that artists and intellectuals in Mexico who employ a theoretical discourse with a historical evolution completely different from that of Latinos in the United States should radically change their notions of identity overnight. In Mexico, your position would be seen as ethnocentric. There has to be a less categorical way of dealing with differences. There are many thinkers in Latin America who for a long time have spoken about multicentric notions of identity. The problem is that this kind of thought is not made available in the United States as much as the more conservative thought of writers such as Octavio Paz. I also think that there are many contemporary Mexican artists whose interests are similar to that of Chicanos, and who are exploring processes of hybridization and transidentity. The problem is that the impresarios of "Free Trade Art" are more interested in Magical Realism than they are in a true intercultural dialogue.*

To this I would add that one of the differences between a pragmatic society like that of the United States and a transcendental one such as Mexico's is that, in a pragmatic society, the intellectuals and the artists have to look the way they think. They have to look like what they believe. This is a militant vision of ethnic and sexual identity as lifestyle. It takes place in an urban culture that demands very specific and visibly recognizable ideologies, customs, institutions, and world views, and ways of being, of dressing, and of speaking. In Latin America, I think there is more acceptance of open contradictions. In Mexico, there is gay culture, but it is not necessarily a textual culture, with a "militant" gay lifestyle. There are many gay artists and intellectuals who do not proclaim themselves to be gay. I think that there are many feminists who exist in the same way. The Mexican feminist doesn't stop wearing makeup, dressing well, or getting along with men. Latin American women have been bothered by the separatism of American feminism, which proposes a society without men.

CF: You are advocating a dangerous double standard. Your arguments in favor of repressing open expression of gay identity and feminism sound very patriarchal. I doubt that *machistas* have to veil their "masculinity" to avoid offending Mexican women. And it has been extremely convenient for Latin American men to reduce American feminism to stereotypes about appearance, which is misogynist, and about separatism, which is actually embraced by few feminists anywhere, even in the United States. It makes it much easier to reject feminism when it posed in such a simplistic manner. The Left in Latin America has always been suspicious of feminism and has dismissed it as sectarian and "imported" from Europe and America. It has systematically treated issues of identity as a national question, not as an intergroup problem within societies. For intellectuals in Latin America, who are for the most part *criollos* and male, it is much more convenient to employ spatial paradigms such as center and margin. These models allow anyone to consider themselves distanced from the "center," as nondominant, and as marginal, which ultimately means that any privileged person from a Latin American elite can categorize him- or herself as geographically oppressed, without having to question his or her relationship to other races and classes—or to the opposite sex—in his or her country. That is a strategy. You hide the differences within the society so that the majority of intellectuals can claim to be themselves representative, in an omnipotent way, of their locales. That is why the questions about power relations that minorities in the United States ask are so threatening. We demand equity in sexual and ethnic representation. We always ask, where is your Latino or African American representative? How many women are participating in this event? If you ask this of a Cuban or a Mexican, they get annoyed or laugh. They simply do not want to enter into that level of dialogue. They see it as facile; but in this context, those questions help to break the stronghold that the elite has in cultural institutions.

"El Altar," by Yolanda Andrade, 1991.

GG-P: *The official culture is one thing; that is, what is exported; what reality reflects is another. The case of so-called Neo-Mexican culture is emblematic. We know that, after the Mexico City earthquake of 1985, a cultural convulsion erupted in Mexico. The city fell into ruins, and from those ruins emerged the need to look inward: Writers offered themselves as chroniclers, artists auctioned their paintings, musicians sang to heal the wounded conscience of the damned, and journalists felt compelled to deal with the immediate realities. The true hero of the reconstruction, as Felipe Ehrenberg has said, is the Naco, who, to be sure, has never stopped being Neo-Mexican. This is to say that, at that moment, a clear Neo-Mexicaneity emerged from the ruins of Mexico City. Very interesting work emerged that had nothing to do with the dominant culture: the cartoonists of La Jornada, the best days of magazines like La Regla Rota and La Linea Quebrada. That Neo-Mexicaneity emerged from within. It is a Neo-Mexicaneity that has much in common with Chicano culture, which is a culture of crisis, and with border culture, which is a culture of urgency. For the first time in years, there was a great sense of identification among Mexicans, people at the border, and Chicanos. All of a sudden, Super Barrio was becoming friends with Super Mojado. In 1985–86, you could hear a Mexican punkarachi band and a Tex-Mex band on the same stage in one night, and the similarities were striking. But, parallel to this, another form of Neo-Mexicanism emerged in yuppie art milieus, and those who espoused it quickly figured out that ethnicity was fashionable in New York. The more ethnic-looking the object, the better the chance of its selling. So they started to paint the rustic, countrified Mexico of the films of the 1940s and 1950s, using that landscape as a backdrop for their own personal angst. What emerged was a kind of Chicano-style art without the bite, a Chicano version that was too nice.*

CF: I agree with you to a certain extent, but I think that the main source of aesthetic inspiration for these Neo-Mexicans is the pictorial language of Frida Kahlo as well as her conceptual framework, her references to popular art traditions, her use of the *retablo* form, and not so much the cinematography of Mexico's golden age.

GG-P: *For me, the point is that this other Neo-Mexicanism has nothing to do with the delicious rascuachismo of the Nacos and Chicanos whose relationship with popular culture is organic. It has nothing to do with magazines and art galleries. They resemble each other, but the fancy one has no bite. Am I making myself understood?*

CF: These different kinds of difference are part of the postmodern condition. There are many kinds of postmodernism in artistic practices. There is a postmodernism that feeds on urban consumer culture and cultural hybridization. These experimental artists combine "high" culture with popular tendencies of the moment; they might use mass-produced materials and cheap media to subvert their dominant cultural meanings. This kind of postmodernism might be expressed in the work of certain rap artists, for example. There also exists the kind of postmodernism you are talking about, based on an apolitical notion of culture in which everything is equatable with everything, and nothing means anything. In this sense, an American who appropriates Chicano iconography means the same as the Chicano who uses high technology. This other kind of postmodernism is particularly interesting for Americans and Europeans. It is a by-product of postindustrial society. In the so-called First World, there exists at the moment a search for spirituality, and for the "primitive." Capitalist, postindustrial society defines itself by its lack of emotion and ritual. "Exotic" art from the Third World provokes a series of primordial emotions for that society. That art is associated with kitsch. The apolitical appropriation of popular culture by Neo-Mexicans is perfect for gringos: It offers them sentimental iconography, which they so desperately need to fill their spiritual void. On the other hand, Chicano art represents another kind of "primitivism," a more irritating, cruder, and vulgar kind. It is more threatening, and full of political significance that questions the hegemony of Anglo culture. It also reminds middle-class Mexicans that our roots are not in Paris or New York; on the contrary, they are in this land, and are its fruit. That is why, with few exceptions, there is little amicability between Neo-Mexicans and Chicanos.

NORTE: SUR

A PERFORMANCE-RADIO SCRIPT
BY COCO FUSCO AND GUILLERMO GÓMEZ-PEÑA

FEMALE VOICE: This is Norte: Sur. This is about America. America, not only the U.S., but America.

[*Music: Los Electrodomésticos sing: Les deseo de lo más profundo de mi corazón. A todos ustedes y los suyos…*]

MALE VOICE: And now, *queridos radioescuchas,* direct from Santiago de Chile, los Electrodomésticos. We dedicate this song to the newly deposed president, General Augusto Pinochet. The conductor of this machine, one of many conductors…

[*Music: Los Electrodomésticos sing: Así mismo como también, para respetarle Señor conductor de esta máquina, que también cumple un papel importante en nuestra ciudad…*]

[*Latin Musak Jingle*]

AMERICAN RADIO ANNOUNCER: Greetings, friends, this is Meredith James, hostess of MPR's weekly series, *Buscando América.* Today we are going to listen to some daring thoughts about America's changing cultural identity. We have two people in our Miami studio who believe that the United States can no longer be conceived of as separate from Latin America and the Caribbean.

GUILLERMO GÓMEZ-PEÑA: (*Interrupting*) In fact, American identity is a 500-year-old wound that has never healed.

COCO FUSCO: The North and the South aren't bipolar entities anymore. The First and Third worlds, English and Spanish—they are totally intertwined.

MEREDITH JAMES: Wait. I think we're getting ahead of ourselves. We haven't even introduced you yet. As you can tell, listeners, our guests have quite a bit to say about

The program was commissioned by the Festival 2000 of San Francisco in 1990 and was produced by Toucan Productions. It aired on National Public Radio in 1990.

the issue. They are Gwermo Comes-Pinis from Mexico—

GG-P: Guillermo Gómez-Peña, *por favor*. I see myself as a citizen from San Diejuna, really.

MJ: (*Exasperated*) All right then. And we have Coucou Fusco, a Cuban living in New York.

[*Bizarre Flute Music*]

CF: My name is Coco Fusco, and actually, I was born in the U.S. and am genetically composed of Yoruba, Taino, Catalan, Sephardic, and Neopolitan blood. In 1990, that makes me Hispanic. If this were the '50s, I might be considered black.

MJ: How romantic!

[*Cheesy Drumroll*]

GG-P: Would you believe that one of my grandmothers was part German and part British? During the '40s, she wrote bilingual poetry in Mexico City, but no one was into that sort of thing back then. My other grandparents had a mixture of Spanish and Indian blood.

Gómez-Peña and Fusco as "El Aztec High-Tech and La Authentic Santera," from *Norte: Sur,* 1990.
PHOTO BY CRISTINA TACCONE.

MJ: Fascinating, but I'm afraid we have to go back to our subject. Coco, how do you think that your personal story makes you part of America?

MALE VOICE WITH THICK SPANISH ACCENT: *Pregunta de la semana*—how much Spanish can your cultivated ears take?

> [*Music:* Fernando Albuerne sings: *Siento la nostalgia de volverte a ver, más el destino manda y no puede ser. Habana, mi tierra querida…*]

FEMALE VOICE: *Ay, vivir en la música ajena, padecer de nostalgia importada, importar la nostalgia propia, triste condición de nuestras tierras.*

> [*Music:* Romantic guitar music]

CF: *Mi tio abuelo Flaviano escucha a su Frank Sinatra por la Radio Martí.*

GG-P: *Mi padre escuchaba ferviente a Nat King Cole el la XEW, México, D. F.*

CF: *Me acuerdo de mi abuela, bailando en la cocina al ritmo de Los Panchos, escuchando a la WHOM de New York.*

> [*Interference:* CB radio Pirate] [radio breaks in]

PIRATE: This is the voice of Comandante Ruiz broadcasting from Radio Sandino in exile. I must inform the American public that the last elections in Nicaragua were substantially affected by the thirteen million dollars in U.S. aid to Violeta Chamorro's campaign.

> [*Sound of Interference*]

NEWSCASTER: We interrupt this broadcast. In Washington tonight, state officials are meeting with the Motion Picture Association of America to discuss the latest findings of the Rockefeller Report on the export of American entertainment to Bolivia, Colombia, Peru, Nicaragua, Paraguay…

> [*Music:* Mexican singing a parodic version of "I Wanna Hold Your Hand": *O ye, dame tu mano, quiero rascarme aquí, quiero rascarme aca, quiero rascarme aquí…*]

> [*Music:* Mexican version of "Shake Rattle 'n' Roll"]

> [*Music:* La Lupe sings "Fever": *Fever de mañana, fiebre en la noche azul. Todo el mundo tiene fiebre, eso bien que lo sé yo. Tener fiebre no es de ahora, hace mucho tiempo que empezó. Dame tu fiebre…*]

> [*Stadium Crowds Cheer*]

TEACHER'S VOICE WITH ECHO: *La calcutización, la tijuanización, la fronteri-zación, la tropicalización, la rascuachización, la picuización…*This is bilingual radio a continental infection, and there's no antidote for it.

> [*Music:* Latin Musak with lots of horns]

VOICES THAT SOUND LIKE THOSE OF A TV AD: *Para los niños en América Latina, la primera figura de autoridad es una "miss." Ya después, llamar a la reina de la belleza "Miss Universo" no representa ningún problema.*

Kids in Caracas love Kellogg's cornflakes for breakfast

En Chile, los corn chips se llaman "Crispies."

In Cuba, all detergent is "Fab."

En México, el pan para sandwiches es "Wonder" o "Bimbo."

In Costa Rica, the automatic teller is called "Anglomatic."

Sadly enough, *en California, Colorado, Arizona y Florida*, English Only was approved.

But what will happen to words like barbecue, lasso, or even salsa?

Linguofuturologists predict that chile con carne will be renamed pepper steak and will be served at McDonald's, and Speedy Gonzalez will become Speedy Gordon and will be featured in Cyberpunk movies.

[*Music:* Speedy Gonzalez]

RADIO ANNOUNCER: This is radio frontera FM, spoiling your dinner as always, 200 megahertz *en todas las direcciónes.*

[*Music:* 1950s Latin orchestra]

MALE VOICE WITH THICK SPANISH ACCENT: *Queridos radioescuchas, les habla Joaquín Esteban Taylor, ministro de cultura de Panama.* Some of you have expressed concern that we may be losing our culture. It is true that the U.S. dollar is our official currency, and that our president was sworn in at a U.S. military base. *Pero les aseguro que seguimos tan panameños y tan latinos como siempre.*

[*Music: Medio Evo's nonsensical bolero: …y propongo que de una vez y por todas, sea respetado el rumbo que requiere el país nacional, el cual atraviesa por una coyuntura historica indisolu, en cuanto a la estructura que se…*]

[*Music:* Indigenous Mexican music]

VOICE IN MEGAPHONE MUSIC: *Nuestros centros culturales chicanos deben promover el ballet folclórico, el muralismo y el teatro alegórico como expresiones idiosincráticas de nuestra raza, única y auténtica.*

FEMALE VOICE: Due to pressures from the Mexican *secretaria de turismo*, Huichol and Chamula Indian crafts must remain authentic, at least until 1992.

[GG-P *speaks in tongues*]

AUCTIONEER VOICE: 30, 40, 100, 300, no, 3,000 years of Mexican art at the Metropolitan Museum. An adventure in wisdom and pride.

FEMALE VOICE WITH ECHO: Authentic art, authentic nostalgia, quality control. (*Repeats*)

[*Music:* Yomo Toro on guitar]

GG-P: Come to Vieques. Enjoy our tropical warmth.

CF: Rest on our immaculate beaches, the whitest sand on earth.

GG-P: Shop for our colorful crafts.

CF: Date our exotic men and women.

GG-P: Drink our Bacardi rum at sunset on the terrace of your bungalow. Come to Vieques. You will sleep peacefully. You will be protected by the U.S. military bases that occupy most of our island.

MALE VOICE: Call your travel agent or your nearest navy recruitment center.

FEMALE VOICE: This announcement was brought to you by the Borinquen Chamber of Commerce.

[*Music:* Latin Musak jingle]

CF: Well, I would say that my identity has always been a problem for most people. They are constantly trying to change it. When I was born, the nuns in the hospital thought they were doing my parents a favor by classifying me as white. Then my mother got deported just after I was born and took me to Cuba with her, where everyone saw me as a *mulatica clarita*.

GG-P: I am my parent's youngest and darkest child. I was born *morenito y peludo*, a dark and hairy thing at the Spanish Hospital of Mexico City.

MJ: Was this a problem for you, Gwermo?

GG-P: Not really. Ninety percent of all Mexicans were mestizos like me. In a sense, I grew up raceless.

CF: My parents tried to raise me without a sense of race, but that was unrealistic. My *abuela,* who came to live with us in 1963, she was happy that I was light enough for her to call me "*la princesa francesa.*"

MJ: The French princess, you mean?

[*1950's Tango Music*]

GG-P: Now that you say that, Coco, I realize that my world wasn't completely raceless either. I became aware of skin privilege when my slightly darker schoolmates began to treat me with extra respect. To them I was white, sort of.

MJ: But what does it mean to be white in Mexico?

GG-P: To come from "*buena familia,*" to be mysteriously linked to Spain. See, in Mexico, race has more to do with class. But wait, let me ask you something—has anybody here ever asked you what it means to be white here?

MJ: Well, not really. But I'm asking questions. So the, Coco, do you think your parents were trying to hide something from you to protect you?

GG-P: What kind of a question is that?

MJ: Let her answer!

CF: Not exactly. They knew that the Civil Rights movement wasn't going to end racial classification, but they didn't want me to be psychologically impaired by it. They found a private school where they thought I wouldn't have to deal with my race in negative terms. I entered in 1966 as a child of color.

MJ: And?

CF: Segregation had been supplanted by separatism. No one was into the idea of "mixed race." And whenever I took national exams, I had to check an ethnic

"GI Joe Conquering the Cartel," by José Sances and Daniel Galvez, 1990.

background box, and I couldn't find one for myself. So I always marked Other. Chicanos, Puerto Ricans, and Cubans hadn't been lumped together yet.

[*Music:* Kitsch Harps]

MJ: Do you think things got better for you when people started using the word "Hispanic"?

CF: People were still confused about whether I was Black or not. A the end of high-school, three administrators—a black, a Chicano, and a Jew—were deciding if I was eligible for a minority scholarship, The black said no, the Chicano said yes, and the Jew said that I should ask my mother if we had any African ancestors. They weren't convinced by my little Afro. Have you ever thought about your ancestors?

MJ: Well no. Gwermo, didn't you arrive in this country just as Americans started to employ the term "Hispanic"? Do you think that helped them to understand who you were?

GG-P: They had a lot of other terms for me besides "Hispanic." When I crossed the border in '78, I ipso facto became a greaser, a wetback, a meskin. At the time, I didn't understand what those words implied.

MJ: I'm getting really confused. Well, I've just been told that that's about all the time for today. Thank you for joining us for *Buscando America*. Next week, we'll have Professor Malcolm Stevens from Purdue University talking to us about indigenous basket weaving traditions at the Tex-Mex border.

[*Music:* Ranchero Tune]

[*Sound of Ticking Clock*]

PACHUCO VOICE: Sssspanglish, the language of pop-cultural diplomacy… Ssssspanglish is our language, yeah. This is the *voz* of the future, 1992, American glasnost *con safos*.

[*Music:* Tex-Mex tune]

CF: Border lunch menu on the U.S. side. Our specials today are tofu enchiladas, taco salad, fajita pita, barbecue curritos and pizzadillas.

GG-P: Border lunch menu on the Mexican side. Hot-dogs wrapped in bacon and covered with salsa picada, *hamburguesas en mole verde* and Kentucky Fried *tripa*.

FEMALE VOICE: Art menu for the 1990's: Chicano magical realists, Native American conceptual artists, Dominican rappers and Asian performance artists. America is wonderfully strange, and cheap.

MALE VOICE: Hey there, stranger, looking for a fun way to spend the evening? Doesn't matter where you are, you'll always find affordable prices for the cultural Other. A muscular mestizo in Tijuana, only $25. A mulata beauty in Havana, only $35. A Nuyorican in Los Sures, only $15.

FEMALE VOICE: *El otro siempre sabe mejor.*

> [*GG-P speaks in tongues, interspersed names of computer brands such as "IBM" and "MacIntosh."*]

CF: I met a homeless man in Santiago who dressed up as a Mapuche Indian. He wore a sign on his chest that said: "Authentic Indian made in Chile."

GG-P: I remember the "real live Aztec dancers" Niagra Falls who swore they spoke Nahuatl. They performed colorful rituals for the mesmerized tourists. They were actually undocumented ex-mechanics from Mazatlan.

FEMALE VOICE: Yaqui, Seri, Guaycura, Diegueño, Barona, Seminole, Comanchero, Tuscarora. Romantic dots on tourist maps. Romantic words in empty ears; *cambio de canal.*

> [*Music:* Corazón de Melon (*cha-cha-cha*): ...*Corazón de melon, de melon melon melon melon, corazón de melon. Your heart is a watermelon heart, just a watermelon heart...*]

MEXICAN BARKER VOICE: *"Amor Salvaje," el nuevo supervideo de Madonna y Julio Iglesias ya está a la venta en su tienda favorita. En su compra recibirá gratuitamente un paquete con diez simpaticos preservativos para que el "Amor Salvaje" no lo traicione.*

MALE VOICE: Dear listener, do you know the difference between cultural exchange and colonialism? Between vampirism and creative appropriation? We are here to help you figure it out. Today, we are going to talk to Enrique Mendez Orduño, adviser on Latin American Affairs for *Arteamérica,* a new program of the United States Information Agency.

> [*Drum Music*]

MEXICAN RADIO ANNOUNCER: *Nuevas aventuras para toda la familia. Buenos Aires cartelera doble*: "The Terminator" and "The Incredible Hulk." San Francisco double bill: "*Bronson, Vengador Asesino*" and "*Mojados Precolombinos contra la Sico-Migra.*"

> [*Music:* Charlie Parker playing "La Cucaracha"]

> [*Cafeteria Sounds*]

FEMALE VOICE WITH SPANISH ACCENT: That guy was handing out flyers about Latino cultural identity. I wonder if he's been anywhere in Latin America lately. Lots of middle-class women there dye their hair blond.

FEMALE VOICE WITH AMERICAN ACCENT: They are not the only ones who do that sort of thing. I've seen more than a few *gringas progresistas* who wear *huaraches* and *huipiles.*

FEMALE NO.1: OK, OK, I get it; so everybody wants to be the other. Is that the point?

FEMALE NO.2: Or sleep with them. (*They crack up*)

FEMALE NO.1: Really, I'm not kidding—hey, check out that music. La Cucaracha—in Russian!

[*Russian Woman Sings "La Cucaracha"*]

MEXICAN RADIO ANNOUNCER: America is no longer the continent that you imagine. Audio-graffitti FM, *buscando un nuevo lenguage para expresar sus temores y deseos interculturales.*

[*Music:* Game Show Jingle]

MASTER OF CEREMONIES: Hi, everybody out there. It's time for your favorite radio contest, *Pura Bicultura.* We'll play you the sounds, and you just phone in with the answer. Tell us what it is or who's singing it, and you will immediately win an airplane ticket to any city in the American continent with the exception of Havana, of course, ha ha!. Our number is 270-LOCO. LOCO! Here's our first sound of the evening. Hey!

AMERICAN SINGS IN SPANISH WITH THICK ACCENT: *De la Sierra Marenga, cielito lindo, vienen cantando. Un par de ojitos negros, cielito lindo, de contrabando. Ay yay yay, Frito Bandito!*

[*Music:* Game Show Jingle]

FEMALE ANNOUNCER: *Está es radio educación. Construendo un nuevo lenguage para nuestro atormentado continente, América poscolombina.*

[*Sounds of Typewriters*]

MALE NEWSCASTER NO. 1: Good evening. At the top of the news tonight, the American television series *Kojak* is voted the most popular show in the Peruvian Andes.

MALE NEWSCASTER NO. 2: A Colombian drug lord claims his role models are Al Pacino and Marlon Brando.

MALE NEWSCASTER NO. 1: Two Mixteco migrant workers were shot to death by an All-American Death squad in Encinitas, California.

MALE NEWSCASTER NO. 2: A Chicago appellate court decides that the firing of a Guatemalan supermarket cashier for speaking Spanish on the job was not racially motivated.

MALE NEWSCASTER NO. 1: The Pope and the King of Spain are preparing the 500th celebration of the discovery of America. Twelve Latin American countries have decided to participate.

[*Music:* Old-fashioned Circus Band]

CF: 3,000 U.S. citizens live in Guantánamo base, and 17,000 in Vieques.

GG-P: 100,000 homes in Baja, California, are owned by U.S. citizens.

CF: There are 26,000 U.S. troops in the Panama canal zone and 25,000 in Tegucigalpa.

GG-P: The second largest Mexican city is Los Angeles.

CF: The second largest Salvadoran city is Los Angeles.

GG-P: The second largest Puerto Rican city is New York.

CF: The second largest Dominican City is New York.

GG-P: The second largest Cuban city is Miami.

[*An Echo Repeats:* The second largest, the second largest…]

CF: The second largest Nicaraguan city is Miami.

MALE NEWSCASTER NO. 1: This is Trans-American Radio, interrupting your coitus, as always. *Buenas noches.*

[*Music:* Mercado Negro playing "La Cucaracha," punk-style.]

RADIO PIRATA:
COLÓN GO HOME!

A LIVE BROADCAST FROM *LA PINTA DOS*
BY COCO FUSCO AND GUILLERMO GÓMEZ-PEÑA

[*Opening:* Street Sounds and Crowd Noises]

(*Vox Pop interview; each response has a different voice*)

REPORTER: Excuse me could you tell me what you think of Christopher Columbus?

WOMAN: You mean the film or the Broadway musical?

MAN: He was the first illegal alien in the Americas, *que no?*

WOMAN: He discovered this country and that's a great thing.

MAN: I'm Italian. I identify with him completely.

WOMAN: Uh, didn't he begin the slave trade? (*Laughter*)

KID: I saw him on TV the other day. He's boring.

REPORTER: What do you think of all the quincentennial celebrations?

MAN WITH ACCENT: It seems strange to celebrate a funeral.

MAN: I've made my reservations for my trip to Spain—there's a big party over there!

WOMAN: I know, it's the year of the loan, right? (*Cracks up*)

YOUNG MAN: We're turning a very painful history into a bunch of souvenirs. I mean, Columbus pizza, discovery condoms, Columbus survival kits for sailboats—it's terrible.

MAN: I don't give a damn. I need a (BEEP) job!

WOMAN: (*Happy*) Read my T-shirt. "It's Columbus bashing time!"

REPORTER: Do any contemporary celebrities remind you of Columbus?

This program was produced as part of "The Year of the White Bear." It was commissioned by the Los Angeles Festival and The Territory of Art and aired on National Public Radio in 1992–1993.

WOMAN: President Bush?

MAN: Neil Armstrong.

REPORTER: What about Queen Isabella?

MAN: Margaret Thatcher, of course.

REPORTER: Hernan Cortez?

WOMAN: General Schwartzkopf. No, no, Conan the Barbarian.

REPORTER: And Cabeza de Vaca?

MAN: Sorry, I don't speak Spanish.

[*Street Sounds Fade Into Tribu Song* (Cow noises)]

FEMALE VOICE: *Acaso es posible explicar este pais, este presente sin la dolorisima memoria de la colonización del Nuevo Mundo?*

[*Soundbed of Indigenous Tongues (10 seconds) followed by recording of Leon Felipe Poem in Old Spanish about Cortez's arrival.*]

MAN'S VOICE: Discovery, encounter, exchange, invasion, intervention, synthesis, culture clash, culture shock, rupture, genocide, rape…

[*Music:* The Residents: Eskimo (Side 2, no. 2)]

OLD MAN'S VOICE WHISPERING (*Music in background*): I, Bartholome de las Casas, have endless evidence to prove the mild and peaceful temperament of the natives. But our work was to exasperate, ravage, kill, mangle, and destroy. In a short time this land which was so great, so powerful and fertile, was depopulated. My eyes have seen these acts so foreign to human nature, and now I tremble as I write. From 1494 to 1508, over three million people perished from war, slavery, and the mines. Who in future generations will believe this?

[*Music:* European court music]

FEMALE VOICE: *Nuestro continente fue creado por lenguas indigenas*
procreado en espanol
y descreado finalmente en ingles….
Translation please?

MAN: Our continent still has no name.

[*Music:* The Residents: Eskimo (Side 2, no. 2/3)]

CHORUS OF THREE VOICES CHANT:
Ame mmm
América…
Pa-namérica…
Ma-ma-mérica
Nuestra América…Norteamérica

Nor-te-amé-rica
Centroamérica…Zen tu América
Send them to América
Send them to América
Arte América…
Arde América
Are they Américan?
Are they Américan?
América te llama
América se llama

ONE VOICE SINGS:
América en llamas…
América on fire

[*Sounds:* Firefighter's sirens, then B-52 bombers, then postindustrial rock]

CB RADIO STYLE STATIC AND VOICE: Let's get things under control here, Jack.

CB VOICE NO.2: Sure thing, Jack.

[*Music Jingle Begins:* Eric Dolphy]

ANNOUNCER: Good morning friends and welcome to XPR's Voyage to the American Zone, radio for the New World Border—I mean Order, 1992 megahertz above reality. My name is Dwight Christian Windbag, your host for our special program on the 500th anniversary of Christopher Columbus's discovery of America. As you listeners know, artists around the world are creating fascinating works to commemorate this historic occasion. Two of them are with us today in the studio. Nuevoo Latinoo artists Gwermo Comes-Pina and Coocoo Fuscoo are going to key us into the Hispanic perspective on the "Encwayntro."

[*Music Fades Slightly—Becomes Soundbed*]

COCO FUSCO: Desencuentro, I'd say, actually.

GUILLERMO GÓMEZ-PENA: We see this as an opportunity to question expansionist behavior from the Spanish Conquest to the New World Order. We are part of a continental countercelebratory move—

XPR: (*Annoyed*) Did I hear you say ca-ca-countercelebration? What's going on? My press release here says you two are from the Walker Art Center in Minneapolis. You know—fine art, good taste. I thought you guys were… Who are you?

CF: I'm a multi-culti pop semiotician from Cuba York. Guillermo's a post-Mexican borderologo. We're excavating contemporary material culture in search of signs of the Great Columbian Myth.

MPR: Uh, this is too heavy—let's break for a minute while I check with the station manager.

COMMERCIAL VOICE: And now, a message from our sponsor!

[*Music:* Los Machucambos Harp]

SOFT FEMALE: Here at the Christopher Columbus Fiesta Bureau, we believe in creating a total experience of the discovery of America. Not only do we bring you great educational programs like this one—but for the next three weeks we are offering special prices for wonderful quincentenary souvenirs. All products were made by talented and cost-effective workers in our satellite *maquiladoras* throughout the New World. (pause) Make sure your private life stays adventurous by giving the woman you want to conquer some Christa Columbus lingerie in black, mulata, mestiza, and Indian skin colors, and once you've got her ready slap on some of that manly fragrance—La Colonia de Colón. It's guaranteed to make her your slave. (*Woman's giggle*)

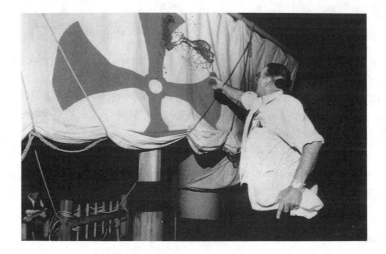

"American Indian Movement activist Vernon Bellecourt
throws a pint of his own blood at a replica caravel at St. Paul's Science Museum, 1992.
© STAR TRIBUNE/MINNEAPOLIS-ST. PAUL.

[*Sounds: Monkeys and Tropical Birds*
Hanraken Drums as Soundbed]

XPR: OK, looks like we have no choice except to continue.

GG-P: We understand that all the marketing *mamadas* around Columbus express a deep anxiety about white America's place in this hemisphere.

XPR: Aha, it's the P.C. Patrol at work—you always manage to ruin the pleasure some of us take in holding certain things about this country sacred. Just like our president said—you are like Puritans who can't sleep at night because some big guy out there might be having fun.

GG-P: *Coquito, este hombre es un verdadero pendejo.*

[*Buzzer Sound*]

COMPUTER VOICE: This is the voice of Airheadedness and Nationalism in Media speaking. We are interupting this program to delete inappropriate language for radio broadcast. This station does not permit the use of Spanish, Spanglish, or any other foreign language. You have been warned.

GG-P: *Chale ches Gabachos. (Horn Noise)*

XPR: Please, let's return to our topic.

CF: Fine. As far as I'm concerned, Columbus is just another one of this country's disposable icons. He's being wheeled out to stand for everything the white minority would like to defend against us—the new multicultural barbarians. So what we get is a mass-scale historical fiction that draws a direct line from the New World to the New World Order.

XPR: I don't see the connection really.

GG-P: The U.S. is riddled with social and economic problems and is on the decline as a world power. It's sense of self is very fragile, and that makes this a perfect time for self-aggrandizing myths. You know what I'm talking about, man.

XPR: (*Nervous*) Let's try to keep it light, folks. This is the culture hour after all. How about telling our listeners about your art exhibit at the Walker? It has such a wonderful title—isn't it *The Year of the White Bear*? Is it connected to the Chinese Calendar?

GG-P: No. The White Bear was the name the Paez Indians of Colombia gave to the Spaniards when they first saw them. (*He laughs*)

XPR: But there are no white bears in Colombia.

GG-P: They imagined them.

CF: We tend to forget that both cultures developed myths about the other— the thing is that the indigenous peoples based their myths on the violence they experienced at the hands of Europeans.

XPR: Could you be more concrete and less propagandistic?

GG-P: Yes, the Amerindians in Surinam called the Europeans the *panekitis*, or the "people who kill their brothers." The Aztecs called the Spaniards *teules*, meaning "arrogant outsiders."

CF: Their descendants still call tourists *gringos* because of their "We can buy any-thing in this greasy little country" attitude.

XPR: (*Exasperated*) Isn't that reverse racism?

STUDIO ENGINEER VOICE: (*Muffled*) Uh, excuse but you guys have been talking for five minutes and you're still on the same old subject. You wanna liven it up a little, since you've only got a couple of minutes left?

CF: OK, Mr. Windbag, what are we supposed to be celebrating? The slave trade, contraband, and piracy that made Europe rich?

XPR: Hey, we don't want a moral dilemma here. We just want to have a nice fiesta for Columbus.

COMPUTER VOICE: Watch it, pal—your English is slipping.

XPR: Oops. Sorry. Well, uh, let's try to pull ourselves together.

[*Music:* Latin Musak—Old Album]

MALE VOICE WITH THICK ACCENT: In Mexico we have a saying—*Mi casa es su casa*—which means, My country is yours. The next time you are contemplating making a foreign investment, look into the advantages of the Free Trade Agreement. No taxes, low overhead, and lots of salsa. While you're down there, enjoy our free trade cocktail: free water from Canada, and cheap oil from Mexico, all served in an American glass—*Caramba!*

[*Sound:* Excerpt From Mexican Radio
Static, Then Sounds of Wind, Seagulls and Waves]

MALE VOICE WITH PUERTO RICAN ACCENT: Hello, America. This is Radio Pirata: Colón, Go Home, reporting to you from the deck of the ex-official caravela la Pinta Dos, which was on its way to Santo Domingo before we high-jacked it. We have dropped the crew off at Cape Verde and are continuing our transatlantic voyage to Haiti, where we will liberate 2,000 political prisoners and transport them to the sanctuary city of San Francisco. Meanwhile we will be entertaining you with more of our kind of news about the re-discovery…

[*Music:* Tribu]

NASAL MALE VOICE: In 1492, an Aztec sailor
named Noctli Europzin Tezpoca
departed from the port of Veracruz
with a small flotilla of wooden rafts
Three months later
he discovered a new continent
and named it Europzin after himself
In November 1512,
omnipotent Aztecs
began the conquest of Europzin
in the name of thy Father Tezcatlipoca

Lord of Cross-cultural Misunderstandings

[*Music Begins:* A Lighter Shade of Brown]

NASAL MALE VOICE: *Y entonces el desmadre se comenzó a multiplicar* logo-rhythmically and *logaritmicamente*

[*Tribu Track is Broken by Postindustrial Music*]

COMPUTER VOICE: We will not tolerate this intervention. We have located you on our radar system and have succeeded in jamming your signals. May our legitimate program proceed. Tape rolling...

[*Music:* Perez Prado Mambo And Sounds of Rolling Waves]

MASTER OF CEREMONIES: Hello, all of you out there. It's a beautiful day here at Conquista Beach in the Dominican Republic, where we are enjoying the 500th version of our Miss Discovery beauty contest—and on this beautiful we are distributing free posters of your superstar saints donated by the Vatican and 500 cases of Diet Cola sent to us by the European Common Market. Our judges from the local Jesuit Mission have come up with a marvelous set of questions for our exotic contestants. The lucky winner will receive a temporary green card and a round trip plane ticket to Columbus, Ohio, where she'll get to work for six months as tour guide at the new Discoveryland Amusement Park.

We're down to six *finalistas, damas y caballeros,* and aren't they just heavenly creatures, every one of them. Tell us, Kukiya, what was it like the first time you saw white people?

KUKIYA: (*With strange accent; she articulates carefully*) It was not long ago. I was so happy because they gave me gifts of mirrors. Then they showed me how to pour some white powder on them in little lines. I breathed it into my nose—

MC: Uh, well that's nice, dear. Let's let you rest and go on to Lila. How do you feel today?

LILA: (*Also accented, but speaks faster*) I believe that this celebration will bring knowledge about our beautiful island to the entire world and that this will help us to participate in the global economy.

MC: That's what I like to hear.

LILA: We have spectacular beaches and bungalows. My father can pick you up at the airport and bring you to our cozy *bohio* in his bamboo canoe.

MC: Did you hear that, America? This is paradise!

LILA: My mother will cook for you. My brother and I will be ready for you every night at 11:00 P.M. in case you're into crosscultural ménage à—

MC: (*Interrupts*) Well, yes, thank you, Lila, we'll have to break now for a commercial...

[*Latin Musak:* Les Luthiers]

FEMALE COMMERCIAL VOICE NO.2: Let's talk woman-to-woman. It's a cruel truth that this society just doesn't appreciate mature women. But not every culture is like ours, thank God. Those suave men in Latin America just love us American girls, no matter what our age or size is. We were forbidden fruit for five hundred years, but times have changed. So it's time for you to discover Latin love. We offer fabulous trips to the Caribbean for single women who want a daring adventure with an appreciative and dark-skinned man. You'll be whisked away on a blind date by a certified, AIDS-free, bilingual Latino stud. Our *mucho macho* men are guaranteed to make you feel like a million without ever asking you for a green card. All they want is your, uh… So call Mestizaje Dating Services today!

[*Song Ends:* Soundbed for Interview Begins: La Bolivariada Drums]

XPR: Ok, we're back in Studio Three conversing with Coocoo Fiusco and Gwermo Comes-Pina. So now really you two, don't you think it's time to shed all that anger? I mean, isn't rage kind of passe?

GG-P: You mean, isn't it time to forget history, right?

XPR: Yeah. I mean, no.

GG-P: We're not suggesting that all European-descended people be deported. We recognize that most of us on this continent are the product of a mixing of the Old and New Worlds—and I don't only mean culturally, I also mean genetically, even though most Anglos have a hard time acknowledging that they probably have some African or Native American ancestry.

XPR: I beg your Mexican pardon!

CF: Look, if we're going to deal with cultural identity in this country, we have to face our own hybridity and figure out why there have been such strong efforts to deny it for all these years. Think about how the news deals with race these days— they're only interested in racial conflict. Latino gangs, interracial riots, sex scandals involving black athletes…

GG-P: There seems to be a fear that if "whites" don't control everyone else anymore, we're headed for social chaos. So we need a new Papa Columbus to bring order back to the wild urban jungles of contemporary America.

XPR: Right—wait a second, I mean—there's also a lot to be excited about. The world is becoming more interconnected than ever, and as a result, more intercultural. Now that should appeal to you Nuevoo Latinoos. (*Voice begins to reverberate*) Soon there will be no reason for you to fight, because thanks to free trade and global media, we will all buy the same, eat the same, think the same, and dream the same. (*Hypnotic echo continues: Buy the same, eat the same, think the same, dream the same.*)

[*Sounds:* Soldiers Marching]

[*Music:* Bolivariada]

MILITARY CHANTS IN CRESCENDO (Three voices interlocking with echoing phrase): New World Justice, New World Order, New Word Order
New World Odor, New Disorder,
New World Orders,
Free Trade, Free Trade Art,
Utopia, Utopia, 92, 92

[*Sound of Soccer Game in Crescendo*]

CADENCE CALL:
New World Order is the Best
Old World Order put to Rest

[*Soccer Game Blends into Sounds of Auditorium Crowd*]

Gómez-Peña and Fusco as "El Aztec High-Tech and La Miss Discovery,"
from *The New World (B)order*, Dance Theatre Workshop, New York City, 1993.
PHOTO BY HIMARI DUGATANI.

COMMENTATOR WHO SOUNDS LIKE A PREACHER: Ladies and Gentlemen and all good and God-fearing people of America, every day the minds of hundreds of thousands of young people are being polluted in colleges across this blessed land by the communist, East Coast establishment intellectuals. Now I use the word intellectual, but can hardly conceive of their anti-American drivel as rational thinking. I'm going to play you just a little bit of this venom so you can hear what your hard-earned dollars are paying for. It was recorded by a heroic student who works for us undercover at Boston University:

ACTIVIST FEMALE PROFESSOR: Washington has criminalized everybody who threatens the hegemony of the New World Order. This includes the handful of rebellious countries left in the Third World, but also the minority populations of the U.S. *All forms of sexual, political and cultural opposition are regarded as—* (*Abruptly terminates*)

[*Classical Music:* Les Luthiers]

MALE VOICE (*Macho style*): Tired of being screamed at by ungrateful minorities and hysterical feminists? Sick of listening to the leftist rhetoric of those affirmative action pimps? Fed up with counter-Columbus demonstrators? Don't worry, you're not the only one who feels this way, and it doesn't mean you're a bigot. You're just experiencing compassion fatigue. You've had enough of a beating. For a quick recovery, call Dr. James Lord at 1-800-AMERICA. Call today—and take your country back.

[*Soundbed*: Caribbean Drums]

CF: The right wing sure is giving radicals a lot of airtime. That professor was right on the mark. In fact, the Spanish Inquisition used the same strategies as Washington. Not much about labor has changed, either. *La Nueva España* used to have *encomiendas*. Now Latin America has *maquiladoras*.

COMPUTER VOICE: Translation, please!

GG-P: *Váyase al carajo*. Back then the colonial governments outlawed native languages.

CF: Now the U.S is pushing English Only.

GG-P: *A la chingada con el inglés oficial*.

COMPUTER VOICE: One more unamerican word and you'll be on a plane back to Mexico. We don't mess around with your kind. You probably don't event have a green card.

GG-P: Yes, I do.

COMPUTER VOICE: You've proven to be excessively resistant to assimilation. You are unwilling to forget, forget, forget (*Turns into orders*) FORGET, FORGET, FORGET,...

[*Sound:* Concerto Grosso by Les Luthiers (30 seconds)]

VOICE WITH MEGAPHONE:
Dear Spanish Inquisition
Dear Border Patrol
Dear American Culture
For 500 years we have been invisible to you.

Tu, vous se sabe de nada
For 500 years we've been remembering
Recordar, desandar, performear
Recordar, desandar, performear

    [*Sound:* Church Bells]

The following section consists of two separate tracks: One is the the female voice, slow and poetic. The other is three male voices, one overlapping the other.

FEMALE VOICE:
It's October 12, 1992,
in Mexico Tenochtitlan
I listen to an old radio show
and feel a 500-year-old vertigo

Cansada estoy,
y cansada permanezco
por los siglos de los siglos,
let me loose.

La otra historia
desconocida
por ustedes
las otras voces
que te producen
pánico
las otras culturas
que poco a poco
te devoran
aquí estan
aquí estamos
aquí estaremos
por los siglos
de los siglos
let me loose

MALE VOICES:
It's 1494 and Taino Cacique Caonabo is organizing the first guerilla war against the Spainiards at Hispaniola.

It's 1522 and slaves in Hispaniola have destroyed the sugar harvest in rebellion against Columbus's son.

It's 1553 and Pedro de Valdivia and his soldiers have been annihilated by the Araucanian chief Lautaro.

It's 1605 and the maroons of Palmares are beginning the longest-surviving society of runaway slaves in the Americas.

[*Music:* Misa Dos Quilombos Begins]

MALE VOICES:

It's 1676 and Wampanoag chief Metacom is driving his forces toward Boston to stop the Puritans.

It's 1742 and Juan Santos Atahualpa Apo Inca has called for an indigenous insurrection to end slavery and expel the Spaniards holding power in Peru.

It's 1761 and Mayan leader Canek is beginning a revolt against the white rulers in Yucatan.

It's 1762 and Chief Pontiac and his confederacy of eighteen tribes have held British troops at Fort Detroit in the longest siege in American history.

It's 1780 and the Inca leader Tupac Amaru II has won a victory against Spanish troops in Peru.

It's 1793 and the Haitian leader Toussaint L'Ouverture is beginning the first black revolution against white rule in this hemisphere.

[*Music Blends into Static Noise*]

COMPUTER VOICE: Please excuse the delay in the termination of this insufferable program. We are experiencing a crisis in our national identity management system. We have finally located the transmitter and shut it down. Proceed.

[*Music:* La Bolivariada: Middle of Cassette: Drum]

XPR: Listen, you two little radio terrorists, aren't you willing to admit that things in pre-Hispanic times weren't always so groovy? What makes you think that everything was so hunky-dory in the Aztec Empire? I've read that most societies in Mesoamerica were pretty decadent and violent by the time that we arrived.

GG-P: That doesn't negate that the Europeans brought a categorically different kind of warfare to the hemisphere—it's called *genocidio*. (*Horn noise*)

XPR: Oh, quiet, Gwermo. So, Coco, wouldn't you at least concede that there was some internal conflict in the Americas?

CF: Sure, but Europe was also at war with itself. It was overcrowded and overrun with diseases. The Conquest was driven by a scramble for wealth. Everyone was looking for a way out. Nobody really knew where they were going, so they created utopian fantasies about America that didn't leave much space for anyone but them.

XPR: So, what's wrong with utopia and competition? Sounds very American to me.

GG-P: Are you ever going to accept that there might have been something wrong? You guys are always worried that someone is going to pin the blame on you.

XPR: Isn't that the way Latin Americans feel, too?

GG-P: No. The hoopla down there isn't connected to an obsessive concern with identity like it is in the U.S. That debate was over ages ago. Everyone knows that official celebrations organized by government agencies are just publicity ploys to attract tourism and foreign investment.

XPR: There you go, trying to blame us Americans for everything again. The truth is that Cortez conquered Tenochtitlan with the help of native Mexicans, not gringos. What do you say to that?

CF: Whites have always employed people of color to punish other people of color, and there are always some self-hating types who will do the dirty work. That's part of the Columbian legacy.

GG-P: Look at Clarence (BEEP)—he's a perfect example.

XPR: My god, I'm going to lose my job.

GG-P: You brought it up, man.

XPR: (*Furious*) You sound like Fidel Kaddafi on acid. You're taking advantage of—

COMPUTER VOICE: Having trouble?

XPR: No, no—that's OK. (*Clears his throat*) I'm just going to zap them. Take that, you multi-culti monsters!!

[*Music: Static Sound Then Postindustrial Music Into Sounds of Breeze, Boat Horns, and Seagulls*]

"The Governor's Nightmare," by Enrique Chagoya, 1994.
PHOTO COURTESY OF THE ARTIST.

MALE VOICE WITH PUERTO RICAN ACCENT: This is Radio Pirata: Colón Go Home!, reporting from the middle of the Pacific Ocean. We're back again after having been so rudely interrupted. With us on the deck is the warrior for gringostroika with a message.

MALE VOICE (PACHUCO):
It's October 12, 1992,
off the shore of California
the tribe and I are about to land
in a low-rider *caravela*
a huge banner reads
500 años de genocidio
y aquí andamos todavía, vida mia
I grab a high-powered megaphone
and adopt a heroic position
(Begins speaking with megaphone)
hello America-ca-ca-ca
(Helicopter sounds begin in crescendo)
soy Cristobal Cogelon
unofficial chronicler
de la Pinta Dos
and I just discovered you
therefore you exist
per omnia saecula speculorum
con safos

[*Speech Rises From Beneath Helicopter Sounds*]

MALE VOICE: Here at the INS (Immigration and Naturalization Service) we understand immigration since that's how our ancestors arrived to this land of opportunity. What we have on our hands at present, however, is a problem of a different order. Gone are the days of reasonably regulated entry that was beneficial to all. What we now have is a full-scale invasion into America by the poor peoples of the world, a flood of homeless, uneducated, job-stealing criminals that is threatening our national sovereignty.

VOICE (*Begins to echo*)
Our natural sovereignty
Our national security
Our national identity
Our natural identity
Our national security
Our natural security

Our personal security
Our personal identity

FEMALE TELEPHONE REGULAR: Hello, hello. I don't know who I am anymore, or where I am. The airwaves are open again. The radio universe is empty. (*She screams*)

[*Sound of Winds Blowing*]

[*Music:* La Bolivariada (Side 2, beginning)]

MALE VOICE:
I woke up exhausted on stage
not knowing exactly where I was
what a beautiful paradox I thought
the first Americans came from Russia
40,000 years ago
what brave illegal aliens
who dared to cross the border of ice
they walked
all the way down
to the Valley of Anahuac
all the way down
to the bottom of my psyche

The following section is divided into two tracks. In the first, there is a female voice; In the second, three male voices overlapping.

FEMALE:
Dream about the future of your America
Euro America
Your own America
Su América
Suya
Sudamérica
Suda y sangra
Latinoamérica despierta
Hispanoamérica dormida
Iberoamérica borracha querida
borrame del mapa
(*Sound of crying then in erotic voice*)
Adonde estoy
Adonde estamos

Estamos Unidos en América
Estar dos unidos
Estar dos sumidos
el uno en el otro
Norte
Sur
Este
Oeste
Europa
Asia
Africa
América
Where Chingadas are we?

MALE NEWSCASTER VOICES:

It's 1838 and Rafael Carrera and his 4,000 rebels march into Guatemala City to contest the rule of wealthy landowners.

It's 1839 and fifty-four Africans on the slave ship *Amistad* have declared mutiny and are attempting to sail back to Africa.

It's 1848 and Cecilio Chi is leading fifteen thousand Mayans to the first battle of the Caste War against the whites that rages in the Yucatan for eighty years to follow.

It's 1873 and Yaqui leader Cajeme is organizing a separate Indian state within Mexico.

It's 1876 at Little Big Horn and General George Armstrong Custer and his troops suffer the worst defeat in U.S. military history against Native peoples at the hands of Crazy Horse.

It's 1901 and black activist Ida B. Wells begins a national campaign to stop lynchings of African Americans.

It's 1926 and Augusto Cesar Sandino returns from Mexico to start his fight against American business' hold on Nicaragua.

It's 1931 and massive demonstrations in El Salvador have led to the release of imprisoned activist leader Farabundo Martí.

It's 1956 and Rosa Parks is starting the American Civil Rights movement on a bus in Montgomery, Alabama.

It's 1964 and Malcolm X puts a petition to the United Nations charging the U.S. government with genocide against twenty-two million black Americans.

It's 1973 and Sioux at the Pine Ridge Reservation occupy Wounded Knee for seventy-one days forcing the U.S. government to negotiate with them.

[*Music Begins:* Punk Song—No Mas Presos]

MALE NEWSCASTER VOICES:

It's 1976 and Chico Mendes and Wilson Pinheiro organize protests to save the Amazonian rain forests.

It's 1988 and Paulinho Paiakan, a Kayapo militant from the Amazon, speaks before the World Bank in defense of the rain forests and indigenous rights.

It's 1992, and over fifteen million supporters around the world have petitioned the U.S. government for the release of Ojibway-Sioux activist Leonard Peltier, known to many as the American Mandela...

[*Music Dissolves into Tribu*]

[*No Soundbed*]

CF: Europe owns no other continent

GG-P: Eurown discovery,

CF: not continent

GG-P: disco-

CF: very strange

GG-P: co-

CF: *descubrimiento,*

GG-P: *descubro*

CF: *miento*

GG-P: I lie to you

CF: we don't lie together

GG-P: in the end

CF: we never lie together

GG-P: *vecinos abismales*

CF: still undiscovered
to one another

GG-P: not quite *carnales* yet

CF: not quite connecting

GG-P: you are here
against my will

CF: I am here
against yours

GG-P: we are damned
to repeat

CF: *la conquista y liberación
del Nuevo Mundo*

CF: This is Coco Fusco and Guillermo Gómez-Peña, speaking to you from the territory of arteamérica. *Buenas Noches.*

ENDNOTES

EL DIARIO DE MIRANDA

1. José Enrique Rodó, *Ariel,* trans. Margaret Sayers Peden (Austin, Texas: University of Texas Press, 1988).

2. Roberto Fernández Retamar, "Caliban: Notes on the Discussion of Culture in Our America" in *Caliban and Other Essays,* trans. Edward Baker (Minneapolis: University of Minnesota Press, 1989), pp. 3–45. Lamming and Césaire are cited in Retamar's book: George Lamming in "The Pleasures of Exile" (London: 1960); Aimé Césaire in "Une tempête: Adaptation de 'La Tempête' de Shakespeare pour un théâtre nègre" (Paris: 1969).

3. Octave Mannoni, *Prospero and Caliban: The Psychology of Colonization* trans. Pamela Powesland (Ann Arbor: University of Michigan Press, 1990); Originally published as *Psychologie de la Colonisation* (Paris: Editions du Seuil, 1950).

THE OTHER HISTORY OF INTERCULTURAL PERFORMANCE

1. Franz Kafka, *The Basic Kafka* (New York: Washington Square Press, 1979), 245.

2. Robert Rydell, *All the World's a Fair: Visions of Empire at American International Exhibitions, 1876–1916* (Chicago: University of Chicago Press, 1984).

3. Richard D. Altwick, *The Shows of London* (Cambridge, Mass.: Belknap Press, 1978).

4. Tristan Tzara, *Seven Dada Manifestos and Lampisteries,* trans. Barbara Wright (London: J. Calder, 1992), 57–58.

5. James Clifford, *The Predicament of Culture* (Cambridge, Mass.: Harvard University Press, 1988).

6. Jerome Rothenberg, "New Models, New Visions: Some Notes Towards a Poetics of Performance," in *Performance in Postmodern Culture*, ed. Michel Benamou and Charles Caramello (Madison, Wisconsin: Coda Press, 1977), 15.

7. Ibid.

8. Homi Bhabha, "The Other Question: Difference, Discrimination and the Discourse of

Colonialism," in *Out There: Marginalization and Contemporary Culture*, ed. Russell Ferguson, Martha Gever, Trinh T. Minh-ha, and Cornel West (Cambridge, Mass.: MIT Press, 1990) 71–88.

9. Frantz Fanon, "The Negro and Psychopathology," in *Black Skin, White Masks*, trans. Charles Lam Markmann (New York: Grove Press, 1967), 141–209.

10. Octave Mannoni, *Prospero and Caliban: The Psychology of Colonization*, trans. Pamela Powesland (Ann Arbor: University of Michigan Press, 1990).

11. Roger Bartra, *El Salvaje en el Espejo* (Mexico: Ediciones Era S.A. de C.V., 1992).

12. *Chicago Sun Times*. January 7, 1993

13. *Cambio 16*. January 19, 1992.

WHO'S DOIN' THE TWIST?

1. Richard Fung, "Working Through Cultural Appropriation," *Fuse Magazine*, vol. XVI, nos. 5-6 (summer 1993): 16–24.

2. Ibid.

3. Kobena Mercer. "Black Hair/Style Politics," *Out There: Marginalization and Contemporary Cultures*, ed. Russell Ferguson, Martha Gever, Trinh T. Minh-ha, and Cornel West (The New Museum of Contemporary Art and MIT Press, 1990), 247–264.

4. For more historical information, see Robert Rydell's *All the World's a Fair: Visions of Empire at American International Exhibition, 1876–1916* (Chicago: University of Chicago Press).

5. Jack Weatherford, *Native Roots: How the Indians Enriched America* (New York: Ballantine Books, 1991), 171–173.

6. Mike Davis, *City of Quartz: Evacuating the Future of L.A.* (New York: Verso, 1990).

7. Chandra Talpade Mohanty, "Under Western Eyes: Feminist Scholarship and Colonial Discourse," in *Third World Women and the Politics of Feminism*, 51–80.

8. Luis Martin, *Daughters of the Conquistadores* (New Mexico: University of New Mexico Press, 1983), 280–309.

9. Dick Hebdige, *Subculture and the Meaning of Style* (London: Methuen Press, 1979), 45.

10. Mercer, ibid.

11. bell hooks, "Eating the Other," in *Black Looks: Race and Representation* (Boston: South End Press, 1992), 21–40.

12. "Is Paris Burning?" in *Black Looks*, and Judith Butler's "Gender is Burning," in *Bodies that Matter* (New York: Routledge, 1993), 121–140.

13. Fung, ibid.

14. Butler, ibid.

UNCANNY DISSONANCE

1. Michele Wallace, *Invisibility Blues: From Pop to Theory* (New York: Verso Press, 1990), 229.

2. Roland Barthes, *Writing Degree Zero*, trans. Annette Lavers and Colin Smith (New York: Hill and Wang, 1968), 48–49.

3. Yasmin Ramirez Harwood, catalogue essay for *Centric 38, Lorna Simpson* exhibition

at The University Art Museum, California State University at Long Beach, January 30–April 6, 1990.

ESSENTIAL DIFFERENCES

1. Homi K. Bhabha, "Sly Civility," *October*, no. 34 (fall 1985), 73.

2. While concentrating on images of women might seem arbitrary, it is important to keep in mind the centrality of female representations to the iconography of *la mexicanidad;* identity is guaranteed by the mother, who, as the archetype *la chingada*, has been violated by the foreign invader.

3. *Malinchismo* refers to the inclination toward favoring the foreign, a term derived from the legends surrounding La Malinche, the indigenous woman who became the lover and interpreter of the Spanish conquistador Hernán Cortés.

4. Roger Bartra, *La jaula de la melancolia: identidad y metamórfosis del mexicano* (The cage of melancholy: identity and metamorphosis of the Mexican) (Mexico City: Grijalbo, 1987).

5. Carlos Monsiváis, catalog essay, *Yolanda Andrade: los velos transparentes, las transparencias veladas* (Yolanda Andrade: transparent veils, veiled transparencies) (Villahermoso, Mexico: Gobierno del Estado de Tabasco, 1988).

6. Eugenia Parry Janis, "Her Geometry," in *Women Photographers*, ed. Constance Sullivan (New York: Harry N. Abrams, Inc., 1990), 24–25.

7. An earlier version of this essay was presented at the San Francisco Museum of Modern Art on January 17, 1991, at the conference "Gender and Modernism: American and European Photography between the Two World Wars."

RICAN/STRUCTIONS

1. See Lucy Lippard, "Coming to Life," *Rican/Structed Convictions*, exhibition catalog, New York, Exit Art, 1989, p.10.

2. In a recent work called *Neorican Convictions* (1989), Sánchez also takes issue with the mythology of martyrdom. Sprawled across an American flag that appears to be drained of color by a bleeding heart is an excerpt from a statement by Sánchez's brother Samuel, an independence movement activist, in response to a grand jury subpoena. In his statement Samuel Sánchez recounts the systematic violence, a type of enforced martyrdom, against Puerto Ricans in the United States.

3. The text inscribed in *Cultural, Racial, Genocidal Policy* reads, in part: "More than one-third of all Puerto Rican women of childbearing age were sterilized by a program which the United States planned, billed as a means to combat overpopulation and unemployment. This continues to be the highest rate of genocidal sterilization in the world."

A BLACK AVANT-GARDE?

1. The Metro Cinema occupies a place analogous to that of the Film Forum in New York City.

2. Menelik Shabazz was the first black British independent filmmaker to screen his film commercially in London. *Burning an Illusion* opened in 1982.

3. I have chosen to limit my discussion of the black workshops to Black Audio and Sankofa because the debates around them and their filmic strategies set them apart from the rest of the black workshop sector. Other black workshops in England are: Cardiff, Macro, Star, Retake, and Ceddo. The last two are also London-based, and I conducted interviews with their members as part of my research. I should mention here that Ceddo also produced a documentary about racially motivated riots, entitled *The People's Account* (1986). It was commissioned by Channel 4, but has not been aired as of this writing due to an unresolved conflict involving Channel 4 and the Independent Broadcasting Authority (IBA). The IBA found the original version of the documentary unacceptable for its accusations against the British state, even after Channel 4 lawyers had submitted requests for minor changes and had them attended to. When I was conducting research for this article in the summer of 1987, the IBA was insisting on a balancing program to accompany the documentary, and on the right to cancel the airing of both if they did not approve of the balancing program.

4. Although there had been outbreaks of violence in the 1970s and earlier in protest of harassment by police and right-wing groups, and in protest of the state's strategic neglect of racial injustice, the riots that took place in 1981 marked a watershed moment in the history of British race relations. The first disturbances in Britain were immediately related to the suspicious deaths of three black youths. But what began in the Brixton area of London spread to urban ghettos in most of the industrial centers of London, lasting an entire summer. The scale of the protests, as I mention later in the article, made it impossible for the government and the media to ignore the situation. Sociological investigations into the conditions of blacks in Britain, such as the Scarman Report, were a direct governmental response to these events. The cultural policies of the GLC and new attention to race in many British cultural institutions were other responses.

5. For an in-depth discussion of this, see Paul Gilroy, *There Ain't No Black in the Union Jack: The Cultural Politics of Race and Nation* (London: Century Hutchinson Ltd., 1987), chap. 3; see also Cecil Gutzmore, "Capital, 'black youth' and crime," in *Race & Class* XXV, no. 2 (autumn 1983), 13–30; and Lee Bridges, "Policing the Urban Wasteland" in the same issue, 31–48.

6. Channel 4 started broadcasting in 1982. It is government-subsidized but funded by a number of sources, including advertising and subscription payments. When it was set up it was supposed to commission and air a variety of voices, including those of ethnic minorities, the independent filmmaking sector, foreign programming, and nontraditional formats. The actual percentage of airtime and monies allocated to the independent sector has been exaggerated in the United States. Most of what would be considered innovative programming is shown on two one-hour weekly slots ("Eleventh Hour" and "People to People") at off-peak hours.

7. For an in-depth discussion of this, see Franco Bianchini, "GLC R.I.P.: Cultural Politics in London, 1981–1986," *New Formations* (summer 1987), 103–117.

8. Sociology departments in the more progressive British Polytechnics (such as Portsmouth,

Middlesex, and South Bank) have a quite different course of study from their American counterparts. Theory and Research Methods are distinct branches of study, and it was within the theory rubric that Black Audio members John Akomfrah, Reese Auguiste, Lina Gopaul, and Avril Johnson encountered the critical writings that would later inform their creative work.

9. This list is not exhaustive. The work of Birmingham's Center for Contemporary Cultural Studies and London's Institute for Race Relations is also extremely important. The filmmakers are also interested in the work of many black American essayists, particularly June Jordan.

10. For more about Bhabha's relation to Lacan and Fanon, see "Of Mimicry and Man: The Ambivalence of Colonial Discourse," *October*, no. 28 (spring 1984), 118–124. Also see Franz Fanon, *Black Skin, White Masks*, trans. Charles Lam Markmann (New York: Grove Press, 1967).

11. See Gilroy, *There Ain't No Black in the Union Jack*, and *The Empire Strikes Back* (London: Hutchinson, 1982).

12. Julian Henriques, "Realism and the New Language," *Artrage* no. 13 (summer 1986), 32–37.

13. Jim Pines, interview with the author, London, July 1987.

14. Attile, "Young, British and Black," 14.

15. In 1985, riots in Handsworth and Broadwater Farm were set off by the deaths of Cynthia Jarrett and Cheryl Groce. Police entered the Jarrett home and began to question Ms. Jarrett, who suffered from a heart condition and began to feel ill when she was questioned. The police did not respond to the oncoming heart attack. She died shortly thereafter. Ms. Groce was shot by police who were supposedly searching for someone else. The Broadwater Farm riot gained infamy from the killing of a policeman by rioters on the first night.

16. See Gilroy, *There Ain't No Black in the Union Jack*, chap. 5.

17. Ibid., chap. 6, 69.

18. The Black Audio Film Collective, "Handsworth Songs: Some Background Notes," 1987, 4.

PERMISSIONS

"El Diario de Miranda/Miranda's Diary" originally appeared in *The Subversive Imagination*, ed. Carol Becker (New York: Routledge, 1994) and *The Michigan Quarterly Review*, Vol. 33, No. 3, Summer 1994.

"Pan American Post Nationalism" originally appeared in *Black Popular Culture*, ed. Gina Dent. © 1992 by Dia Center for the Arts. Reprinted by permission of Bay Press, Inc.

"Passionate Irreverence: The Cultural Politics of Identity" originally appeared in the 1993 *Biennial Exhibition* catalogue. © 1992 Whitney Museum of American Art, New York.

"The Other History of Intercultural Performance" originally appeared in *The Drama Review* 38, I (T141), Spring 1994.

"Andres Serrano Shoots the Klan: An Interview with Andres Serrano" originally appeared in High Performance, Issue No. 55, Vol. 14, No. 3, Fall 1991.

"Vernacular Memories' originally appeared in Art in America Magazine, Brant Publications, December 1991.

"Rican/Structions" originally appeared in Art in America Magazine, Brant Publications, February 1990.

"Uncanny Dissonance" originally appeared in the Lorna Simpson exhibition catalogue published in 1991 by the Colgate University Gallery of the Department of Art and Art History. It subsequently appeared in *Third Text*, No. 22, Spring 1993.

"Essential Differences: Photographs of Mexican Women" originally appeared in *Afterimage*, Vol. 18, No. 9, April 1991.

"Traces of Ana Mendieta" appeared in *Poliester*, No. 4, Winter 1993. An earlier version of this article, entitled "For Ana Mendieta," was published in *The Portable Lower East Side*, Vol. 5, Nos. 1 & 2, 1988.

"The American Blues of Catalina Parra" originally appeared in the artist's exhibition catalogue published in 1991 by INTAR Gallery.

"A Black Avant-Garde? Notes on Black Audio Film Collective and Sankofa" was published in the 1988 monograph, *Young, British and Black*, by Hallwalls Contemporary Arts Center, Buffalo, NY. An earlier version of the essay, entitled "Black Filmmaking in Britain's Workshop Sector," appeared in *Afterimage*, Vol. 15, No. 7, February 1988.

An earlier version of "Bilingualism, Biculturalism, and Borders," entitled "The Border Art Workshop/El Taller de Arte Fronterizo," appeared in *Third Text*, No. 7, Summer 1989.

INDEX

ABOUT THE AUTHOR

Born in New York City, Coco Fusco is an
interdisciplinary artist, curator, and writer
whose articles have been published in the
United States, Latin America, and Europe,
including the *Los Angeles Times*, *The Nation*,
Art in America and *The Village Voice*.
She lives in Los Angeles.